GROUNDS OF NATURAL PHILOSOPHY

broadview editions
series editor: Martin R. Boyne

Engraved frontispiece portrait of Margaret Cavendish from *The Philosophical and Physical Opinions* (1655). Published by permission of the Provost and Fellows of King's College, Cambridge. The inscription reads: "Studious She is and all Alone / Most visitants, when She has none, / Her Library on which She look's / It is her Head her Thoughts her Books. / Scorninge dead Ashes without fire / For her owne Flames doe her Inspire."

GROUNDS OF NATURAL PHILOSOPHY

Margaret Cavendish

edited by Anne M. Thell

broadview editions

BROADVIEW PRESS – www.broadviewpress.com
Peterborough, Ontario, Canada

Founded in 1985, Broadview Press remains a wholly independent publishing house. Broadview's focus is on academic publishing; our titles are accessible to university and college students as well as scholars and general readers. With 800 titles in print, Broadview has become a leading international publisher in the humanities, with world-wide distribution. Broadview is committed to environmentally responsible publishing and fair business practices.

Library and Archives Canada Cataloguing in Publication

Title: Grounds of natural philosophy / Margaret Cavendish ; edited by Anne M. Thell.
Names: Newcastle, Margaret Cavendish, Duchess of, 1624?-1674, author. | Thell, Anne M., editor.
Series: Broadview editions.
Description: Series statement: Broadview editions | Originally published: London : A. Maxwell, 1668. | Includes bibliographical references.
Identifiers: Canadiana (print) 20190225335 | Canadiana (ebook) 20190225343 | ISBN 9781554813872 (softcover) | ISBN 9781770487314 (PDF) | ISBN 9781460406878 (HTML)
Subjects: LCSH: Physics—Early works to 1800. | LCSH: Philosophy of nature—Early works to 1800.
Classification: LCC B1299.N273 G76 2019 | DDC 192—dc23

Broadview Editions
The Broadview Editions series is an effort to represent the ever-evolving canon of texts in the disciplines of literary studies, history, philosophy, and political theory. A distinguishing feature of the series is the inclusion of primary source documents contemporaneous with the work.

Advisory editor for this volume: Colleen Humbert

Broadview Press handles its own distribution in North America:
PO Box 1243, Peterborough, Ontario K9J 7H5, Canada
555 Riverwalk Parkway, Tonawanda, NY 14150, USA
Tel: (705) 743-8990; Fax: (705) 743-8353
email: customerservice@broadviewpress.com

For all territories outside of North America, distribution is handled by Eurospan Group.

Broadview Press acknowledges the financial support of the Government of Canada for our publishing activities.

Canada

Typesetting by Aldo Fierro
Cover design by Aldo Fierro

PRINTED IN CANADA

For Archibald

Contents

Contents

Acknowledgements

This critical edition would not be possible without two Singapore Ministry of Education Tier 1 Grants administered by The Faculty of Arts and Social Sciences at National University of Singapore (R-103-000-164-115 and R-103-000-131-112). I am immensely grateful for this institutional support, which enabled all of the archival research necessary to execute this project. I am also grateful for the comments and suggestions of a lively group of Cavendish scholars, who have been steadfast in their support of this edition. I am especially indebted to Deborah Boyle and Lisa Walters, who were both generous enough to offer rigorous comments on the introduction as well as various other aspects of the project. I must also thank James Fitzmaurice, who patiently and sagely answered my many questions about Cavendish's copy texts, her handwriting, and the dissemination of her work. In addition, Sarah Hutton and Emma Wilkins offered initial suggestions about Cavendish's philosophical milieu that proved extremely fertile in the long term. I am grateful also to Stephen Tabor at The Huntington Library for sharing his wealth of knowledge about the Bridgewater collection, as well as The British Library's exceptional Rare Books staff, who helped solve many a mystery regarding provenance, handwriting, and family connections. Special thanks are also due to my anonymous readers at Broadview Press, who offered constructive and timely feedback that improved immeasurably this edition. Finally, I am sincerely grateful to Stephen Latta at Broadview, whose faith in this project sustained its publication, from the initial pitch to the minutest details of the final draft.

Introduction

"[W]ho knows but after my honourable burial, I may have a glorious resurrection in following ages, since time brings strange and unusual things to passe." So speculates Margaret Cavendish (1623–73) in her epistle dedicatory to *The Philosophical and Physical Opinions* (1655), on which *Grounds of Natural Philosophy* (1668) is based.[1] This comment was delivered along with copies of *The Philosophical and Physical Opinions* to the university libraries at Oxford and Cambridge and demonstrates both Cavendish's great ambition and her simultaneous resignation that she would never be appreciated or even accepted during her own lifetime, in large part due to the era's disparaging views toward female intellect (or the "careless neglects, and despisements of the masculine sex"). Although she recognized that it was "unusual for a woman to present a Book to the University," she explains her "vainglorious" act by suggesting that such audacity is the very thing that makes us human: "I am to be pardoned, since there is little difference between man and beast, but what ambition and glory makes." As this Broadview Edition signals, Cavendish has gained the "resurrection" for which she long hoped and is now read widely by students and scholars of the period. Finally, then, Cavendish has risen to "Fame[']s Tower" and her ideas "Live in Many Brains."[2]

Born the eighth and final child of a wealthy, Royalist family in Colchester, England, in 1623, Cavendish was a prolific author and philosopher whose career spanned some of the most tumultuous years of British history, including the English Civil Wars (1642–49), which resulted in the beheading of Charles I (r. 1625–49) and, during the subsequent Interregnum (1649–60), more than a decade of exile for prominent English Royalists like Cavendish, who could not return home until the 1660 Restoration of Charles II (r. 1660–85).[3] She also lived at a time of

1 Cavendish, *The Philosophical and Physical Opinions* (1655) (hereafter *PPO*), sig. B2[v]–[B3r].

2 Cavendish, "A True Relation" 62; *Sociable Letters* 142.

3 The Interregnum lasted from 1649 until 1660 and is the only period in British history when there was no reigning monarch. During this time, England, Wales, Ireland, and Scotland became the English Commonwealth.

unprecedented scientific development—or what is sometimes called the "Scientific Revolution"—that took root in England through the work of Francis Bacon (1561–1626) and was formalized in the Restoration period in The Royal Society of London, a fellowship of philosophers and scientists (then called "natural philosophers") who advanced the systematic study of nature via Baconian ideals of observation, experiment, and induction. Cavendish was deeply interested in the philosophical and scientific developments of her era, and she ultimately proved to be one of the most astute critics of the aims and methods of early English experimental science.

Like many women of the seventeenth century, Cavendish received no formal education. However, after her 1645 marriage to William Cavendish (1592–1676), marquis and eventual duke of Newcastle, she was privately tutored by William's brother, Charles Cavendish (c. 1591–1654). Later, in the post-Restoration period, she read widely and deeply in both ancient and contemporary philosophy.[1] While in exile during the Interregnum (first in Paris and later in Antwerp), the Cavendish family became a hub of English intellectuals abroad. They hosted regular salons and dinners that were attended by renowned thinkers like René Descartes (1596–1650), Kenelm Digby (1603–65), Thomas Hobbes (1588–1679), Pierre Gassendi (1592–1655), and Marin Mersenne (1588–1648). Although Cavendish denies having conversations with these men—she was always, she insists, "naturally Bashfull"—she was certainly familiar with them and their work.[2] Indeed, as her later philosophy indicates, she read contemporary and ancient philosophy with great diligence and set herself in direct dialogue with the leading thinkers of her day. She also corresponded with intellectual figures like Joseph Glanvill (1636–80), Constantijn Huygens (1596–1687), and Walter Charleton (1619–1707).

Like many natural philosophers of her era, Cavendish's interests were wide-ranging: in her prolific writings, which range from

---

1 Cavendish begins earnestly to engage with other philosophers in her 1664 *Philosophical Letters*; for details about her "reading of Philosophical Authors" see Cavendish, *The Life*, sig. a2r; *Observations* 11, 13; Whitaker 254–56, 263.

2 "A True Relation" 52. Yet Cavendish elsewhere admits that much of her intellectual growth occurred via "visiting and entertaining discourse." See Fitzmaurice, "Margaret Cavendish Writing Fiction." See also Whitaker 94–97.

poetry to philosophy to science fiction, she investigates the nature of all things, including the entire gamut of natural phenomena as well as humans and their beliefs and tendencies. This lack of specialization is characteristic of the philosophical inquiry of the seventeenth century, when more discrete disciplines had yet to coalesce and "natural philosophy"—or what we would now call "science"—took place within the broader rubric of "philosophy" and studied all aspects of nature, from botany to oceanography to cosmology, as well as mathematics, metaphysics, and theology. Even those philosophers who ultimately became major figures in the traditional canon of the history of philosophy—Hobbes and Descartes, for example—participated in a wide range of natural philosophical debates along with contemporaries who were just as important at the time but are less well known today (e.g., Robert Boyle [1627–91], Charleton, Ralph Cudworth [1617–88], Digby, Jan Baptist van Helmont [1580–1644; see Appendix C2], Robert Hooke [1635–1703], Henry More [1614–87; see Appendix C1], and Henry Power [1623–68]).[1] Moreover, the philosophical debates that we now privilege are not necessarily the same as those that most concerned these authors at the time. We must keep these historical nuances in mind as we read and contextualize *Grounds of Natural Philosophy.*

Grounds is important to Cavendish's philosophical oeuvre not only because it is her final and most concise statement of philosophy but also because its gradual composition from the early 1650s until 1668 spans the duration of Cavendish's writing career and demonstrates her development as a thinker and writer. Technically speaking, *Grounds* is what Cavendish calls a "Second," "much altered" edition of her most important early work, *The Philosophical and Physical Opinions*, which was published in 1655. But the story is not quite so simple. First of all, *The Philosophical and Physical Opinions* is itself a composite work, as it incorporates Cavendish's first philosophical treatise, *Philosophicall Fancies* (1653). Furthermore, *Grounds* is not really the second edition of *The Philosophical and Physical Opinions*, as this proclamation ignores the 1663 edition, which revises extensively the original and paves the way for *Grounds* in 1668. Indeed, *Grounds* resembles the 1663 *Philosophical and Physical Opinions* far more than it does the original, 1655 edition. Yet *Grounds* also stands apart from both of its predecessors in that

1 On the multifarious interests of these not yet canonic philosophers, see Hutton, "Margaret Cavendish and Henry More," esp. 186–87.

it is more succinct, organized, and professional; here Cavendish has streamlined her work and confidently expresses her later, more developed system of organic materialism, while also exploring a variety of speculative topics. She also demonstrates more control over her famously quirky style, which includes staging wars in her mind and frequent apostrophes to her readers. Even though *Grounds* might be seen as its own, separate text, its long evolution means that we need to keep in our view not just the philosophical debates that were current at the time of its publication in 1668 (e.g., experimentalism and chemical philosophy), but also those which were taking place in the early 1650s (e.g., atomism). This long view also allows us to isolate major changes in Cavendish's own thinking as she develops as a philosopher and engages with emerging philosophical debates.

Grounds of Natural Philosophy was published just two years after the first edition of *Blazing World* and *Observations upon Experimental Philosophy*, which were published together in 1666. While its arguments about nature are generally in accordance with those we find in her other philosophical treatises of the 1660s, including *Observations* and *Philosophical Letters* (1664), *Grounds* focuses on the "nature of nature," or, in other words, on defining nature and natural phenomena (rather than offering, say, a sustained critique of experimental philosophy, as we find in *Observations*). It provides an analytic account of the base substance and mechanics of all natural matter, from the tiniest organisms to the motions of the planets, and, at just 311 folio pages, is more approachable than many of her other works. Cavendish also devotes three substantial sections to health and the human body, cataloguing ailments and their ultimate causes. In addition, she includes a fascinating and lengthy appendix that makes up nearly a quarter of *Grounds* and explores more conjectural ideas like the possibility of alternate worlds; "Restoring-Beds, or Wombs" that bring life to annihilated bodies; and the distinctions between nature and God (with this section constituting Cavendish's most sustained effort to reconcile her materialist philosophy and Christianity). In outlining her most advanced philosophical program and, at the same time, entertaining wildly speculative concepts, *Grounds* also illustrates Cavendish's ongoing investment in the philosophical value of imaginative thought.

The actual publication of Cavendish's philosophy is unique and deserves some mention here. Throughout the 1650s, when Cavendish published her earliest philosophical and poetical writings, she was in exile in Europe. In November 1651, however, she returned from Antwerp to England on personal business regarding the recovery of the Newcastle estates, since, as a Royalist, William Cavendish could not return without pledging fealty to the Commonwealth (women, with the exception of queens, were not considered political subjects). During this visit, which lasted until early 1653, she managed to publish *Poems and Fancies* and *Philosophicall Fancies* (which were originally meant to be published together, much like her later works, *Observations* and *Blazing World*). It was highly unusual for a woman to publish, and even more unusual for her to publish philosophy, especially under her own name, and that Cavendish independently managed this feat is a testament to her ambition and tenacity. The 1650s in fact saw a steady stream of her publications, with *The World's Olio* and *The Philosophical and Physical Opinions* appearing in 1655 and, in 1656, *Nature's Pictures*. It is perhaps significant that later in the 1660s, when she returned to England, she chose to publish her most mature work—including *Observations*, *Blazing World*, and *Grounds*—with Anne Maxwell, one of the few women running publishing houses in seventeenth-century London. As a wealthy aristocrat, Cavendish could afford to publish her work in beautiful, calf-bound volumes and, in bestowing these on illustrious friends and university libraries, she arranged as far as possible for them to occupy a place in the great annals of literature and philosophy that were, of course, dominated by men. If not rewarded with contemporary accolades, she was determined to see herself into posterity with the publication and dissemination of her books.

Given this tremendous effort, it might be surprising that it has taken this long for Cavendish to be taken seriously by historians of philosophy and science. But, then again, the odds were stacked against her: ridiculed by many contemporaries for violating gender norms and participating in the period's intellectual debates, as well as for her extravagant public persona and dress, Cavendish also adopted a complicated writing style and skeptical, sometimes bellicose voice (although stylistically she shares many traits with Thomas Hobbes, who deeply influenced her work).[1] Later critics were no kinder: she was considered an

1 On the possibility that Cavendish was more read and appreciated than scholars have previously assumed, see Walters, *Margaret Cavendish*. On her reception, see also Whitaker 159–61.

eccentric across the nineteenth and early twentieth centuries, with even Virginia Woolf castigating her work as the product of "loneliness and riot."[1] But with the wholesale adoption by literary critics of Cavendish's *Blazing World*, a now canonic science fiction that offers a pointed critique of seventeenth-century experimental science, and ongoing scholarship that has recovered the timeliness and salience of many of her philosophical contributions, she is now taught and read with increasing frequency. Like many philosophers, Cavendish changed her stance on various topics across her career; by the time she published *Grounds* in the 1660s, however, she had developed a coherent natural philosophy that contributes in important ways to the period's philosophical debates. Although some of her ideas seem outlandish today (and were not widely influential at the time), her philosophy is deeply syncretic and anticipates the work of many of the more famous men who succeeded her, from John Locke (1632–1704) to Gottfried Leibniz (1646–1716) to Donald Davidson (1917–2003).[2]

As many recent scholars have noticed, Cavendish is a thinker uniquely in and out of her time; she contributes directly to a wide range of contemporary debates yet also manages to critique them with surprising distance and acumen. Although invested in the great issues of her age, she is surprisingly able, due perhaps to both her natural skepticism and her marginal position as a female philosopher, to peek around the corners of hegemonic discourse and to poke holes in dominant methods and theories.[3] She is, then, a unique voice of the Restoration period who engages with the major players of the time—Bacon, Boyle, Charleton, Descartes, Gassendi, Hobbes, Hooke, More, van Helmont—while also forwarding an alternative model of nature that resonates with today's readers. Indeed, in many ways, Cavendish speaks directly to us: we are her interlocutors, the readers of "after-Ages" who will find specific aspects of her work—her staunch separation of faith and knowledge, for

1 Woolf 61.

2 On how Cavendish anticipates later theories of mind, see Cunning, "Cavendish." On Cavendish and Leibniz specifically, see Wilson. On Cavendish and Baruch Spinoza (1632–77), see Detlefsen, "Atomism," esp. 202–03, 239–40.

3 For more on gender and Cavendish's position on the "intellectual margins," see Keller.

instance, or her insistence on the sentience of nature—almost uncannily modern.[1] For this, she has long waited.

***

While the 1655 *Philosophical and Physical Opinions* marks Cavendish's early turn away from atomism and toward an understanding of nature as a continuous network of living matter, *Grounds* outlines in clearer terms her more mature philosophical program. In *Grounds*, she combines certain aspects of ancient philosophy—including the doctrine of the four elements of air, fire, earth, and water—with newer, seventeenth-century ideas about motion and matter.[2] Specifically, *Grounds* expresses what is often called "organic materialism," which entails that all of nature is material, perceptive, self-knowing, self-moving, and alive. Cavendish's materialism is in fact thorough-going: she claims that all things are composed of a base substance, or "matter," and denies the existence in nature of souls or "immaterial substances" (a concept that is, to Cavendish, oxymoronic). In this pan-psychic or hylozoistic vision of the universe, where all matter is living, thinking, and moving, Cavendish opposes mechanical accounts of nature, which, in the tradition of Descartes and Hobbes, tend to explain all natural phenomena via the collision of inert parts. However, as Sarah Hutton notes, she does not "dispense with the basic ingredients of the Hobbesian world: matter in motion."[3]

Matter in Motion

The fundamental tenet in *Grounds* is Cavendish's absolute form of materialism, which aligns her with Hobbes but distances her from most other thinkers of the period, especially Neoplatonists

1 Cavendish, "A True Relation" 63. While Cavendish seems forward-thinking in many ways, she does at times side with ancient authority, especially in the realm of medicine. See Broad, "Cavendish."

2 While today a discussion of natural phenomena like the four elements or the motion of the planets might seem unrelated to philosophy, these questions were central to philosophical inquiry of the period (see, for instance, Part IV of Descartes's *Principles of Philosophy* [1644] or the final chapters of Hobbes's *De Corpore* [1655]).

3 Hutton, "In Dialogue" 426.

like More and dualists working in the wake of Descartes.[1] Indeed, Cavendish opens *Grounds* with her chapter "Of Matter," recognizing that this is a distinguishing element of her work. As the author announces, "there cannot be any Substances in Nature, that are between Body, and no Body: Also, Matter cannot be figureless, neither can Matter be without Parts" (p. 65). This stalwart materialism was a somewhat risky proposition in the late seventeenth century, as scientists were already under attack for their presumed hubris in attempting to know comprehensively nature and, by extension, God's ways. Denying souls or incorporeal substances in nature was even riskier, as this created a certain tension between natural philosophy and Christianity (and led to thinkers like Hobbes facing charges of atheism).[2] Cavendish tends to sidestep this problem by suggesting that the "divine soul" and religious matters more generally are not "natural"—or part of nature—and therefore beyond the scope of natural philosophical inquiry. By contrast, the "human" or "natural soul" she considers an especially pure form of matter, but material no less; similarly, thoughts and imaginations are also material in that they are embodied in the material motions of the mind. Like Hobbes, Cavendish also employs her materialism to counter the increasingly popular notion of the vacuum, or entirely empty space: "Body and Place is but one thing" (p. 67).[3] In sum, Cavendish admits no exceptions to her materialism besides potentially divine entities that humans cannot perceive or understand.

This elemental substance, matter, is composed of three "degrees" or elements that have distinct functions but remain

---

1 Henry More was a leading member of a group of seventeenth-century Anglican divines called the "Cambridge Platonists," who were invested in reviving and modernizing the work of Plato (c. 428–348 BCE) and Neoplatonist philosopher Plotinus (c. 204–270 CE). In her materialist natural philosophy Cavendish was opposed to More in almost every way, although she did share his belief that nature was alive (vitalism). See Hutton, "Margaret Cavendish." Cartesian dualism proposes that the mind and body are separate entities and attributes a causal role to the incorporeal mind in matters of voluntary motion and perception.

2 For instance, in 1662 More argues that all of nature is pervaded by "Spirit" and that disbelief in such substances is "a dangerous Prelude to Atheism." See Appendix C1, p. 247.

3 In *PPO* (1655), Cavendish was still open to the possibility of a vacuum in nature; by the 1660s, however, she adamantly denies it.

both inseparable and irreducible. That is, however many times matter is divided into smaller and smaller parts—a process that is potentially "infinite" (p. 68)—the admixture of the three degrees of rational, sensitive, and inanimate remains. The "Rational Parts," which are the purest, most "agil and free," and most self-aware, choreograph the decisions and actions of the other parts, while also assembling knowledge of the whole; the "Sensitive Parts," or "Labouring Parts," perceive their surroundings and move all three degrees of matter along their course; finally, the "Inanimate Parts," which lack self-motion, serve as a kind of base material that the sensitive parts use to "form, build, or compose themselves ... into all kinds and sorts of Creatures" (p. 67).[1] Again, although the rational, sensitive, and inanimate parts have distinct roles and compositions, they are indivisible from each other in all natural substances and remain "one united material Body" that "move[s] together as one Body" (pp. 66, 67). In this, Cavendish's natural philosophy cuts against the grain of Cartesian dualism (which posits mind and body as two separate entities), while it also resists the corpuscularianism—a theory that envisions all matter composed of minute particles that could potentially be divided from one another—that pervades the work of Boyle, Descartes, Gassendi, Locke, and van Helmont.[2] For her, matter is infinitely "dividable, and compoundable" into an infinite variety of forms, and smaller and smaller parts, but never distilled into *separate* parts (with the three degrees of matter remaining commingled in

1 Confusingly, Cavendish claims that even inanimate matter "hath life and self-knowledge"; however, it is not *self-moving* and therefore lacks "perceptive knowledge" (*Observations* 39).

2 While atomism and corpuscularianism both posit that all matter is composed of minute particles, seventeenth-century thinkers tended to prefer the term "corpuscle" over "atom" because the latter had associations with Epicureanism and therefore atheism. Most corpuscularianists also believed that these minute particles could in theory be divided and in this way contributed to the development of modern chemistry. For more on Cavendish's critique of "chymical philosophy," see Clucas, "Margaret Cavendish's Materialist Critique"; Wilkins, "'Exploding.'" See also Cavendish, *Observations* 227–41.

even the smallest quantities) (p. 74).[1] This tripartite substance composes "all kinds and sorts of Creatures, as Animals, Vegetables, Minerals, Elements, or what Creatures soever there are in Nature," which take shape via "the Associations of Parts, into particular Societies, which we name, *Particular Creatures*" (pp. 67, 208). Taken together, the aggregate whole of this blended matter makes up the totality of the universe and is both infinite and eternal.[2] Moreover, because all things are made of this combination of rational, sensitive, and inanimate matter, all things know, perceive, and move. For instance, a rock knows, perceives, and moves, but in its own distinct way and according to its own principles.

Another fundamental tenet of Cavendish's materialist natural philosophy is continual motion: all things exist and take on their unique forms—or what Cavendish often calls "Societies"—via the "figurative motions" of sentient matter. Of course, motion was also central to the doctrines of other seventeenth-century philosophers, especially the mechanists, who proposed that nature operates "like a machine" and thus according to a set of fundamental laws based on the collision of parts. But Cavendish consciously wrote against mechanist accounts of nature by suggesting that matter moves with "natural Free-will," or by its own conscious action, rather than involuntary reaction (p. 117). That is, because all matter is intelligent, perceptive, and has the capacity for self-motion, it chooses to move itself in certain ways rather than obeying laws of brute force. As Cavendish elaborates, there are "occasional" causes—or events that spur action, like a billiards cue hitting a ball—but the primary cause for all motion, and hence all life and natural change, is self-directed and volitional (so, in this analogy, the ball moves itself). Despite this constant, self-directed motion, nature still functions in a well-ordered,

---

1 However, Cavendish explores the conjectural possibility of the rational parts separating from the other parts in her Appendix to *Grounds*. See pp. 186–222.

2 In the seventeenth century, these eternal and infinite qualities were often associated with God; however, Cavendish elucidates that nature is material (or "a Body") while God is immaterial, and thus they are infinite and eternal in different ways. See Cavendish, *Philosophical Letters* 8–13; see also Detlefsen, "Margaret Cavendish"; Mendelson, "God of Nature"; Boyle, *The Well-Ordered Universe* 106–14, and "Margaret Cavendish."

harmonious, and rational manner because its parts are wise enough to understand that a "sympathetical" system—where matter agrees to move in mutually beneficial ways—is better for all things that exist within that system (p. 100). Importantly, then, Cavendish collapses ontology and epistemology by suggesting that natural matter exists only insofar as it moves and knows: "Nature ... being Self-moving, causes Infinite Variety, by the altered Actions of her Parts; every altered Action, causing both an altered Self-knowledg, and an altered Perceptive Knowledg" (p. 149). In all this, Cavendish has some ancient precedents: motion is innate, as in Epicurean philosophy, while occasional motion—where matter moves itself based on its perception of a given situation—might also have links to Stoic thought.[1]

Vitalism

Cavendish's natural philosophy is technically "vitalist" in that she posits that everything in nature—all "things, or Creatures"—is composed of living substance (p. 213). In fact, for Cavendish, there is no real death in nature, as the matter that animates a certain form or "society" simply disperses and then migrates into new forms (a process that is often magnificent: "for, what Human would not be a glorious Sun, or Starr?" [p. 205]). We should note, however, that "vitalism" encompasses a heterogeneous and often conflicting array of philosophical doctrine. For instance, Cavendish's belief that nature is a living entity loosely aligns her with other seventeenth-century vitalists like Anne Conway (1631–79), Francis Glisson (1597–1677), More, and van Helmont, whose theories animate nature and therefore refute

1 Stoic philosophy was developed by ancient Greek philosopher Zeno of Citium (c. 300 BCE); several of its propositions about nature became popular in the "neo-Stoic" movement of the late Renaissance. On Cavendish's indebtedness to Stoic philosophy, see O'Neill, "Margaret Cavendish" and "Introduction." Based on the work of Greek philosopher Epicurus (341–270 BCE), Epicurean philosophy was explained by Roman poet Lucretius (c. 99–55 BCE) in his *De rerum natura* and gained popularity in early-modern England with the rediscovery of this text. Although Cavendish remained a committed materialist, she diverged from Epicurean thought in abandoning atomism and embracing vitalism.

the pervasive mechanism of Boyle, Hobbes, and Descartes.[1] Yet unlike these thinkers, Cavendish refuses to imbue matter with any kind of spiritual substance. Cavendish's vitalism also connects at least obliquely to Stoic philosophy, which envisions all matter infused with *pneuma*, or a living substance that binds all things.[2] However, she diverges from both ancient precedent and seventeenth-century vitalism in her uncompromising materialism: Cavendish admits no immaterial "soul" or "Spirit of Nature," nor any animating quality that is not material.[3] In her system, spirits are superfluous because matter is innately mobile and intelligent (with the source of motion and thought internal to matter). Thus, she offers a unique brand of material vitalism that stands apart from other animate theories of the period, while also presaging the work of thinkers like Spinoza and Leibniz.

Perception and Panpsychism

One of the most pressing questions that seventeenth-century philosophers explored had to do with the nature of thought as well as the substances that do or can think.[4] Cavendish responds to this question in a unique way by collapsing the categories of mind and body and suggesting that thought and perception are fundamental operations of all living matter. Indeed, another defining characteristic of Cavendish's mature natural philosophy, and specifically *Grounds*, is her contention that all of nature is perceptive, self-knowing, and self-aware. This panpsychism means that all elements of nature are conscious and infused with rational knowledge. From our fingernails to the oceans and planets, everything that exists moves, perceives, and knows. Moreover, everything

---

1 Unlike other vitalists, seventeenth-century Neoplatonists like More and Cudworth retained Descartes's dualistic structure of mind and matter, although they emphasized that this relationship was flexible and mediated by an organic link (or "Spirit"). As Wilkins has pointed out, Cavendish seems to be the first philosopher to criticize More's "Spirit of Nature" in print. Cavendish also found absurd van Helmont's notion of gasses, a "category of existence between spirit and substance" ("'Exploding'" 865–66).

2 On specific similarities, see O'Neill, "Introduction" xxi–xxii.

3 On this distance between Cavendish's vitalism and the "mysticism we might associate with vitalist thought," see Killeen.

4 On these "watershed" questions, see Anstey; see also Walters, *Margaret Cavendish* 163–65.

perceives both itself and its surroundings and *decides* to act in certain ways, meaning that nature has not only sentience but also free will.[1] However, while all nature thinks and perceives, the type of knowledge and knowledge production varies from creature to creature; that is, "there are different Knowledges, in different Creatures," with the knowledge and perception of "Animal-kind," for instance, differing from that of "Mineral-kind." These "different Knowledges" are explained via the varied "Corporeal Motions" of self-moving matter. Cavendish also points out that this natural differentiation is not necessarily hierarchical: "none can be said to be *least knowing*, or *most knowing*: for, there is (in my opinion) no such thing as *least* and *most*, in Nature: for, several kinds and sorts of Knowledges, make not Knowledg to be more, or less; but only, they are different Knowledges proper to their kind" (p. 148). This radical pluralizing of knowledge means that knowledge is not always intelligible from one creature to another. For example, humans cannot perceive and know what a rock perceives and knows. By the same token, no single creature can ever attain "infinite perceptive knowledg" (p. 176). We cannot know perfectly another creature (or what it knows), nor nature in its entirety.

Cavendish's focus on the cogent, perceptive nature of all matter, as well as the "natural Free-will" with which it operates, undermines the very premise of Baconian science because it refuses to envision nature as an inert object of inquiry (p. 117). Instead, nature is a living network of thinking substance, which muddies the subject-object binary that sustains experimental science. A conscious entity, nature also moves, thinks, and perceives in ways that call into question the ethics of manipulating or "torturing" its products, as Cavendish famously expounds in *Grounds*: "Human Creatures ... wast their Time and Estates, with Fire and Furnace, cruelly torturing the Productions of

1 There is ongoing debate surrounding Cavendish's thoughts on free will, specifically whether her stance on the freedom of bodies is of the libertarian or the compatibilist variety. For the libertarian interpretation, see Boyle, "Freedom and Necessity" and *The Well-Ordered Universe* 105–14; and Detlefsen, "Atomism" and "Margaret Cavendish." For a compatibilist reading, see Cunning, *Cavendish*, esp. 210–26, and "Margaret Lucas Cavendish." On free will as it relates to political theory and theology, and on nature as nominally free within certain prescribed limits, see Walters, *Margaret Cavendish* 138–94, esp. 178–80.

Nature, to make their Experiments" (pp. 213–14).[1] Moreover, since humans are simply one tiny part of a vast, continuous, and all-encompassing natural system, we lack the perspective to perceive and understand it completely; this, too, directly undermines the Baconian goal of assembling a comprehensive "history" or account of all natural phenomena. Cavendish's panpsychism therefore has interesting parallels with modern critiques of the Anthropocene and, specifically, eco-criticism. It also aligns with certain feminist critiques of the history of science.[2]

According to Cavendish, all natural matter produces knowledge in two primary ways: self-knowledge, which is "interior" knowledge, and perception, which is the knowledge of "exterior parts." This latter topic was a point of great debate in late-seventeenth-century natural philosophy—and is still debated by philosophers and neuroscientists today—and Cavendish considers it extensively in *Grounds*. Like her natural philosophy in general, her theory of perception draws together elements of ancient and contemporary thought and is based, unsurprisingly, on the figurative corporeal motions of natural matter. For her, perception occurs when one creature encounters and gains knowledge about the external parts of another: "*Perception* is a sort of Knowledg, that hath reference to Objects; that is, Some Parts to know other Parts" (p. 68). Yet Cavendish makes a conscious departure from mechanical theories of perception, which were based on actual collision or contact between particles: "Objects are not the cause of Perception; for the cause of Perception is Self-motion." While Cavendish concedes that perception could not likely occur without external objects to perceive, she is careful to indicate that those objects do not and cannot cause perception; instead, perception is a defining feature of the living substance that composes the universe: "corporeal motions cannot be without Parts, and so not without Perception" (p. 69). In her non-mechanical explanation, perception occurs when the sensitive parts "copy or pattern" the animating motions of external things and then convey this

1 Cavendish likely had in mind several recent and well-publicized experiments conducted by The Royal Society of London, including blood transfusions between dogs and the dissection of live animals. She might also be referring to alchemists like van Helmont, who employed "Fire and Furnace" in their experiments. For more on the ethics of consuming animals, see pp. 204–05.

2 See Keller.

knowledge to the rational parts. Hence, Cavendish specifies that perception is actually a two-fold process, or what she calls "Double Perception": "Sensitive Perception" entails sensitive matter "patterning" the motions of another object, and, in the next step, "Rational Perception" occurs when rational matter copies those motions of the sensitive (p. 69). As Cavendish sees it, rational matter is actually better at perceiving because it is "freer, (being not a painful Labourer) [and] can more easily make an united Perception, than the Sensitive.... Whereas the Sensitive makes but Perceptions in part, of one and the same Object" (p. 69). This means that rational perception has a certain supervisory and combinational power—a role not unlike that of "understanding" in later Lockean metaphysics—that sensitive perception lacks. Or, as Deborah Boyle suggests, "rational perception is a kind of consciousness of the sensitive perception."[1] Indeed, Cavendish argues that the rational and sensitive parts can perceive each other (even though they remain indivisible).

We might be inclined to imagine that the sensitive parts of any creature are located in the sensory organs—or, for instance, that humans "pattern" images via the eyes. This assumption is sometimes encouraged by Cavendish herself, who tends to create confusing analogies between the human body and organic matter (with the brain analogous to rational matter and the eyes and muscles like sensitive matter). But this is not the case. Our eyes certainly perceive, but all of our other parts do, too. For example, our lungs "perceive" via "Respirations; which is one sort of Human Perception: for, all Parts of all Creatures, are perceptive one way, or another." Even "Artificial [or manmade] Productions are Perceptive," while the general phenomenon of perceptive imitation also explains things like imprints in the snow, cooling winds, mirror reflections, and remedies for disease (p. 184). As Cavendish clarifies, not all perception is "patterning," and there are likely many types of perception that humans do not and cannot know.[2] However varied and pervasive, though, perception is always limited because it can offer only superficial information: "Exterior Parts of one Creature, can but perceive the Exterior Parts of another Creature." Knowledge of "Interior Parts" can only by formed via the always provisional

1 *The Well-Ordered Universe* 77.

2 Michaelian 41.

"Conceptions" of rational matter: "for, neither the Sense, nor Reason, can perceive what is not present, but by rote, as after the manner of Conceptions" (p. 77).

Conception is a kind of mirror opposite of perception: that is, while perception operates on "Foreign Parts" or "present Objects," conceptions "have no such strict dependency" and are therefore more free and autonomous (p. 95). In conception, rational matter works upon its "own Parts," performing more complex cognitive activities by reflecting on and recombining the information received from sensitive matter, as well, we assume, as its various forms of self-knowledge. Technically, the sensitive parts can also conceive, but less proficiently—and often in "an irregular manner; as when a Human Creature is in some violent Passion, Mad, Weak, or the like Distempers" (p. 95). Conception, then, occurs when rational or sensitive parts "do move by Rote, and not by Example," and this type of thought is always more fecund than perception: "it is to be noted, That the Rational parts can move in more various Figurative Actions than the Sensitive; which is the cause that a Human Creature hath more Conceptions than Perceptions; so that the Mind can please it self with more variety of Thoughts than the Sensitive with variety of Objects" (p. 95). Conception includes a broad range of mental activities, including consideration, conjecture, memory, "Fancies, Imaginations, *&c.*," dreaming, understanding, worrying, and all "such Actions of the Mind, as concern not Forrein Objects" (p. 100). For instance, Cavendish describes dreaming in *Grounds* as a type of conception whereby the rational corporeal motions "act by rote, ... making mixt Figures of several Objects" (p. 112). Similarly, she describes imagination as an autonomous, joyful pursuit, one "easier and more delightful" than perception (p. 111), that occurs when rational matter is liberated from patterning external objects and instead creates novelty of its own accord (with these fancies remaining, of course, material, or at least embodied in the material motions of the mind). Thus, "Man can enjoy Worlds of [his] own making, without the assistance of the Sensitive Parts ... but certainly, as the pleasures of the Rational Parts are beyond those of the Sensitive, so are their Troubles" (p. 103). This account of imagination is directly at odds with that of Hobbes, who sees imagination as a kind of "decaying sense" that is inferior to rational thought.[1] However,

1 Hobbes, *Leviathan* 41–51.

it does correspond loosely with Hobbes's view of pleasure as unimpeded vital motion.[1]

Unlike perception and, obliquely, conception, self-knowledge has nothing to do with external objects and is instead "innate and fixt."[2] In her later work, Cavendish identifies at least three types of self-knowledge.[3] First, all organic matter is self-aware and thus recognizes how it exists and moves in any given moment. As Cavendish explains, "If Nature were not Self-knowing, Self-living, and also Perceptive, she would run into Confusion: for, there could be neither Order, nor Method, in Ignorant motion; neither would there be distinct kinds or sorts of Creatures, nor such exact and methodical Varieties as there are: for, it is impossible to make orderly and methodical Distinctions, or distinct Orders, by Chances" (p. 68).[4] Second, all parts of nature recognize how they are supposed to behave given their own unique natures (or "actions proper to their Compositions," which are governed by "Natural Rules") (p. 74).[5] In *Grounds*, Cavendish demonstrates this point by likening the human body to a commonwealth: "for, every Part, or Corporeal Motion, knows its own Office; like as Officers in a Common-wealth, although they may not be acquainted with each other, yet they know their Employments" (p. 91). In the healthy human body, "every Part knows his own Work, [and] there is Order and Method" (p. 80). Although free to act as it chooses ("every Creature may chuse whether they will

1 Sarasohn, *Natural Philosophy* 59.

2 Cavendish, *Observations* 16.

3 While this applies to all matter, Cavendish can perceive only what is perceivable to humans and therefore cannot describe the "infinite several Self-knowledges and Perceptions" that must arise from the "infinite ... Corporeal Figurative Motions" of nature (p. 91). For details on these three types of self-knowledge, see Boyle, *The Well-Ordered Universe* 104–14.

4 See also *Observations* 159–60.

5 On this "knowledge how," see Michaelian 46–47 and Detlefsen, "Margaret Cavendish," esp. 427–31. There is some debate among historians of philosophy about whether Cavendish does indeed endorse a normative account of nature, whereby different entities know both what they do and what they should do and decide to act accordingly. For instance, see Boyle, *The Well-Ordered Universe* 23–30, which advocates the normative interpretation, and Lascano's review of Boyle's book, which questions this reading. See also Detlefsen, "Atomism."

follow those [Natural] Rules"),[1] organic matter naturally inclines toward harmonious and orderly behavior due to "Self-love, ... which is an innate Nature," recognizing that "sympathetical" motions better preserve its existence (or "its Interior, or Innate Nature or Figure"), as well as "an united Love" for its own "Society" and "a Rational Fear of a disuniting, or dissolving" (pp. 100, 130). Finally, in addition to knowing itself and its environs, and knowing how to move so as to maintain order and harmony, Cavendish also suggests that self-knowledge includes the knowledge of the existence of God (even if we cannot know details about God's essence).[2] All of these types of self-knowledge are "interior" and "innate."

In light of the pervasive knowledge that suffuses natural matter, we might turn once more to the question of causation and free will: Cavendish distinguishes between conception and perception by claiming that conception operates "by Rote, and not by Example," whereas perception occurs because of some external trigger—or is "occasioned" (p. 95). She explains motion, and all natural change, in a similar way (e.g., when a bat hits a ball, the ball perceives the bat as an "occasion" to move). We should note, however, that Cavendish does not suggest that "occasioned" actions are involuntary. Instead, there are certain prompts or conditions that lead matter to "chuse" to act, with intent and volition, in a certain way (p. 191). As Deborah Boyle explains, "both occasioned and voluntary actions arise through free acts of will."[3] The real distinction between voluntary and occasioned motions is that voluntary motions move entirely at their own discretion and according to their own designs, whereas occasioned motions occur when matter decides to move when confronted

---

1 Here Cavendish discusses religion and distinguishes between "Natural Rules" that creatures choose to obey, and "Divine Prescriptions and Rules, [that] must be" abided (p. 191). Elsewhere, she emphasizes that "Corporeal Motions" are not "bound" to their prescribed "Works" (p. 81). See also pp. 97–98, 158.

2 Cavendish's suggestion that humans have innate knowledge of the existence of God has clear parallels with Descartes's claim that knowledge of God is "innate" because God "placed that idea within [us], so that it would be, as it were, the mark of the master craftsman impressed in his own work." See *Meditations* 64. See also More, esp. 26–32.

3 *The Well-Ordered Universe*, 101. For a contrasting view, see Cunning, *Cavendish* 210–42.

with specific objects, actions, or situations. They are therefore a response of sorts, but not an obligatory one. This account of perception and volitional action obviously counters mechanical and specifically Hobbesian understandings of nature.[1] It also opens the possibility that natural matter might choose to violate natural "Rules," as well as its own natural inclinations. Since organic matter is governed by "Self-love" and "united Love," however, it is uncertain why nature does occasionally cause discord or "*put her self to pain*" (p. 117).[2] In *Grounds*, Cavendish suggests that this happens due to "some Irregularities" in certain parts; when there are disagreements between parts; or when certain parts are compelled to go along with the irregular motions of others (p. 91).[3] She also suggests that humans are far more likely than other creatures to violate the natural order because of their ambition: our actions are often guided by "desires that cause strife and disorder on a scale not seen in the rest of the natural world."[4]

The Limited Knowledge of Finite Beings

As noted across this introduction, Cavendish emphasizes that natural creatures can never attain complete or "perfect knowledg" of themselves, other creatures, or the totality of nature (p. 187): "there is no single Creature in Nature, that is able to know the perfectest Truth."[5] "Human Creatures," specifically, cannot "know any otherwise, but in part: for, being composed of parts, ... he can have but a parted knowledg." This is "parted knowledg" both because it is partial, or incomplete, and also because it is literally "composed of parts," with the "different composed part[s] of his Body, [creating] different sorts of Self-knowledg, as also, different sorts of Perceptions" (p. 93). That is to say, all creatures contain a kind of kaleidoscopic knowledge that they aggregate but do not perfectly unite. Yet while we cannot attain comprehensive knowledge or totalizing perspectives, and lack perceptive access to both the interior

1 See O'Neill, "Introduction" 82; Hutton, "In Dialogue."

2 For more on these "deviant actions," see Detlefsen, "Margaret Cavendish" 428, which argues that natural and divine laws are suggestions, not requirements.

3 This in turn complicates the freedom of certain parts; see Boyle, *The Well-Ordered Universe* 115–17.

4 Boyle, *The Well-Ordered Universe* 118–19.

5 *Philosophical Letters* 244–45.

parts of other creatures and the largesse of nature, we can still conceive and imagine what those entities are like. Indeed, for a rationalist like Cavendish, conception and imagination play a vital role in filling in the gaps of what we do not or cannot perceive.[1] This same caveat holds true for the pursuit of natural philosophy: we cannot know all of nature, but, with our perspectival contingencies always in mind, we can make informed hypotheses about natural phenomena.[2]

Cavendish's emphasis on the partial and conjectural nature of human knowledge has suggestive parallels with modern notions of "situatedness," or the recognition that our capacity to know certain things arises from a particular time, place, and situation. It also contrasts sharply with the quest for comprehensive knowledge that characterizes the earliest and most enthusiastic phases of British empiricism, when authors like Bacon, Hooke, and Thomas Sprat (1635–1713) championed the transparency and ultimate knowability of "Nature's endless treasury."[3] Cavendish reminds these men—in *Grounds*, and in her other Restoration work like *Observations* and *Philosophical Letters*—that human observers are not above nature but rather just one small part of a vast, living, and infinitely varied system that exists in a state of continual transformation. As Cavendish argues, even Nature cannot know herself perfectly:

> Although Nature knows her self, and hath a free power of her self; ... yet, Nature cannot be an upright, and just Judg of her self, and so not of any of her Parts; because every particular part is a part of her self. Besides, as she is Self-moving, she is Self-changeing, and so she is alterable: Wherefore, nothing can be a perfect, and a just Judg, but something that is Individable, and Unalterable, which is the

1 For a similar claim about imagination, see Hobbes, *The English Works* 458–59.

2 See Cavendish, "An Epistle to the Unbeleeving Readers in Natural Philosophy," *PPO* (1655), 51–53. See also Boyle, *The Well-Ordered Universe* 109.

3 Cowley, "To the Royal Society." Of course, many other seventeenth-century philosophers believed that human knowledge can only be probabilistic, especially Robert Boyle, Charleton, and Glanvill. See Clucas, "Variation"; and Siegfried, "City of Chance."

> Infinite GOD, who is Unmoving, Immutable, and so Unalterable; who is the Judg of the Infinite Corporeal Actions of his Servant Nature. (p. 71)

Put simply: There is no comprehensive viewpoint available to finite creatures—or even "Nature her self"—from which to "Judg" the whole. Only "the Infinite GOD," who is not only supernatural but also "Unmoving" and "Immutable"—that is, static—can see and understand the infinite workings of his productions as they exist and transform. As *Grounds* continually reminds readers, there is much that we cannot "possibly conceive or imagine," in terms of both inner essences and the totalities of the cosmos (p. 205).

Of course, for Cavendish, our inability to access "perfect knowledg" extends also to God, which results in a kind of radical fideism (or the belief "that God is unknowable and therefore cannot be understood by human reason"[1]). According to Cavendish, there are in fact several obstacles in human attempts to know God: first, we are natural, material creatures and thus cannot perceive or have substantive knowledge about "a supernatural, immaterial" entity like God.[2] Furthermore, God is not only immaterial but also infinite and therefore beyond the comprehension of finite beings. For these reasons, across her early work Cavendish is relatively uninterested in discussing religious matters, which fall outside the scope of "Pure natural Philosophy" and belong instead to "Theology."[3] Such dichotomizing aligns her with Hobbes but distinguishes her sharply from Neoplatonists like More, neo-Epicureans like Charleton, and vitalists like van Helmont, who were all invested in integrating natural philosophy and Christianity. Cavendish recognized

---

1 Sarasohn, *Natural Philosophy* 35–36. For more on Cavendish and knowledge of God, see Cunning, *Cavendish*, esp. 106; Sarasohn, "Fideism"; Mendelson, "God of Nature"; Siegfried, "God and the Question." Cavendish follows Hobbes in dichotomizing religion and natural philosophy but, unlike him, frequently proclaims her faith and argues that Christianity and natural philosophy *can* coexist. See Clucas, "'A double Perception.'" See also Hutton, "In Dialogue" 428; Hobbes, *Elements of Philosophy* 411.

2 *Observations* 88. For more on knowledge of the existence of God versus knowledge of God himself, see *Observations* 88–90.

3 *PPO* (1663), sig. b2[v].

that her material vitalism might be viewed as incompatible with orthodox Christianity and thus asked readers to "account me not an Atheist, but beleeve as I do in God Almighty."[1] And, in her later work of the 1660s, "she takes greater pains to establish the boundaries between God and Nature, and between theology and natural philosophy."[2] In *Grounds*, for instance, she suggests that Nature has self-knowledge and power, and exists in a perpetual state of transformation, but is "limited" because it cannot create, annihilate, or transform the material into the immaterial (like God) (p. 71). She also suggests that Nature carries out God's will (and thus that God is the source of natural laws).[3] In addition, she incorporates innate knowledge of God into self-knowledge: all creatures know God's existence, "even if we cannot know the essence of that being."[4] Despite her careful treatment of God's supremacy in *Grounds*, Cavendish's emphasis on God's unknowability borders on agnosticism. Her philosophy explores

---

1 *PPO* (1655), sig. a[3r]. Alarmist attitudes toward atheism accelerated in seventeenth-century England, with "atheism" functioning as "an umbrella term" for "many different forms of heterodoxy," including denial of the immortality of the soul and materialism of the type that Hobbes and Cavendish espoused. Epicurean philosophy in particular was attacked because it did not acknowledge divine first causes and posited the dissolution of soul after death. See Sarasohn, *Natural Philosophy* 86; see also Sheppard 90–136.

2 Clucas, "'A double Perception'" 122.

3 This might, as Boyle suggests, problematize the free will of Nature (*The Well-Ordered Universe* 110–14). But Cavendish might also suggest that Nature has a conditional free will, which, like the human version, is a "gift from God" and not absolute. See Clucas, "'A double Perception'" 122; Walters, *Margaret Cavendish*, esp. 175–76.

4 Boyle, *The Well-Ordered Universe* 107. Boyle and Siegfried disagree with other scholars—including Cunning, Detlefsen, and Sarasohn—that Cavendish's ontology "absolutely preclude[s]" knowledge of God, suggesting instead that she makes allowances for some knowledge of God (Detlefsen, "Margaret Cavendish" 434). See Boyle, *The Well-Ordered Universe* 107–14; Siegfried, "God and the Question" 72.

"Nature's Fundamental actions" and "Productions," but not "GOD's Decrees" (pp. 118, 188).

Bodily Health and Disease

The first and second editions of *Philosophical and Physical Opinions* and *Grounds of Natural Philosophy* are not only philosophical but also medical texts.[1] Although Cavendish pared down the medical sections of *Grounds* compared to the first and second editions of *Philosophical and Physical Opinions* and does not discuss remedies as she does in those earlier texts, at least a quarter of *Grounds* is devoted to the etiology of human disease. Here she catalogues what she calls "Fundamental Diseases"—pain, sickness, weakness, dizziness, faintness, numbness, "Deadness," and "Fainting and Swounding"—as well as a wide range of specific disorders, from bubonic plague to gout (pp. 121–22). Unsurprisingly, Cavendish believes that our bodies function just as the rest of nature does, and she accounts for health and illness via the regular or irregular motions of self-moving matter. She also engages two models of physiology that were competing for prominence in late-seventeenth-century England. The first is Galenic medicine, which adopted the humoral theory of Greek physician, surgeon, and philosopher Galen (130–210 CE). The second, more modern school of thought to which Cavendish responds is now called "iatrochemistry" and was based on the work of the Swiss physician, alchemist, and astrologist Paracelsus (1493/94–1541) and, in the seventeenth century, Flemish chemist and physician Jan Baptist van Helmont. More broadly speaking, Cavendish wrote at a transitional moment in the history of English understandings of the human body, as new, mechanical theories of physiology began to supersede humoral ones. For instance, William Harvey's (1578–1657) discovery of the circulation of blood contributed to mechanist views of bodily function, yet much remained unknown and traditional concepts of humors and "animal spirits" persisted well into the eighteenth century.

The dominant model of medicine in Cavendish's era, Galenism posited that the body contains four humors—blood,

1 In the seventeenth century, medical knowledge fell under the larger rubric of "natural philosophy," as we see in the work of many who were not trained physicians (e.g., Robert Boyle, Descartes, and Hobbes). However, healing and traditional remedies were often considered the domain of women.

phlegm, yellow bile, and black bile—which were each associated with some combination of the four qualities of hot, cold, moist, and dry.[1] Illness occurred when these humors became unbalanced, and hence remedies involved the application of contraries; for instance, excess cold and dryness could be treated by remedies that were hot and moist. By contrast, Paracelsian and Helmontian medicine propounded the therapeutic use of metals (e.g., arsenic, mercury, or antinomy). Although based on Paracelsianism, Helmontian medicine was more radical than its predecessor in that it rejected entirely traditional notions of the humors and the four elements. From the 1650s onwards, English thinkers and practitioners were increasingly exposed to this chemical alternative to Galenism, and, by the mid-1660s, the controversy between the two schools reached its apex in England.[2] While notorious on the continent for his belief in "natural magic," van Helmont gained great traction in England, especially after 1649, when Charleton, a prominent English philosopher and friend of Cavendish, published English translations of his work (with several other English translations to follow). Cavendish knew van Helmont's *Oriatrike, or Physick Refined* (1662) and was deeply critical of his "Paradoxical Opinions," his "strange," "harsh," and perplexing terminology, and his prolixity,[3] as well as his "mixture of Divinity, and natural Philosophy."[4] She is more amenable to Galenic medicine, or

---

1 However, we must note that "there was no single set of beliefs to which the followers of Galen all adhered." Although Galenism was endorsed by The Royal College of Physicians, most of the nation's practitioners would have combined humoral theories with traditional, homeopathic treatments, and even some elements of iatrochemistry (Boyle, *The Well-Ordered Universe* 216–18).

2 Broad, "Cavendish" 51; Boyle, *The Well-Ordered Universe* 218–19. In Cavendish's era, this conflict was fuelled by the exigencies of the Great Plague of 1665–66.

3 *Philosophical Letters* 384, 234, 239, 379. See also Clucas, "Variation." In *Philosophical Letters,* Cavendish criticizes Helmontianism but not Paracelsianism (see, for example, 351); in *Observations,* however, she rejects both (see especially 231). For details, see Boyle, *The Well-Ordered Universe* 224–25.

4 *Philosophical Letters* 248. Like Paracelsus, van Helmont based "his chemical philosophy on a close, literal reading of the Bible" (Broad, "Cavendish" 52). See also Clucas, "Margaret Cavendish's Materialist Critique."

"the old approved and practised way of the Schools," likely because it is more compatible with her organic materialism.[1] She might also have sided with Galenism because it was endorsed by elite practitioners, while Helmontianism was often associated with "the ranks of the Puritans."[2]

In *Grounds,* then, Cavendish demonstrates that she is up to date with medical developments and tends to espouse humoral theory while veering away from iatrochemistry. But she also liberally adapts Galenism and subordinates it to her own philosophical system. For Cavendish, bodily health constitutes the "regular" and "well-ordered" motions of organic matter within a particular body or "society"; that is, all the motions of all of the various parts communicate and function as they should and are therefore free from "Disorder" (pp. 91, 120). By contrast, she accounts for disease via the irregular motions of organic parts, which cause "Uproar and Confusion" (p. 130). In addition, the body contains "many sorts of Humours"—including but not limited to the four traditional ones—that are "so necessary, that the Body could not well subsist without them; yet, a Superfluity of them is as dangerous." These humors are distinct from other parts because they "may be divided ... without danger to the whole Body; so that they are somewhat like Excremental parts" (p. 118). Thus, Cavendish abides by humoral theory in suggesting that a build-up or imbalance of humors can lead to disease, but only insofar as this leads to the irregular motion of organic matter: "There are many sorts of Human Diseases; yet all sorts of Diseases are Irregular Corporeal Motions" (p. 121). While minor "Errors" in the self-motion of matter occur all the time—for example, "when one man cannot readily remember another man, with whom he had formerly been acquainted, it is an Error; and such small Errors, the Sense and Reason do soon rectifie"—"high Irregularities" cause more serious problems like "Madness, Sickness, and the like" that are not so easily corrected (p. 108).

Cavendish explains consumption, for instance, by the irregular "Wasting and Dis-uniting of the Fundamental Parts" that "steal away by degrees; and so, by degrees, the Society of a Human Creature is dissolved" (p. 134). She traces madness to the irregular motions of either sensitive or rational matter (or both)

---

1 *Philosophical Letters* 384.

2 Boyle, *The Well-Ordered Universe* 221.

that cause misconceptions and misperceptions.[1] Illness spreads by what Cavendish calls "Imitation," whereby organic matter "imitates" or "copies" the actions of other parts (within that same "society" or between different creatures). Like her theory of perception, this theory of contagion presumes the conscious action of organic matter: "Infection is an act of Imitation: for, one Part cannot give another Part a Disease, but only that some imitate the same sort of Irregular Actions of other Parts; of which some are near adjoining Imitators, and some occasion a general Mode" (i.e., some are localized, some systemic) (p. 132). Far from the passive reception of disease, here the cogent, self-moving parts mimic or are persuaded by the irregular motions of other parts (and such other parts can be internal parts, people, objects, food, "Vapours," "Poysons," etc.). Again like perception, some diseases are "occasioned" (or triggered) and some are voluntary (when a body spontaneously decides to move irregularly). Indeed, characteristically resisting "universal explanations," Cavendish specifies that not all irregular motion stems from "patterning"; for instance, irregularity might also occur due to an unprompted "Decay of the Vital Parts" (p. 135).[2] She also suggests the rational parts of a creature can cause illness by "Conceit"; that is, the sensitive parts "take a pattern from the Rational," which collapses the occasional and spontaneous in that organic matter directs itself awry (p. 130).[3] We should note, however, that irregular motions are not unnatural: "Nature poysing her Actions by Opposites, there must needs be Irregularities, as well as Regularities" (p. 96). Instead, "they are not *typical*."[4]

Another important facet of Cavendish's account of human physiology is her view of "generation" (or what we would now call reproduction). In the Aristotelian tradition, women were considered passive matter—or the vessel that nourished human life but did not contribute to its form. By contrast, both Galenic and Paracelsian doctrines presumed that both sexes contributed to generation, even if their specific contributions remained mysterious. In *Grounds*, Cavendish

1 And, since all nature is sentient, all parts can literally go mad. See p. 128.

2 Boyle, *The Well-Ordered Universe* 234.

3 Many others believed that the imagination could have physically deleterious results, especially in the case of a woman and her developing fetus; see Broad, "Cavendish" 56.

4 Boyle, *The Well-Ordered Universe* 228.

eradicates gender from this conversation by suggesting that all parts of natural matter contribute to "Production" because its "Self-moving Parts, or Corporeal Motions, are the Producers of all Composed Figures, such as we name *Creatures*." In other words, generation is "only a Society of particular Parts, that joyn into particular Figures, or Creatures" (p. 80). If an association of moving parts makes up the "Fabricks of all Creatures," then these material parts are both "Producer" and "produced": "No Animal, or Vegetable, could be produced, ... without some Corporeal Motions of their Producers; that is, some of the Producer's Self-moving Parts" (pp. 83–84).[1] Furthermore, if life is a fundamental principle of organic matter, then nature is always already living and simply assembles (or dissolves) particular formations. Thus, there is no entirely new matter, and no "annihilation" or death either (Appendix B, p. 236). Instead, natural matter exists in a "perpetual" state of production and dissolution, with its "infinite varieties of Corporeal Figurative Motions" producing "infinite varieties" of "Productions" (p. 83).

In the arena of medicine, and especially her privileging of Galenism over newer, chemical alternatives, Cavendish is decidedly "old guard," as Jacqueline Broad has illustrated. However, some of Cavendish's medical thinking can be seen to anticipate or at least loosely correlate with modern medical knowledge. For instance, she sided with van Helmont in viewing illness as a material entity rather than a humoral imbalance, which prefigures contemporary understandings of disease.[2] Moreover, Cavendish's theory of imitation has some currency in light of contemporary genetics, as we now understand that the operations of our genes and cells can malfunction and spread this corruption to other parts. Her material theory of mind also aligns loosely with contemporary neuroscience, which approaches the mind as a material entity and mental illness as a disorder of transmission (with certain synapses misfiring, or, in Cavendish's terms, a miscommunication between material, moving parts). That said, medical beliefs vary drastically from age to age and place to place and cannot be understood as a simple teleology. Instead, we must view *Grounds* within the

1 Concepts of heredity remained elusive well into the eighteenth century. For more on resemblances between "Producers" and "Off-springs," see pp. 83–84.

2 Broad, "Cavendish" 53.

context of seventeenth-century English medical practice, and specifically Galenism, Paracelsianism, and Helmontianism.

Writing Style and Form

Cavendish's writing style is idiosyncratic, even taking into account the significant differences between seventeenth-century and modern philosophical writing.[1] Her tone, especially, is skeptical and bemused, sometimes veering toward biting satire and sometimes playful or even slapstick humor. By the 1660s, she had also developed an even more acute awareness of the limits of any single perspective and a certain defensiveness about being misinterpreted or attacked, as evinced in various stylistic quirks (e.g., the resounding phrases "mistake me not," "in my opinion," and "I cannot possibly conceive").[2] Cavendish also emphasizes her common-sense approach to metaphysics and her lack of formal education, or "want of Learning," which are important aspects of her anti-scholasticism (p. 157).[3] Another distinctive tendency is her staging of "Warrs" or "Disputes amongst the Parts of [her] Mind," which transforms contemplation into dramatic spectacle (p. 117). Along the same lines, Cavendish habitually records dialogues between the parts of her mind in order to weigh multiple or even conflicting opinions; this, too, creates a kind of multi-dimensionality, or a theatre of differing perspectives that compete to isolate the most likely principles.[4] To be sure, conversations were a common feature of both ancient and early modern European philosophy. But Cavendish employs this mode distinctly by not simply forwarding her own views—although she remains committed to organic materialism—but instead demonstrating the fundamental uncertainty of human knowledge and the infinite possibilities of nature. Such "Warrs" and dialogues also serve to open debates to readers: we, too, must decide, based on only imperfect knowledge, what might or

---

1 On Cavendish's writing in the context of the "essayistic probabilism of mid-seventeenth-century philosophical discourse," see Clucas, "Variation."

2 "Mistake me not" appears 23 times in *Grounds*; "in my opinion" appears 38 times, with 13 of these instances as parenthetical asides.

3 As Cavendish specifies, "Principles ought to be easie, plain, and without any difficulty to be understood" (*Philosophical Letters* 242). On her anti-scholasticism, see Clucas, "Variation"; Siegfried, "City of Chance"; Wilkins, "Margaret Cavendish."

4 On how these internal disputes might critique the Cartesian theory of mind, see Siegfried, "God and the Question" 69.

might not be true. For Cavendish, the practice of philosophy does not depend on scholastic training or pedantic terminology but instead on natural "Wit" and "Contemplation" (p. 54). She "rejects in advance any claims to absolute discursive authority," insisting instead that anyone with "sense and reason" can observe and hypothesize about nature (p. 53).[1]

Epistemology and style also collide, sometimes uncomfortably, in the radical symmetry of Cavendish's natural philosophy, which is, in essence, a theory of everything. For her, all natural matter knows, thinks, and moves, which creates a dizzying imbrication of macro and micro whereby all parts of nature consist of the same base substance that operates in the same way (although Cavendish does emphasize the infinitely varied effects of the infinitely varied motions of organic matter). For instance, the moon is made of the same stuff as Cavendish's quill; similarly, human bodies typify all rational, living matter. Cavendish's rhetorical and epistemological investment in this uniformity—however versatile the productions of continuous, uniform matter—can work both for and against her. That is, such patterning serves as an alluring epistemological position and powerful rhetorical tool, but it can also flatten distinctions and negate complexity. In *Grounds*, Cavendish often illustrates bodily malfunctions via natural phenomena—for example, "shaking palsies" occur after illness "as when a House shakes in a great Wind, or Storm"—which can collapse distinctions between significantly different phenomena (p. 114). Similarly, she frequently compares physiological operations to learned social responses: "for it is, many times, amongst the Interior Motions of the Body, as with the Exterior Actions of Men" (p. 120). On one hand, this makes sense, as the same basic principles govern all things. On the other hand, this is an imperfect analogy, as it elides the procedures of, say, the stomach and a courtier, as well as the accumulative behavioral complexity that might occur when matter aggregates into highly specialized compounds. Yet this occasional exuberance in exposition only foregrounds the fact that natural symmetry is a crucial aspect of Cavendish's philosophy.

One other important feature of Cavendish's writing across her career is her ample use of paratextual materials, including

1 Clucas, "Variation" 204. While Cavendish can "lapse into moments of veridical insistence" (204), on the whole she resists dogmatism.

prefatory epistles, poems, and epilogues. In *Grounds*, Cavendish pares down this material, eliminating the multiple epistles that appeared in the original *Philosophical and Physical Opinions*. Yet *Grounds* includes a lengthy and important appendix in which she discusses speculative ideas that fall beyond the scope of her more formal philosophy. In fact, the appendix often reads like science fiction rather than philosophy—or, perhaps more aptly, philosophy as fiction: here we find the outer fringes of what is knowable spun out in dramatic form. Indeed, we find Cavendish at play—with ideas she finds exciting, with her readers, with her own philosophical system—in a way that emphasizes the imaginative dimensions of philosophy.

She begins the appendix with a discussion of immaterial substances, including God (with this initial section in standard chapter format like the rest of *Grounds* rather than the more experimental conversation structure that characterizes the rest of the appendix), and, in Part Two, the possibility of "other sorts of Worlds" so different that we cannot perceive them. The other worlds she goes on to investigate consist of potential loopholes in her natural philosophy—for instance, purely rational worlds (which cannot exist in nature because of the commixture of rational, sensitive, and inanimate matter) and purely regular or irregular worlds (which again cannot exist in nature and are not the same, she emphasizes, as heaven and hell). Cavendish also explores how exactly material creatures might re-form after resurrection, an attempt to reconcile materialism and Christianity that instead tends to illuminate the friction between the two doctrines. Across the appendix, Cavendish is deeply interested in the procreative function of nature, and the sites and materials that might galvanize or restore life (as well as what she calls the "Root of Human Life") (p. 216), while she also continuously employs the warring motif and eventually pushes this experimental rubric even further with a tongue-in-cheek formal "Discourse" between the parts of her mind: "*Dear Associates ...*" (p. 222). Finally, after weighing at length the possible composition and oceanic location of "Restoring-Beds, or Wombs," Cavendish stages a bizarre conflict: the thoughts located in her pineal gland—often thought to house the soul[1]—appear suddenly and accuse her former thoughts of blindly searching after the impossible (and, specifically, the

---

1 E.g., for Descartes, the pineal gland was the seat of the soul. For a useful overview, see Lokhorst.

pursuit of the fabled "Philosopher-Stone") (p. 222). Angered, her original thoughts castigate these newcomers.

This silly, stagey personification of cogitation seems at first an unexpected conclusion to *Grounds of Natural Philosophy*. Yet it might also provide the perfect ending, as Cavendish foregrounds the radically provisional nature of human knowledge by making light of her *own* thinking and writing and, specifically, opening her philosophy to charges of pure fantasy.[1] In other words, she anticipates and dramatizes the condemnation of her own system to illustrate its radical contingency, which is, of course, an essential aspect of her philosophical thinking.

---

1 Cavendish recognized the fine line between philosophy and fiction and often accused others like More of pure fabrication. See Wilkins, "'Exploding.'"

Margaret Cavendish: A Brief Chronology

1623 Margaret Lucas, later Cavendish, born at St. John's Abbey near Colchester in Essex. She is the eighth and final child of Thomas Lucas and Elizabeth Leighton.

1625 Margaret's father, Thomas Lucas, dies.

Accession of Charles I, who weds Henrietta Maria of France.

1626 Francis Bacon dies.

c. 1630 Thomas Hobbes begins teaching natural philosophy to William Cavendish, Earl (and later Marquis and Duke) of Newcastle, and his brother, Charles Cavendish.

1631 Anne Finch, later Conway, born.

1641 René Descartes publishes *Meditations on First Philosophy.*

1642 Beginning of the English Civil War.

Margaret's home at St. John's Abbey plundered by anti-Royalist mob.

Hobbes publishes *De Cive.*

1643 Margaret moves to Oxford to live with her sister and later joins the court of Queen Henrietta Maria.

Elizabeth Cavendish, first wife of William, dies.

William becomes Marquis of Newcastle.

1644 William is defeated by Oliver Cromwell at the Battle of Marston Moor and flees to Hamburg.

Henrietta Maria and her court flee to Paris.

Descartes publishes *Principles of Philosophy.*

1645 Margaret meets William in court in Paris. They marry in December.

1647 Deaths of Margaret's mother (Elizabeth Lucas), sister, niece, and illegitimate brother.

1648 Sir Charles Lucas, Margaret's youngest brother, executed by Parliamentary troops after the siege of Colchester.

Margaret and William live briefly in Rotterdam and then settle in Antwerp.

1649 Charles I executed and English monarchy dissolved. Commonwealth reign commences.

William Cavendish declared traitor to Parliament and his estates confiscated.

1650 Walter Charleton translates and publishes Jan Baptist van Helmont's medical treatises in *A Ternary of Paradoxes.*

Around this time, Lucy Hutchinson translates into English verse Lucretius' ancient Epicurean text, *On the Nature of Things.*

1651 Margaret travels to London to petition Parliament for income from William's sequestered estates; she is denied.

Hobbes's *Leviathan* published.

1653 Margaret returns to Antwerp after arranging for the London publication of *Poems, and Fancies* and *Philosophicall Fancies.*

Henry More publishes *An Antidote against Atheism.*

English translation of William Harvey's 1628 *On the motion of the Heart and Blood in Animals.*

1654 Walter Charleton publishes *Physiologia Epicuro-Gassendo-Charletoniana,* based on Pierre Gassendi's *Animadversiones* (1649).

Charles Cavendish dies.

1655 Publication of *The World's Olio* and *The Philosophical and Physical Opinions.*

1656 *Nature's Pictures* published, which includes the autobiographical "A True Relation of My Birth, Breeding, and Life."

1657 Margaret corresponds with Constantijn Huygens.

1658 Death of Oliver Cromwell.

William publishes *The New Method and Extraordinary Invention to Dress Horses and Work Them According to Nature.*

1659 More publishes *The Immortality of the Soul.*

1660 Restoration of Charles II.

The Cavendishes return to England, first to London and then to Welbeck Abbey in Nottinghamshire.

A small group of philosophers form a "College for the Promoting of Physico-Mathematical Experimental Learning" (which will, in 1663, gain a royal charter as The Royal Society of London for Improving Natural Knowledge).

1661 Joseph Glanvill publishes *The Vanity of Dogmatizing.*

Robert Boyle publishes *The Sceptical Chymist.*

1662 *Orations of Divers Sorts* and *Playes* published.

Van Helmont's *Oriatrike, Or, Physick Refined* is published (the English translation of his 1648 *Ortus Medicinae*).

Joseph Glanvill publishes *Lux Orientalis ... Concerning the Prœexistence of Souls.*

1663 Second edition of *The Philosophical and Physical Opinions* published.

1664 *CCXI Sociable Letters*, *Philosophical Letters*, and the second edition of *Poems and Fancies* published.

1665 William and Margaret become Duke and Duchess of Newcastle.

Robert Hooke publishes *Micrographia: or Some Physiological Descriptions of Minute Bodies.*

The Great Plague of London, the last major occurrence of bubonic plague in England.

1666 *Observations upon Experimental Philosophy* and *Blazing World* published.

The Great Fire of London.

1667 Margaret attends a meeting of The Royal Society of London (30 May). She also publishes *The Life of the Thrice Noble … William Cavendishe.*

1668 *Grounds of Natural Philosophy* and *Plays, Never before Printed* published. The second editions of *Observations*, *Blazing World*, and *Poems and Fancies* published.

1671 Second editions of *Nature's Pictures* and *The World's Olio* published.

1673 Margaret dies suddenly on 15 December.

1674 In January, Margaret is entombed in Westminster Abbey.

1676 William edits and publishes *Letters and Poems in Honour of the Incomparable Princess, Margaret, Dutchess of Newcastle.*

William dies on 25 December and is entombed next to Margaret.

A Note on the Text

Grounds of Natural Philosophy has a long and complicated publication history that spans more than two decades. The text is derived from one of Cavendish's earliest statements of natural philosophy, *The Philosophical and Physical Opinions*, which was published in London in 1655 by John Martyn and James Allestry (eventual printers to The Royal Society of London). This first edition of *The Philosophical and Physical Opinions* consists of five parts and 210 chapters, along with numerous epistles and poems by the author; the first part, containing 58 chapters, is in fact a reprinting of *Philosophicall Fancies* (1653), Cavendish's first philosophical work. Over the following decade, Cavendish made significant changes to *Philosophical and Physical Opinions* as her thoughts on materialism, vitalism, and hylozoism evolved, and she republished the text in 1663 with William Wilson. This second, "Enlarged, ... Reformed and Corrected" version appeared with seven parts and 262 chapters, with many of the epistles excised or updated and a few new ones added.[1] Finally, Cavendish engaged printer Anne Maxwell to publish *Grounds of Natural Philosophy* in 1668, which she confusingly announces on the title page as "the *Second Edition*, much altered from the *First*, which went under the Name of Philosophical and Physical Opinions." As the third—not second—iteration of her ideas, *Grounds* is so much altered from the original, 1655 *Philosophical and Physical Opinions* that it might be considered an entirely new text. However, if we keep in our view the second, 1663 edition of *PPO*, the transformation appears more gradual. Indeed, taken together, the three texts open a unique window into the evolution of Cavendish's metaphysics from 1653 until 1668, which marks the end of her publishing career.

The copy-text for this Broadview edition of *Grounds of Natural Philosophy* is held at The British Library (shelf-mark 31 f.5) and contains the author's emendations. This copy seems to have been either Cavendish's personal copy of *Grounds* or a presentation copy that she, or a scribe, hand-corrected. While the text cannot be traced directly to Cavendish, there are some indications that it might have been hers. It arrived at The British

1 *PPO* (1663), sig. b[1r].

Library from the collections of George III and, before that, The Bridgewater Library. Founded by Sir Thomas Egerton in the Elizabethan era, this collection was passed down along the Egerton-cum-Bridgewater line; the Egertons and Cavendishes were connected via Elizabeth Cavendish, William Cavendish's daughter (and Margaret Cavendish's step-daughter), who in 1641 married John Egerton, Second Earl of Bridgewater.[1] However, because Cavendish regularly sent copies of her texts to friends, fellow philosophers, and university libraries, it could also be one of many presentation copies that were hand-corrected.[2] In either case, the emendations were certainly directed by Cavendish, as they correspond almost exactly with the annotations in several other extant copies of *Grounds*.[3] Moreover, the handwriting in this copy might also be hers, since it seems to match the handwriting in The British Library copy of *Nature's Pictures* (shelf-mark G.11599), which eighteenth-century book collector Sir Thomas Grenville catalogued as belonging to the author, as well as several other presumed instances of her handwriting.[4] In her earlier texts, Cavendish included Errata pages and often made sure that these changes were integrated into those copies to which she had access. In *Grounds*, however, there is no Errata page, so these handwritten emendations are the only record we have of her intended corrections. I have incorporated these edits into

1 Some duplicates from the Bridgewater Library were auctioned by Thomas King in 1802 and 1804—including this copy of *Grounds*—but the rest remained in the family and, in 1917, passed into the collections of The Huntington Library. See Tabor.

2 For details on the beneficiaries of her books, and the hundreds of presentation copies now available at Oxford and Cambridge, see Poole. For more on Cavendish's process of hand-correction, see Fitzmaurice, "Margaret Cavendish on Her Own Writing." Finally, on her accelerating efforts to control the quality of her printed books, see Whitaker 251.

3 For instance, those copies held at The Bodleian Library, The Folger Shakespeare Library, The Huntington Library, and King's College Cambridge.

4 E.g., another copy of *Nature's Pictures* at The British Library (841.m.25), which is said to feature Cavendish's handwriting, as well as *Poems, and Fancies* (79.h.10.), which notes corrections "by the author."

the main text and also footnoted them so that they are evident to the reader.

Throughout this edition, I have preserved Cavendish's idiosyncratic spelling and grammar. However, I have used modern typography and have silently corrected obvious printing errors, of which there are few. These include a problem with chapter numeration in Part 6 (in both the Table of Contents and the text proper); three missing chapter titles in the original Table of Contents; two misnumbered chapters in Part 3 of the Appendix; a repeated phrase in Part 11, Chapter 15; and typos in several words (e.g., "actious," changed to "actions," and "shaging palsies," changed to "shaking palsies"). For clarity, I have also standardized the use of possessives throughout the text, which Cavendish employs haphazardly. The rest of the text is as Cavendish printed it in 1668, with her later, handwritten emendations flagged in the footnotes.

GROUNDS
OF
Natural Philoſophy:
Divided into
THIRTEEN PARTS:
WITH AN
APPENDIX
CONTAINING
FIVE PARTS.

The *Second Edition*, much altered from the *Firſt*, which went under the Name of
PHILOSOPHICAL
AND
PHYSICAL OPINIONS.

Written by the
Thrice Noble, Illuſtrious, and Excellent Princeſs,
THE
DUCHESS of *NEWCASTLE.*

LONDON,
Printed by *A. Maxwell*, in the Year 1668.

To all the UNIVERSITIES IN EUROPE.

Most Learned Societies,

ALL Books, without exception, being undoubtedly under your Jurisdiction, it is very strange that some Authors of good note, are not asham'd to repine at it; and the more forward they are in judging others, the less liberty they will allow to be judg'd themselves. But, if there was not a necessity, yet I would make it my choice, To submit, willingly, to your Censures, these *Grounds of Natural Philosophy*, in hopes that you will not condemn them, because they want *Art*,[1] if they be found fraught with *Sense* and *Reason*. You are the *Starrs of the First Magnitude*, whose Influence governs the *World of Learning*; and it is my confidence, That you will be propitious to the Birth of this beloved Child of my Brain, whom I take the boldness to recommend to your Patronage; and as, if you vouchsafe to look on it favourably, I shall be extreamly obliged to your Goodness, for its everlasting Life:[2] So, if you resolve to Frown upon it, I beg the favour, That it be not buried in the hard and Rocky Grave of your Displeasure; but be suffer'd, by your gentle silence, to lye still in the soft and easie Bed of Oblivion, which is incomparably the less Punishment of the Two. It is so commonly the error of indulgent Parents, to spoil their Children out of Fondness, that I may be forgiven for spoiling This, in never putting it to suck at the Breast of some Learned Nurse, whom I might have got from among your Students, to have assisted me; but would, obstinately, suckle it my self, and bring it up alone, without the help of any Scholar:[3] Which having caused in the First Edition, (which was published under the name of *Philosophical and Physical Opinions*) many Imperfections; I have endeavoured in this Second, by many Alterations and Additions, (which have forc'd me to give it another Name) to correct them;[4]

1 I.e., rhetorical skill and polish.

2 Cavendish often describes her texts as progeny or "children" who will live forever.

3 Unlike other women philosophers of the period, such as Anne Conway (1631–79), Cavendish did not have a philosophical mentor, nor did she receive a formal education.

4 *The Philosophical and Physical Opinions* was published in 1655 and then revised and republished in 1663. In *Grounds*, Cavendish further revises these ideas to the extent that they must be published under "another Name." See A Note on the Text (p. 47).

whereby, I fear, my Faults are rather *changed* and *encreased*, than *amended*. If you expect fair Proportions in the Parts, and a Beautiful Symmetry in the Whole, having never been taught at all, and having read but little; I acknowledg my self too illiterate to afford it, and too impatient to labour much for Method. But, if you will be contented with *pure Wit*, and the Effects of *meer Contemplation*; I hope, that somewhat of that kind may be found in this Book, and in my other *Philosophical*, *Poetical*, and *Oratorical Works*: All which I leave, and this especially, to your kind Protection, and am,

Your most humble Servant,

and Admirer,

MARGARET NEWCASTLE.

A TABLE *of the* CONTENTS.

The Eleventh Part.

The Twelfth Part.

The Thirteenth Part.

APPENDIX.

The First Part.

The Second Part.

The Third Part.

GROUNDS OF Natural Philosophy.

THE FIRST PART.

CHAP. I.
Of MATTER.

Matter is that we name *Body*; which Matter cannot be less, or more, than Body: Yet some Learned Persons are of opinion, That there are Substances that are not Material Bodies. But how they can prove any sort of Substance to be no Body, I cannot tell: neither can any of Nature's Parts express it, because a Corporeal Part cannot have an Incorporeal Perception. But as for Matter, there may be degrees, as, *more pure*, or *less pure*; but there cannot be any Substances in Nature, that are between Body, and no Body: Also, Matter cannot be figureless, neither can Matter be without Parts. Likewise, there cannot be Matter without Place, nor Place without Matter; so that Matter, Figure, or Place, is but one thing: for, it is as impossible for One Body to have Two Places, as for One Place to have Two Bodies; neither can there be Place, without Body.[1]

CHAP. II.
Of MOTION.

Though Matter might be without Motion, yet Motion cannot be without Matter; for it is impossible (in my opinion) that there should be an Immaterial Motion in Nature: and if Motion is corporeal, then Matter, Figure, Place, and Motion, is but one thing, *viz.* a corporeal figurative Motion. As for a First Motion, I cannot conceive how it can be, or what that First Motion should be: for, an Immaterial cannot have a Material Motion; or, so strong a Motion, as to set all the Material Parts in Nature, or this World, a-moving; but (in my opinion) every particular part moves by its own Motion: If so, then all the Actions in Nature are self-corporeal, figurative Motions.[2] But this is to be noted, That as there is

---

1 By contrast, *PPO* (1655) opens with "Of Motion and Matter." Here, the specific focus on "Matter" indicates the centrality of materialism in Cavendish's later philosophy.

2 For Cavendish, all nature is material and all matter exists in a state of constant, self-orchestrated motion. Rather provocatively, she also muses that "First Motion"—the original force that set nature on its course—could not be immaterial. In this, she directly opposes René Descartes (1596–1650; see, for instance, *Principles of Philosophy*, Part II: 36).

but one Matter, so there is but one Motion; and as there are several Parts of Matter, so there are several Changes of Motion: for, as Matter, of what degree soever it is, or can be, is but Matter; so Motion, although it make Infinite Changes, can be but Motion.

CHAP. III.

Of the degrees of MATTER.

Though Matter can be neither more nor less than Matter; yet there may be degrees of Matter, as *more pure*, or *less pure*; and yet the purest Parts are as much material, in relation to the nature of Matter, as the grossest: Neither can there be more than two sorts of Matter, namely, that sort which is Self-moving, and that which is not Self-moving. Also, there can be but two sorts of the Self-moving Parts; as, that sort that moves intirely without Burdens, and that sort that moves with the Burdens of those Parts that are not Self-moving: So that there can be but these three sorts; Those parts that are not moving, those that move free, and those that move with those parts that are not moving of themselves: Which degrees are (in my opinion) the Rational Parts, the Sensitive Parts, and the Inanimate Parts; which three sorts of Parts are so join'd, that they are but as one Body; for, it is impossible that those three sorts of Parts should subsist single, by reason Nature is but one united material Body.[1]

CHAP. IV.

Of VACUUM.[2]

In my opinion, there cannot possibly be any *Vacuum*: for, though Nature, as being material, is divisible and compoundable; and, having Self-motion, is in perpetual action: yet Nature cannot divide or compose *from* her self, although she may move, divide, and compose in her self: But, were it possible Nature's Parts could wander and stray in, and out of *Vacuum*, there would be a

---

1 Although nature consists of a continuous network of self-moving, sentient matter, which cannot be divided into "single parts" (like atoms), Cavendish envisions three "degrees" of matter—the rational, sensitive, and inanimate—that each have specific properties (described in subsequent chapters).

2 The existence of vacuums—or entirely empty space—became a point of great controversy in the late seventeenth century. As a committed materialist, Cavendish, like Thomas Hobbes (1588–1679), denies this possibility. For the opposite view, see Jan Baptist van Helmont (1580–1644), *Oriatrike* 81–86.

Confusion; for, where Unity is not, Order cannot be: Wherefore, by the Order and Method of Nature's corporeal Actions, we may perceive, there is no *Vacuum*: For, what needs a *Vacuum*, when as Body and Place is but one thing; and as the Body alters, so doth the Place?

CHAP. V.

The difference of the Two Self-moving Parts of Matter.

The Self-moving Parts of Nature seem to be of two sorts, or degrees; one being purer, and so more agil and free than the other; which (in my opinion) are the Rational Parts of Nature. The other sort is not so pure; and are the Architectonical Parts, which are the Labouring Parts, bearing the grosser Materials about them, which are the Inanimate Parts; and this sort (in my opinion) are the Sensitive Parts of Nature; which form, build, or compose themselves with the Inanimate Parts, into all kinds and sorts of Creatures, as Animals, Vegetables, Minerals, Elements, or what Creatures soever there are in Nature: Whereas the Rational are so pure, that they cannot be so strong Labourers, as to move with Burdens of Inanimate Parts, but move freely without Burdens: for, though the Rational and Sensitive, with the Inanimate, move together as one Body; yet the Rational and Sensitive, do not move as one Part,[1] as the sensitive doth with the Inanimate. But, pray mistake me not, when I say, the Inanimate Parts are grosser; as if I meant, they were like some densed Creature; for, those are but Effects, and not Causes: but, I mean gross, dull, heavy Parts, as, that they are not Self-moving; nor do I mean by Purity, Rarity; but Agility: for, Rare or Dense Parts, are Effects, and not Causes: And therefore, if any should ask, Whether the Rational and Sensitive Parts were Rare, or Dense; I answer, They may be Rare or Dense, according as they contract, or dilate their Parts; for there is no such thing as a Single Part in Nature: for Matter, or Body, cannot be so divided, but that it will remain Matter, which is divisible.[2]

---

1 In the corrected text, Cavendish crossed out the word "Inanimate," which appeared before "Part."

2 Cavendish argues that natural matter endlessly divides and recombines into organisms or "societies," a process that drives natural change; however, the three degrees of elemental matter cannot be divided, even in the smallest quantities. By "rare," she means airy or ephemeral rather than uncommon.

CHAP. VI.

Of Dividing and Uniting of Parts.

Though every Self-moving Part, or Corporeal Motion, have free-will to move after what manner they please; yet, by reason there can be no Single Parts, several Parts unite in one Action, and so there must be united Actions: for, though every particular Part may divide from particular Parts; yet those that divide from some, are necessitated to join with other Parts, at the same point of time of division; and at that very same time, is their uniting or joining: so that Division, and Composition or Joining, is as one and the same act. Also, every altered Action, is an altered figurative Place, by reason Matter, Figure, Motion, and Place, is but one thing; and, by reason Nature is a perpetual motion, she must of necessity cause infinite Varieties.

CHAP. VII.

Of Life and Knowledg.

All the Parts of Nature have Life and Knowledg; but, all the Parts have not Active Life, and a perceptive Knowledg, but onely the Rational and Sensitive: And this is to be noted, That the variousness, or variety of Actions, causes varieties of Lives and Knowledges: For, as the Self-moving parts alter, or vary their Actions; so they alter and vary their Lives and Knowledges; but there cannot be an Infinite particular Knowledg, nor an Infinite particular Life; because Matter is divisible and compoundable.

CHAP. VIII.

Of Nature's Knowledg and Perception.

If Nature were not Self-knowing, Self-living, and also Perceptive, she would run into Confusion: for, there could be neither Order, nor Method, in Ignorant motion; neither would there be distinct kinds or sorts of Creatures, nor such exact and methodical Varieties as there are: for, it is impossible to make orderly and methodical Distinctions, or distinct Orders, by Chances: Wherefore, Nature being so exact (as she is) must needs be Self-knowing and Perceptive: And though all her Parts, even the Inanimate Parts, are Self-knowing, and Self-living; yet, onely her Self-moving Parts have an active Life, and a perceptive Knowledg.

CHAP. IX.

Of PERCEPTION in general.

Perception is a sort of Knowledg, that hath reference to Objects; that is, Some Parts to know other Parts: But yet Objects are not the cause of Perception; for the cause of Perception is Self-motion. But some would say, *If there were no Object, there could be no Perception.* I answer: It is true; for, that cannot be perceived, that is not: but yet, corporeal motions cannot be without Parts, and so not without Perception. But, put an impossible case, as, That there could be a single Corporeal Motion, and no more in Nature; that Corporeal Motion may make several Changes, somewhat like *Conceptions*, although not *Perceptions*: but, Nature being Corporeal, is composed of Parts, and therefore there cannot be a want of Objects. But there are Infinite several manners and ways of Perception; which proves, That the Objects are not the Cause: for, every several kind and sort of Creatures, have several kinds and sorts of Perception, according to the nature and property of such a kind or sort of Composition, as makes such a kind or sort of Creature;[1] as I shall treat of, more fully, in the following Parts of this Book.

CHAP. X.
Of Double PERCEPTION.

There is a *Double Perception* in Nature, the Rational Perception, and the Sensitive: The Rational Perception is more subtil and penetrating than the Sensitive; also, it is more generally perceptive than the Sensitive; also, it is a more agil Perception than the Sensitive: All which is occasioned not onely through the *purity* of the Rational parts, but through the *liberty* of the Rational parts; whereas the Sensitive being incumbred with the Inanimate parts, is obstructed and retarded. Yet all Perceptions, both Sensitive and Rational, are in parts; but, by reason the Rational is freer, (being not a painful Labourer) can more easily make an united Perception, than the Sensitive; which is the reason the Rational parts can make a Whole Perception of a Whole Object: Whereas the Sensitive makes but Perceptions in part, of one and the same Object.[2]

---

1 Perception is therefore a general phenomenon that occurs across nature, which is sentient and self-aware. For more details on her theory of perception, see Appendix B.

2 Thus, while all perception occurs "in parts," rational matter has the combinational power to create a "united" or "Whole Perception of a Whole Object." For more on "Double Perception," see the Introduction (p. 25) and Appendix B.

CHAP. XI.

Whether the Triumphant Parts can be perceived distinctly from each other.

Some may make this Question, *Whether the Three sorts of Parts, the Rational, Sensitive, and Inanimate, may be singly perceived*? I answer, Not unless there were single Parts in Nature; but, though they cannot be singly perceived, yet they singly perceive; because, every Part hath its own motion, and so its own perception. And though those Parts, that have not self-motion, have not perception; yet, being joined, as one Body, to the Sensitive, they may by the Sensitive Motion, have some different forms of Self-knowledg, caused by the different actions of the Sensitive parts; but that is not *Perception*. But, as I said, the *Triumphant Parts* cannot be perceived distinctly asunder, though their Actions may be different: for, the joining, or intermixing of Parts, hinders not the several Actions; as for example, A Man is composed of several Parts, or, (as the Learned term them) *Corporeal Motions*; yet, not any of those different Parts, or Corporeal Motions, are a hindrance to each other: The same between the *Sensitive* and *Rational Parts*.

CHAP. XII.

Whether Nature can know her self, or have an Absolute Power of her self, or have an exact Figure.

I was of an opinion, That Nature, because Infinite, could not know her Self; because Infinite hath no limit. Also, That Nature could not have an Absolute Power over her own Parts, because she had Infinite Parts; and, that the Infiniteness did hinder the Absoluteness: But since I have consider'd, That the Infinite Parts must of necessity be Self-knowing; and that those Infinite Self-knowing Parts are united in one Infinite Body, by which Nature must have both an United Knowledg, and an United Power. Also, I questioned, Whether Nature could have an Exact Figure, (but, mistake me not; for I do not mean the Figure of Matter, but a composed Figure of Parts) because Nature was composed of Infinite Variety of Figurative Parts: But considering, that those Infinite Varieties of Infinite Figurative Parts, were united into one Body; I did conclude, That she must needs have an Exact Figure, though she be Infinite: As for example, This World is composed of numerous and several Figurative parts, and yet the World hath an exact Form and Frame, the same which it would have if it were Infinite. But, as for Self-knowledg, and Power, certainly God hath given them to Nature, though her

Power be limited: for, she cannot move beyond her Nature; nor hath she power to make her self any otherwise than what she is, since she cannot create, or annihilate any part, or particle: nor can she make any of her Parts, Immaterial; or any Immaterial, Corporeal: Nor can she give to one part, the Nature (*viz.* the Knowleg, Life, Motion, or Perception) of another part;[1] which is the reason one Creature cannot have the properties, or faculties of another; they may have the like, but not the same.

CHAP. XIII.

Nature cannot judg her self.

Although Nature knows her self, and hath a free power of her self; (I mean, a natural Knowledg and Power) yet, Nature cannot be an upright, and just Judg of her self, and so not of any of her Parts; because every particular part is a part of her self. Besides, as she is Self-moving, she is Self-changeing, and so she is alterable: Wherefore, nothing can be a perfect, and a just Judg, but something that is Individable, and Unalterable, which is the Infinite GOD, who is Unmoving, Immutable, and so Unalterable; who is the Judg of the Infinite Corporeal Actions of his Servant Nature. And this is the reason that all Nature's Parts appeal to God, as being the only Judg.

CHAP. XIV.

Nature Poyses, or Balances her Actions.

Although Nature be Infinite, yet all her Actions seem to be *poysed*, or *balanced*, by Opposition; as for example, As Nature hath dividing, so composing actions: Also, as Nature hath regular, so irregular actions; as Nature hath dilating, so contracting actions: In short, we may perceive amongst the Creatures, or Parts of this World, slow, swift, thick, thin, heavy, leight, rare, dense, little, big, low, high, broad, narrow, light, dark, hot, cold, productions, dissolutions, peace, war, mirth, sadness, and that we name *Life*, and *Death*; and infinite the like; as also, infinite varieties in every several kind and sort of actions: but, the infinite varieties are made by the Self-moving parts of Nature, which are the Corporeal Figurative Motions of Nature.

1 In *Grounds*, Cavendish is careful to distinguish Nature and God, suggesting that Nature has self-knowledge and power but is "limited" in that it cannot create, annihilate, or transform fundamental aspects of matter (like God).

CHAP. XV.

Whether there be Degrees of Corporeal Strength.

As I have declared, there are (in my Opinion) Two sorts of Self-moving Parts; the one Sensitive, the other Rational. The Rational parts of my Mind, moving in the manner of Conception, or Inspection, did occasion some Disputes, or Arguments, amongst those parts of my Mind.[1] The Arguments were these: *Whether there were degrees of Strength, as there was of Purity, between their own sort, as, the Rational and the Sensitive?* The Major part of the Argument was, *That Self-motion could be but Self-motion: for, not any part of Nature could move beyond its power of Self-motion.* But the Minor part argued, *That the Self-motion of the Rational, might be stronger than the Self-motion of the Sensitive.* But the Major part was of the opinion, *That there could be no degrees of the Power of Nature, or the Nature of Nature: for Matter, which was Nature, could be but Self-moving, or not Self-moving; or partly Self-moving, or not Self-moving.* But the Minor argued, *That it was not against the nature of Matter to have degrees of Corporeal Strength, as well as degrees of Purity: for, though there could not be degrees of Purity amongst the Parts of the same sort, as amongst the Parts of the Rational, or amongst the Parts of the Sensitive; yet, if there were degrees of the Rational and Sensitive Parts, there might be degrees of Strength.* The Major part said, *That if there were degrees of Strength, it would make a Confusion, by reason there would be no Agreement; for, the Strongest would be Tyrants to the Weakest, in so much as they would never suffer those Parts to act methodically or regularly.* But the Minor part said, that they had observed, *That there was degrees of Strength amongst the Sensitive Parts*. The Major part argued, *That they had not degrees of Strength by Nature; but, that the greater Number of Parts were stronger than a less Number of Parts. Also, there were some sorts of Actions, that had advantage of other sorts. Also, some sorts of Compositions are stronger than other; not through the degrees of innate Strength, nor through the number of Parts; but, through the manner and form of their Compositions, or Productions.* Thus my Thoughts argued; but, after many Debates and Disputes, at last my Rational Parts agreed, That, If there were degrees of Strength, it could not be between the Parts of the same degree, or sort; but, between the Rational and Sensitive; and if so, the Sensitive was Stronger, being *less pure*; and the Rational was more Agil, being *more pure*.

---

1 Cavendish often stages "disputes" within her mind in order to assess theoretical possibilities. For instance, see *Observations* 23–42. See also Introduction (p. 38).

CHAP. XVI.

Of Effects, and Cause.

To treat of Infinite Effects, produced from an Infinite Cause, is an endless Work, and impossible to be performed, or effected; only this may be said, That the Effects, though Infinite, are so united to the material Cause, as that not any single effect can be, nor no Effect can be annihilated;[1] by reason all Effects are in the power of the Cause. But this is to be noted, That some Effects producing other Effects, are, in some sort or manner, a Cause.

CHAP. XVII.

Of INFLUENCE.

An *Influence* is this; When as the Corporeal Figurative Motions, in different kinds, and sorts of Creatures, or in one and the same sorts, or kinds, move sympathetically: And though there be antipathetical Motions, as well as sympathetical; yet, all the Infinite parts of Matter, are agreeable in their nature, as being all Material, and Self-moving; and by reason there is no *Vacuum*, there must of necessity be an Influence amongst all the Parts of Nature.

CHAP. XVIII.

Of FORTUNE and CHANCE.

Fortune, is only various Corporeal Motions of several Creatures, design'd to one Creature, or more Creatures; either to *that* Creature, or *those* Creatures Advantage, or Disadvantage: If Advantage, Man names it *Good Fortune*; if Disadvantage, Man names it *Ill Fortune*. As for *Chance*, it is the visible Effects of some hidden Cause; and *Fortune*, a sufficient Cause to produce such Effects: for, the conjunction of sufficient Causes, doth produce such or such Effects; which Effects could not be produced, if any of those Causes were wanting: So that, *Chances* are but the Effects of *Fortune*.

CHAP. XIX.

Of TIME and ETERNITY.

TIME is not a Thing by it self; nor is *Time* Immaterial: for, *Time* is only the variations of Corporeal Motions; but *Eternity* depends not on Motion, but of a Being without Beginning, or Ending.

---

1 In Cavendish's metaphysics, nothing in nature is annihilated and nothing is entirely new, either; instead, matter combines, dissolves, and recombines into new forms. See also Part 3, and Part 4, Chapter XIII (pp. 79–85, 88).

THE SECOND PART.

CHAP. I.
Of CREATURES.

All *Creatures* are Composed-Figures, by the consent of Associating Parts; by which Association, they joyn into such, or such a figured Creature: And though every Corporeal Motion, or Self-moving Part, hath its own motion; yet, by their Association, they all agree in proper actions, as actions proper to their Compositions: and, if every particular Part, hath not a perception of all the Parts of their Association; yet, every Part knows its own Work.

CHAP. II.
Of Knowledg and Perception of different kinds and sorts of Creatures.

There is not any Creature in Nature, that is not composed of Self-moving Parts, (*viz.* both of Rational and Sensitive) as also of the Inanimate Parts, which are Self-knowing: so that all Creatures, being composed of these sorts of Parts, must have a Sensitive, and Rational Knowledg and Perception, as Animals, Vegetables, Minerals, Elements, or what else there is in Nature: But several kinds, and several sorts in these kinds of Creatures, being composed after different manners, and ways, must needs have different Lives, Knowledges, and Perceptions: and not only every several kind, and sort, have such differences; but, every particular Creature, through the variations of their Self-moving Parts, have varieties of Lives, Knowledges, Perceptions, Conceptions, and the like; and not only so, but every particular part of one and the same Creature, have varieties of Knowledges, and Perceptions, because they have varieties of Actions. But, (as I have declared) there is not any different kind of Creature, that can have the like Life, Knowledg, and Perception; not only because they have different Productions, and different Forms; but, different Natures, as being of different kinds.

CHAP. III.
Of Perception of Parts, and United Perception.

All the Self-moving Parts are perceptive; and, all Perception is in Parts, and is dividable, and compoundable, as being Material; also, Alterable, as being Self-moving: Wherefore, no Creature that is composed, or consists of many several sorts of Corporeal Figurative Motions, but must have many sorts of Perception; which is the reason that one Creature, as Man, cannot perceive another Man any otherwise but in Parts: for, the Rational, and Sensitive; nay, all the Parts of one and the same Creature, perceive their Adjoining Parts, as they perceive Foreign Parts; only, by their close conjunction and near relation, they unite in one and the same actions. I do not say, they always agree: for, when they move irregularly, they disagree: And some of those United Parts, will move after one manner, and some after another; but, when they move regularly, then they move to one and the same Design, or one and the same United Action. So, although a Creature is composed of several sorts of Corporeal Motions; yet, these several sorts, being properly united in one Creature, move all agreeably to the Property and Nature of the whole Creature; that is, the particular Parts move according to the property of the whole Creature; because the particular Parts, by conjunction, make the Whole: So that, the several Parts make one Whole; by which, as Whole Creature hath both a general Knowledg, and a Knowledg of Parts; whereas, the Perceptions of Foreign Objects, are but in the Parts: and this is the reason why one Creature perceives not the Whole of another Creature, but only some Parts. Yet this is to be noted, That not any Part hath another Part's Nature, or Motion, nor therefore, their Knowledg, or Perception; but, by agreement, and unity of Parts, there is composed Perceptions.[1]

---

1 This chapter propounds an important aspect of Cavendish's theory of perception. All parts of all creatures have particular self-knowledge but only limited knowledge of the other parts within that same creature (they "perceive their Adjoining Parts, as they perceive Foreign [or external] Parts"); similarly, the "Whole Creature" has "general Knowledg" of its composite function as well as particular knowledge of its parts and can assemble general perceptions of foreign (external) objects, but it cannot ever attain full or perfect knowledge of another creature. In the same way, humans can never know nature perfectly because we cannot perceive it in its entirety (as explained in Part 2, Chapters VIII and X, and Part 3, Chapter III [pp. 78, 80–81). On this, see also Appendix B.

CHAP. IV.

Whether the Rational and Sensitive Parts have a Perception of each other.

Some may ask the Question, *Whether the Rational and Sensitive, have Perception of each other?* I answer: In my Opinion, they have. For, though the Rational and Sensitive Parts, be of two sorts; yet, both sorts have Self-motion; so that they are but as one, as, that they are both Corporeal Motions; and, had not the Sensitive Parts incumbrances, they would be, in a degree, as agile, and as free as the Rational. But, though each sort hath perception of each other, and some may have the like; yet they have not the same: for, not any Part can have another's Perception, or Knowledg; but, by reason the Rational and Sensitive, are both Corporeal Motions, there is a strong sympathy between those sorts, in one Conjunction, or Creature. Indeed, the Rational Parts are the Designing Parts; and the Sensitive, the Labouring Parts; and the Inanimate are as the Material Parts: not but all the three sorts are Material Parts; but the Inanimate, being not Self-moving, are the Burdensome Parts.[1]

CHAP V.

Of Thoughts, and the whole Mind of a Creature.

As for Thoughts, though they are several Corporeal Motions, or Self-moving Parts; yet, being united, by Conjunction in one Creature, into one whole Mind, cannot be perceived by some Parts of another Creature, nor by the same sort of Creature, as by another Man. But some may ask, *Whether the whole Mind of one Creature, as the whole Mind of one Man, may not perceive the whole Mind of another Man?* I answer, That if the Mind was not joyn'd and mix'd with the Sensitive and Inanimate Parts, and had not interior, as well as exterior Parts, the whole Mind of one Man, might perceive the whole Mind of another Man; but, that being not possible, one whole Mind cannot perceive another whole Mind: By which Observation we may perceive, there are no *Platonick Lovers* in Nature.[2] But some

---

1 Cavendish describes the "inanimate" parts of matter—which are, again, not divisible from the rational and sensitive parts, and can also perceive—as "burdensome" because they lack self-motion.

2 Cavendish often discusses "Platonick" or non-sexual unions, which were a popular topic in the court of Charles I (r. 1625–49), where Cavendish served as a lady-in-waiting to Queen Henrietta Maria (1609–69). For example, see *Blazing World* 113, 133.

may ask, *Whether the Sensitive Parts can perceive the Rational, in one and the same Creature?* I answer, They do; for if they did not, it were impossible for the Sensitive Parts to execute the Rational Designs; so that, what the Mind designs, the Sensitive Body doth put in execution, as far as they have Power: But if, through Irregularities, the Body be sick, and weak, or hath some Infirmities, they cannot execute the Designs of the Mind.

CHAP. VI.

Whether the Mind of one Creature, can perceive the Mind of another Creature.

Some may ask the reason, *Why one Creature, as Man, cannot perceive the Thoughts of another Man, as well as he perceives his exterior Sensitive Parts?* I answer, That the Rational Parts of one Man, perceive as much of the Rational Parts of another Man, as the Sensitive Parts of that Man doth of the Sensitive Parts of the other Man; that is, as much as is presented to his Perception: for, all Creatures, and every part and particle, have those three sorts of Matter; and therefore, every part of a Creature is perceiving, and perceived. But, by reason all Creatures are composed of Parts, (*viz.* both of the Rational and Sensitive) all Perceptions are in parts, as well the Rational, as the Sensitive Perception: yet, neither the Rational, nor the Sensitive, can perceive all the Interior Parts or Corporeal Motions, unless they were presented to their perception: Neither can one Part know the Knowledg and Perception of another Part: but, what Parts of one Creature are subject to the perception of another Creature, those are perceived.

CHAP. VII.

Of Perception, and Conception.

Although the Exterior Parts of one Creature, can but perceive the Exterior Parts of another Creature; yet, the Rational can make Conceptions of the Interior Parts, but not Perception:[1] for, neither the Sense, nor Reason, can perceive what is not present, but by rote, as after the manner of Conceptions, or Remembrances, as I shall in my following Chapters declare: So that, the Exterior Rational Parts, that are with the Exterior Sensitive Parts of an Object, are as much perceived, the one, as the other: but, those

1 That is, one cannot "perceive" the interior parts of another, but one can "conceive" or form ideas about them.

Exterior Parts of an Object, not moving in particular Parties, as in the whole Creature, is the cause that some Parts of one Creature, cannot perceive the whole Composition or Frame of another Creature: that is, some of the Rational Parts of one Creature, cannot perceive the whole Mind of another Creature. The like of the Sensitive Parts.

CHAP. VIII.

Of Human Suppositions.

Although Nature hath an Infinite Knowledg and Perception; yet, being a Body, and therefore divisible and compoundable; and having, also, Self-motion, to divide and compound her Infinite Parts, after infinite several manners; is the reason that her finite Parts, or particular Creatures, cannot have a general or infinite Knowledg, being limited, by being finite, to finite Perceptions or perceptive Knowledg; which is the cause of *Suppositions*, or Imaginations, concerning Forrein Objects: As for example, A Man can but perceive the Exterior Parts of another Man, or any other Creature, that is subject to Human Perception; yet, his Rational Parts may suppose, or presuppose, what another Man thinks, or what he will act: and for other Creatures, a Man may suppose or imagine what the innate nature of such a Vegetable, or Mineral, or Element is; and may imagine or suppose the Moon to be another World, and that all the fixed Starrs are Sunns; which suppositions, Man names *Conjectures*.

CHAP. IX.

Of Information between several Creatures.

No question but there is *Information* between all Creatures: but, several sorts of Creatures, having several sorts of Informations, it is impossible for any particular sort to know, or have perceptions of the Infinite, or Numberless Informations, between the Infinite and Numberless Parts, or Creatures of Nature: Nay, there are so many several Informations amongst one sort (as of Mankind) that it is impossible for one Man to perceive them all; no, nor can one Man generally perceive the particular Informations that are between the particular Parts of his Sensitive Body; or between the particular Informations of his Rational Body; or between the particular Rational and Sensitive Parts: much less can Man perceive, or know the several Informations of other Creatures.

CHAP. X.

The Reason of several kinds and sorts of Creatures.

Some may ask, *Why there are such sorts of Creatures, as we perceive there are, and not other sorts?* I answer, That 'tis probable, we do not perceive all the several kinds and sorts of Creatures in Nature: In truth, it is impossible (if Nature be Infinite) for a Finite to perceive the Infinite varieties of Nature. Also they may ask, *Why the Planets are of a Spherical Shape, and Human Creatures are of an Upright shape, and Beasts of a Bending and stooping shape?* Also, *Why Birds are made to flye, and not Beasts? And for what Cause, or Design, have Animals such and such sorts of shapes and properties? And Vegetables such and such sorts of shapes and properties? And so of Minerals and Elements?* I answer; That several sorts, kind, and differences of Particulars, causes Order, by reason it causes Distinctions: for, if all Creatures were alike, it would cause a Confusion.

CHAP. XI.

Of the several Properties of several Kinds and sorts of Creatures.

As I have said, There are several kinds, and several sorts, and several particular Creatures of several kinds and sorts; whereof there are some Creatures of a mixt kind, and some of a mixt sort, and some of a mixture of some particulars. Also, there are some kind of Creatures, and sorts of Creatures; as also Particulars of a Dense Nature, others of a Rare Nature; some of a Leight Nature, some of a Heavy Nature; some of a Bright Nature, some of a Dark Nature; some of an Ascending Nature, some of a Descending Nature; some of a Hard Nature, some of a Soft Nature; some of a Loose Nature, and some of a Fixt Nature; some of an Agil Nature, and some of a Slow Nature; some of a Consistent Nature, and some of a Dissolving Nature: All which is according to the Frame and Form of their Society, or Composition.

THE THIRD PART.

CHAP. I.

Of Productions in general.

The Self-moving Parts, or Corporeal Motions, are the Producers of all Composed Figures, such as we name *Creatures*: for, though all Matter hath Figure, by being Matter; for it were non-sense to say, *Figureless Matter*; since the most pure Parts of Matter, have Figure, as well as the grossest; the rarest, as well as the densed: But, such Composed Figures which we name *Creatures*, are produced by particular Associations of Self-moving Parts, into particular kinds, and sorts; and particular Creatures in every kind, or sort. The particular kinds, that are subject to Human Perceptions, are those we name Animals, Vegetables, Minerals, and Elements; of which kinds, there are numerous sorts; and of every sort, infinite particulars: And though there be Infinite Varieties in Nature, made by the Corporeal Motions, or Self-moving Parts, which might cause a Confusion: Yet, considering Nature is intire in her self, as being only Material, and as being but one United Body; also, poysing all her Actions by Opposites; 'tis impossible to be any ways in Extreams, or to have a Confusion.

CHAP. II.

Of Productions in general.

The Sensitive Self-moving Parts, or Corporeal Motions, are the Labouring Parts of all Productions, or Fabricks of all Creatures; but yet, those Corporeal Motions, are parts of the Creature they produce: for, Production is only a Society of particular Parts, that joyn into particular Figures, or Creatures: but, as Parts produce Figures, by Association; so they dissolve those Figures by Division: for, Matter is a perpetual Motion, that is always dividing and composing; so that not any Creature can be eternally one and the same: for, if there were no Dissolvings, and Alterings, there would be no varieties of Particulars; for, though the kinds and sorts may last, yet not the Particulars. But, mistake me not, I do not say those Figures are lost, or annihilated in Nature; but only, their Society is dissolved, or divided in Nature. But this is to be noted, That some Creatures are sooner produced and perfected, than others; and again, some Creatures are sooner decayed, or dissolved.

CHAP. III.

Of Productions in general.

There are so many different composed Parts, and so much of variety of Action in every several Part of one Creature, as 'tis impossible for Human Perception to perceive them; nay, not every Corporeal Motion of one Creature, doth perceive all the varieties of the same Society; and, by the several actions, not only of several Parts, but of one and the same Parts, cause such obscurity, as not any Creature can tell, not only how they were produced, but, not how they consist: But, by reason every Part knows his own Work, there is Order and Method: For example, In a Human

Creature, those Parts that produce, or nourish the Bones, those of the Sinews, those of the Veins, those of the Flesh, those of the Brains, and the like, know all their several Works, and consider not each several composed Part, but what belongs to themselves; the like, I believe, in Vegetables, Minerals, or Elements. But mistake me not; for, I do not say, those Corporeal Motions in those particulars, are bound to those particular Works, as, that they cannot change, or alter their actions if they will, and many times do: as some Creatures dissolve before they are perfect, or quite finished; and some as soon as finished; and some after some short time after they are finished; and some continue long, as we may perceive by any Creatures that dye, which I name Dissolving in several Ages; but, untimely Dissolutions, proceed rather from some particular Irregularities of some particular Parts, than by a general Agreement.

CHAP. IV.

Of Productions in general.

The Reason that all Creatures are produced by the ways of Production, as one Creature to be composed out of other Creatures, is, That Nature is but one Matter, and that all her Parts are united as one Material Body, having no Additions, or Diminutions; no new Creations, or Annihilations: But, were not Nature one and the same, but that her Parts were of different natures; yet, Creatures must be produced by Creatures, that is, Composed Figures, as a Beast, a Tree, a Stone, Water, *&c.* must be composed of *Parts*, not a *single Part*: for, a single Part cannot produce composed Figures; nor can a single Part produce another single Part; for, Matter cannot create Matter; nor can one Part produce another Part out of it self: Wherefore, all Natural Creatures are produced by the consent and agreement of many Self-moving Parts, or Corporeal Motions, which work to a particular Design, as to associate into particular kinds and sorts of Creatures.

CHAP. V.

Of Productions in general.

As I said in my former Chapter, That all Creatures are produced, or composed by the agreement and consent of particular Parts; yet some Creatures are composed of more, and some of fewer Parts: neither are all Creatures produced, or composed after one and the same manner; but some after one manner, and some after another manner: Indeed, there are divers manners of Productions, both of those we name *Natural*, and those we name

Artificial; but I only treat of Natural Productions, which are so various, that it is a wonder if any two Creatures are just alike; by which we may perceive, that not only in several kinds and sorts, but in Particulars of every kind, or sort, there is some difference, so as to be distinguished from each other, and yet the species of some Creatures are like to their kind, and sort, but not all; and the reason that most Creatures are in *Species*, according to their sort, and kind, is not only, that Nature's Wisdom orders and regulates her Corporeal Figurative Motions, into kinds and sorts of Societies and Conjunctions; but, those Societies cause a perceptive Acquaintance, and an united Love, and good liking of the Compositions, or Productions: and not only a love to their Figurative Compositions, but to all that are of the same sort, or kind; and especially, their being accustom'd to actions proper to their Figurative Compositions, is the cause that those Parts, that divide from the Producers, begin a new Society, and, by degrees, produce the like Creature; which is the cause that Animals and Vegetables produce according to their likeness. The same may be amongst Minerals and Elements, for all we can know. But yet, some Creatures of one and the same sort, are not produced after one and the same manner: As for example, One and the same sort of Vegetables, may be produced after several manners, and yet, in the effect, be the same, as when Vegetables are sowed, planted, engrafted; as also, Seeds, Roots, and the like, they are several manners, or ways of Productions, and yet will produce the same sort of Vegetable: but, there will be much alterations in replanting, which is occasioned by the change of associating Parts, and Parties; but as for the several Productions of several kinds and sorts, they are very different; as for example, Animals are not produced as Vegetables, or Vegetables as Minerals, nor Minerals as any of the rest: Nor are all Animals produced alike, nor Minerals, or Vegetables; but after many different manners, or ways. Neither are all Productions like their Producers; for, some are so far from resembling their Figurative Society, that they produce another kind, or sort of Composed Figures; as for example, Maggots out of Cheese, other Worms out of Roots, Fruits, and the like: but these sorts of Creatures, Man names *Insects*; but yet they are Animal Creatures, as well as others.[1]

1 Most thinkers of the period, including English physician William Harvey (1578–1657), believed that insects were produced from decaying food, mud, or slime, and hence that living organisms could appear without descent from similar organisms.

CHAP. VI.

Of Productions in general.

All Creatures are Produced, and Producers; and all these Productions partake more or less of the Producers; and are necessitated so to do, because there cannot be any thing New in Nature: for, whatsoever is produced, is of the same Matter; nay, every particular Creature hath its particular Parts: for, not any one Creature can be produced of any other Parts than what produced it; neither can the same Producer produce one and the same double, (as I may say to express my self:) for, though the same Producers may produce the like, yet not the same: for, every thing produced, hath its own Corporeal Figurative Motions; but this might be, if Nature was not so full of variety: for, if all those Corporeal Motions, or Self-moving Parts, did associate in the like manner, and were the very same Parts, and move in the very same manner; the same Production, or Creature, might be produced after it was dissolved; but, by reason the Self-moving Parts of Nature are always dividing and composing *from*, and *to* Parts, it would be very difficult, if not impossible.

CHAP. VII.

Lastly, *Of Productions in general.*

Though all Creatures are made by the several Associations of Self-moving Parts, or (as the Learned name them) *Corporeal Motions*; yet, there are infinite varieties of Corporeal Figurative Motions, and so infinite several manners and ways of Productions; as also, infinite varieties of Figurative Motions in every produced Creature: Also, there is variety in the difference of Time, of several Productions, and of their Consistency and Dissolution: for, some Creatures are produced in few Hours, others not in many Years. Again, some continue not a Day; others, numbers of Years. But this is to be noted, That according to the Regularity, or Irregularity of the Associating Motions, their Productions are more or less perfect. Also, this is to be noted, That there are Rational Productions, as well as Sensitive: for, though all Creatures are composed both of Sensitive and Rational Parts, yet the Rational Parts move after another manner.

CHAP. VIII.

Productions must partake of some Parts of their Producers.

No Animal, or Vegetable, could be produced, but by such, or such particular Producers; neither could an Animal, or

Vegetable, be produced without some Corporeal Motions of their Producers; that is, some of the Producers Self-moving Parts; otherwise the like Actions might produce, not only the like Creatures, but the same Creatures, which is impossible; Wherefore, the things produced, are part of the Producers; for, no particular Creature could be produced, but by such particular Producers. But this is to be noted, That all sorts of Creatures are produced by more, of fewer, Producers. Also, the first Producers are but the first Founders of the things produced, but not the only Builders: for, there are many several sorts of Corporeal Motions, that are the Builders; for, no Creature can subsist, or consist, by it self, but must assist, and be assisted: Yet, there are some differences in all Productions, although of the same Producers; otherwise all the Off-springs of one and the same Producer, would be alike:[1] And though, sometimes, their several Off-springs may be so alike, as hardly to be distinguished; yet, that is so seldom, as it appears as a wonder; but there is a property in all Productions, as, for the *Produced* to belong as a Right and Property to the *Producer*.

CHAP. IX.

Of Resemblances of several Off-springs, or Producers.

There are numerous kinds and sorts of Productions, and infinite manners and ways, in the actions of Productions; which is the cause that the Off-springs of the same Producers, are not so just alike, but that they are distinguishable; but yet there may not only be resemblances between particular Off-springs of the same Producers, as also of the same sort; but, of different sorts of Creatures: but the Actions of all Productions that are according to their own *Species*, are Imitating Actions, but not Bare Imitations, as by an Incorporeal Motion; for if so, then a covetous Woman, that loves Gold, might produce a Wedg of Gold instead of a Child; also, *Virgins* might be as Fruitful as *Married Wives*.[2]

1 Modern notions of heredity did not take shape until a hundred years later, so the precise relationship between parents and offspring posed an ongoing problem to natural philosophers.

2 Hence, we cannot consciously imitate whatever we wish but are instead driven by the natural actions of both our kind and our particular constitutions.

CHAP. X.

Of the Several Appearances of the Exterior Parts of One Creature.

Every altered Action of the Exterior Parts, causes an altered Appearance: As for example, A Man, or the like Creature, doth not appear when he is old, as when he was young; nor when he is sick, as when he is well in health; no, nor when he is cold, as when he is hot. Nor do they appear in several Passions alike: for, though Man can best perceive the Alteration of his own Kind, or Sort; yet, other Creatures have several Appearances, as well as Man; some of which, Man may perceive, though not all, being of a different sort. And not only Animals, but Vegetables, and Elements, have altered Appearances, and many that are subject to Man's perception.

THE FOURTH PART.

CHAP. I.

Of Animal Productions; and of the Differences between Productions, and Transformations.

I understand Productions to be between Particulars; as, some particular Creatures to produce other particular Creatures; but not to transform from one sort of Creature, into another sort of Creature, as Cheese into Maggots, and Fruit into Worms, *&c.* which, in some manner, is like Metamorphosing. So by Transformation, the Intellectual Nature, as well as the Exterior Form is transform'd: Whereas Production transforms only the Exterior Form, but not the Intellectual Nature; which is the cause that such Transformations cannot return into their former state; as a Worm to be a Fruit, or a Maggot a Cheese again, as formerly.[1] Hence I perceive, that all sorts of Fowls are partly Produced, and partly Transformed: for, though an Egg be produced, yet a Chicken is but a Transformed Egg.

---

1 Translation is a key aspect of Cavendish's metaphysics, whereby substances do not die, disappear, or spontaneously appear but rather migrate into new formations. Here she compares this process to that of "transformation," which is more akin to metamorphosis, as she demonstrates via the common belief that worms and maggots arise from putrefied food.

CHAP. II.

Of different Figurative Motions in MAN's Production.

All Creatures are produced by Degrees; which proves, That not any Creature is produced, in perfection, by one Act, or Figurative Motion: for, though the Producers are the first Founders, yet not the Builders. But, as for Animal Creatures, there be some sorts that are composed of many different Figurative Motions; amongst which sorts, is Mankind, who has very different Figurative Parts, as Bones, Sinews, Nerves, Muscles, Veins, Flesh, Skin, and Marrow, Blood, Choler, Flegm, Melancholy, and the like; also, Head, Breast, Neck, Arms, Hands, Body, Belly, Thighs, Leggs, Feet, *&c.* also, Brains, Lungs, Stomack, Heart, Liver, Midriff, Kidnies, Bladder, Guts, and the like; and all these have several actions, yet all agree as one, according to the property of that sort of Creature named MAN.

CHAP. III.

Of the Quickning[1] of a Child, or any other sort of Animal Creatures.

The Reason that a Woman, or such like Animal, doth not feel her Child so soon as it is produced, is, That the Child cannot have an Animal Motion, until it hath an Animal Nature, that is, until it be perfectly an Animal Creature; and as soon as it is a perfect Child, she feels it to move, according to its nature: but it is only the Sensitive Parts of the Child that are felt by the Mother, not the Rational; because those Parts are as the Designers, not the Builders; and therefore, being not the Labouring Parts, are not the Sensible Parts. But it is to be noted, That, according to the Regularity, or Irregularity of the Figurative Motions, the Child is *well shaped*, or *mishaped*.

CHAP. IV.

Of the Birth of a Child.

The reason why a Child, or such like Animal Creature, stays no longer in the Mother's Body, than to such a certain Time, is, That a Child is not Perfect before that time, and would be too big after that time; and so big, that it would not have room enough; and therefore it strives and labours for liberty.

---

1 The period of pregnancy in which the mother can feel the motions of the fetus.

CHAP. V.

Of Mischances, or Miscarriages of Breeding Creatures.

When a Mare, Doe, Hind, or the like Animal, cast their Young, or a Woman miscarries of her Child, the Mischance proceeds either through the Irregularities of the Corporeal Motions, or Parts of the Child; or through some Irregularity of the Parts of the Mother; or else of both Mother and Child. If the Irregularities be of the Parts of the Child, those Parts divide from the Mother, through their Irregularity: but, if the Irregularity be in the Parts of the Mother, then the Mother divides in some manner from the Child; and if there be a distemper in both of them, the Child and Mother divide from each other: but, such Mischances are at different times, some sooner, and some later. As for false Conceptions, they are occasioned through the Irregularities of Conception.

CHAP. VI.

Of the Encrease of Growth, and Strength of Mankind, or such like Creatures.

The reason most Animals, especially Human Creatures, are weak whilst they are Infants, and that their Strength and Growth encreases by degrees, is, That a Child hath not so many Parts, as when he is a Youth; nor so many Parts when he is a Youth, as when he is a Man: for, after the Child is parted from the Mother, it is nourished by other Creatures, as the Mother was, and the Child by the Mother; and according as the nourishing Parts be Regular, or Irregular, so is the Child, Youth, or Man, weaker, or stronger; healthful, or diseased; and when the Figurative Motions move (as I may say for expression sake) curiously, the Body is neatly shaped, and is, as we say, beautiful. But this is to be noted, That 'tis no Greatness, or Bulk of Body, makes a Body perfect; for, there are several sizes of every sort, or kind of Creatures; as also, in every particular kind, or sort; and every several size may be as perfect, one, as the other: But, I mean the Number of Parts, according to the proper size.

CHAP. VII.

Of the several Properties of the several Exterior Shapes of several sorts of Animals.

The several Exterior Shapes of Creatures, cause several Properties, as Running, Jumping, Hopping, Leaping, Climbing, Galloping, Trotting, Ambling, Turning, Winding, and Rowling; also Creeping, Crawling, Flying, Soaring or Towring; Swimming, Diving,

Digging, Stinging or Piercing; Pressing, Spinning, Weaving, Twisting, Printing, Carving, Breaking, Drawing, Driving, Bearing, Carrying, Holding, Griping or Grasping, Infolding, and Millions of the like. Also, the Exterior Shapes cause Defences, as Horns, Claws, Teeth, Bills, Talons, Finns, *&c.* Likewise, the Exterior Shapes cause Offences, and give Offences: As also, the different sorts of Exterior Shapes, cause different Exterior Perceptions.

CHAP. VIII.

Of the Dividing and Uniting Parts of a particular Creature.

Those Parts (as I have said) that were the First Founders of an Animal, or other sort of Creature, may not be constant Inhabitants: for, though the Society may remain, the particular Parts may remove: Also, all particular Societies of one kind, or sort, may not continue the like time; but some may dissolve sooner than others. Also, some alter by degrees, other of a sudden; but, of those Societies that continue, the particular Parts remove, and other particular Parts unite; so, as some Parts *were* of the Society, so some other Parts *are* of the Society, and others[1] *will be* of the Society: But, when the Form, Frame, and Order of the Society begins to alter, then that particular Creature begins to decay. But this is to be noted, That those particular Creatures that dye in their Childhood, or Youth, were never a full and regular Society; and the dissolving of a Society, whether it be a Full, or but a Forming Society, Man names *DEATH.* Also, this is to be noted, That the Nourishing Motion of Food, is the Uniting Motion; and the Cleansing, or Evacuating Motions, are the Dividing Corporeal Motions. Likewise it is to be noted, That a Society requires a longer time of uniting than of dividing; by reason uniting requires assistance of Foreign Parts, whereas dividings are only a dividing of home-Parts. Also, a particular Creature, or Society, is longer in dividing its Parts, than in altering its Actions; because a Dispersing Action is required in Division, but not in Alteration of Actions.

THE FIFTH PART.

CHAP. I.

Of MAN.

Now I have discoursed, in the former Parts, after a general manner, of *Animals*: I will, in the following Chapters, speak

1 Cavendish added this word in the corrected text.

more particularly of that sort we name *Mankind*; who believe (being ignorant of the Nature of other Creatures) that they are the most knowing of all Creatures; and yet a *whole Man* (as I may say for expression-sake) doth not know all the Figurative Motions belonging either to his Mind, or Body: for, he doth not generally know every particular Action of his Corporeal Motions, as, How he was framed, or formed, or perfected. Nor doth he know every particular Motion that occasions his present Consistence, or Being: Nor every particular Digestive, or Nourishing Motion: Nor, when he is sick, the particular Irregular Motion that causes his Sickness. Nor do the Rational Motions in the Head, know always the Figurative Actions of those of the Heel. In short, (as I said) Man doth not generally know every particular Part, or Corporeal Motion, either of Mind, or Body: Which proves, Man's Natural Soul is not inalterable, or individable, and uncompoundable.[1]

CHAP. II.

Of the variety of Man's Natural Motions.

There is an abundance of varieties of Figurative Motions in Man:[2] As, first, There are several Figurative Motions of the Form and Frame of Man, as of his Innate, Interior, and Exterior Figurative Parts. Also, there are several Figures of his several Perceptions, Conceptions, Appetite, Digestions, Reparations, and the like. There are also several Figures of several Postures of his several Parts; and a difference of his Figurative Motions, or Parts, from other Creatures; all which are Numberless: And yet all these different Actions are proper to the Nature of *MAN*.

CHAP. III.

Of Man's Shape and Speech.

The Shape of Man's Sensitive Body, is, in some manner, of a mixt Form: but, he is singular in this, That he is of an upright and straight Shape; of which, no other Animal but Man is:

---

1 When Cavendish discusses the "natural soul," she refers not to the divine soul but to the human mind. The divine soul is supernatural and therefore beyond the scope of natural philosophy.

2 Figurative motions are a key term for Cavendish and refer to the motions of self-moving, self-knowing matter, which are unique from creature to creature and part to part and determine everything about a given entity's existence (including its form, behavior, and potential knowledge).

which Shape makes him not only fit, proper, easie and free, for all exterior actions; but also for Speech: for being streight, as in a straight and direct Line from the Head to the Feet, so as his Nose, Mouth, Throat, Neck, Chest, Stomack, Belly, Thighs, and Leggs, are from a straight Line: also, his Organ-Pipes, Nerves, Sinews, and Joynts, are in a straight and equal posture to each other; which is the cause, Man's Tongue, and Organs, are more apt for Speech than those of any other Creatures; which makes him more apt to imitate any other Creature's Voyces, or Sounds: Whereas other Animal Creatures, by reason of their bending Shapes, and crooked Organs, are not apt for Speech; neither (in my Opinion) have other Animals so melodious a Sound, or Voice, as Man: for, though some sorts of Bird's Voices are sweet, yet they are weak, and faint; and Beast's Voices are harsh, and rude: but of all other Animals, besides Man, Birds are the most apt for Speech; by reason they are more of an upright shape, than Beasts, or any other sorts of Animal Creatures, as Fish, and the like; for, Birds are of a straight and upright shape, as from their Breasts, to their Heads; but, being not so straight as Man; causes Birds to speak uneasily, and constrainedly: Man's shape is so ingeniously contrived, that he is fit and proper for more several sorts of exterior actions, than any other Animal Creature; which is the cause he seems as Lord and Sovereign of other Animal Creatures.

CHAP. IV.

Of the several Figurative Parts of Human Creatures.

The manner of Man's Composition, or Form, is of different Figurative Parts; whereof some of those Parts seem the Supreme, or (as I may say) Fundamental Parts; as the Head, Chest, Lungs, Stomack, Heart, Liver, Spleen, Bowels, Reins, Kidnies, Gaul,[1] and many more; also, those Parts have other Figurative Parts belonging or adjoining to them, as the Head, Scull, Brains, *Pia-mater*,[2] *Dura-mater*,[3] Forehead, Nose, Eyes, Cheeks, Ears, Mouth, Tongue, and several Figurative Parts belonging to those; so of the rest of the Parts, as the Arms, Hands, Fingers, Leggs, Feet, Toes, and the like: all which different Parts, have different

1 I.e., gall bladder.

2 The membranes that protect the spinal cord and brain.

3 The membranes that protect the dural or cranial sinuses.

sorts of Perceptions;[1] and yet (as I formerly said) their Perceptions are united: for, though all the Parts of the Human Body have different Perceptions; yet those different perceptions unite in a general Perception, both for the Subsistence, Consistence, and use of the Whole Man: but, concerning Particulars, not only the several composed Figurative Parts, have several sorts of Perceptions; but every Part hath variety of Perceptions, occasioned by variety of Objects.

CHAP. V.

Of the several Perceptions amongst the several Parts of MAN.

There being infinite several Corporeal Figurative Motions, or Actions of Nature, there must of necessity be infinite several Self-knowledges and Perceptions: but I shall only, in this Part of my Book, treat of the Perception proper to Mankind: And first, of the several and different Perceptions, proper for the several and different Parts: for, though every Part and Particle of a Man's Body, is perceptive; yet, every particular Part of a Man, is not generally perceived; for, the Interior Parts do not generally perceive the Exterior; nor the Exterior, generally or perfectly, the Interior; and yet, both Interior and Exterior Corporeal Motions, agree as one Society; for, every Part, or Corporeal Motion, knows its own Office; like as Officers in a Common-wealth, although they may not be acquainted with each other, yet they know their Employments: So every particular Man in a Common-wealth, knows his own Employment, although he knows not every Man in the Common-wealth. The same do the Parts of a Man's Body, and Mind. But, if there be any Irregularity, or Disorder in a Common-wealth, every Particular is disturbed, perceiving a Disorder in the Common-wealth.[2] The same amongst the Parts of a Man's Body; and yet many of those Parts do not know the particular Cause of that general Disturbance. As for the Disorders, they may proceed from some Irregularities; but for Peace, there must be a general Agreement, that is, every Part must be Regular.

---

1 All parts of humans—and nature more broadly—can perceive and think, not just the brain. In humans, these perceptions coalesce as a "united" or "general Perception," but this is not perfect (e.g., not everything is known to the whole that is known to each of its parts). For more details, see Appendix B.

2 Cavendish often draws on the metaphor of chaos within a commonwealth, which was timely given that she wrote in the aftermath of the English Civil War (1642–49). E.g., see *Observations* 81.

CHAP. VI.

Of Divided and Composed Perceptions.

As I have formerly said, There is in Nature both Divided and Composed Perceptions; and for proof, I will mention Man's Exterior Perceptions; As for example, Man hath a Composed Perception of Seeing, Hearing, Smelling, Tasting, and Touching; whereof every several sort is composed, though after different manners, or ways; and yet are divided, being several sorts of Perceptions, and not all one Perception. Yet again, they are all Composed, being united as proper Perceptions of one Man; and not only so, but united to perceive the different Parts of one Object: for, as Perceptions are composed of Parts, so are Objects; and as there are different Objects, so there are different Perceptions; but it is not possible for a Man to know all the several sorts of Perceptions proper to every Composed Part of his Body or Mind, much less of others.

CHAP. VII.

Of the Ignorances of the several Perceptive Organs.

As I said, That every several composed Perception, was united to the proper use of their whole Society, as one Man; yet, every several Perceptive Organ of Man is ignorant of each other; as the Perception of Sight is ignorant of that of Hearing; the Perception of Hearing, is ignorant of the Perception of Seeing; and the Perception of Smelling is ignorant of the Perceptions of the other two, and those of Scent, and the same of Tasting, and Touching: Also, every Perception of every particular Organ, is different; but some sorts of Human Perceptions require some distance between them and the Object: As for example, The Perception of Sight requires certain Distances, as also Magnitudes; whereas the Perception of touch requires a Joyning-Object, or Part. But this is to be noted, That although these several Organs are not perfectly, or throughly acquainted; yet in the Perception of the several parts of one Object, they do all agree to make their several Perceptions, as it were by one Act, at one point of time.

CHAP. VIII.

Of the particular and general Perceptions of the Exterior Parts of Human Creatures.

There is amongst the Exterior Perceptions of Human Creatures, both particular sorts of Perceptions, and general Perceptions: For, though none of the Exterior Parts, or Organs, have the sense of Seeing, but the Eyes; of Hearing, but the Ears; of Smelling, but the Nose; of Tasting, but the Mouth: yet all the Exterior Parts have the Perception of Touching; and the reason is, That all the Exterior Parts are full of pores, or at least, of such composed Parts, that are the sensible Organs of Touching: yet, those several Parts have several Touches; not only because they have several Parts, but because those Organs of Touching, are differently composed.[1] But this is to be noted, That every several part hath perception of the other parts of their Society, as they have of Foreign parts; and, as the Sensitive, so the Rational parts have such particular and general perceptions. But it is to be noted, that the Rational parts, are parts of the same Organs.

CHAP. IX.

Of the Exterior Sensitive Organs of Human Creatures.

As for the manner, or ways, of all the several sorts, and particular perceptions, made by the different composed parts of Human Creatures; it is impossible, for a Human Creature, to know any otherwise, but in part: for, being composed of parts, into Parties, he can have but a parted knowledg, and a parted perception of himself: for, every different composed part of his Body, have different sorts of Self-knowledg, as also, different sorts of Perceptions; but yet, the manner and way of some Human Perceptions, may probably be imagined, especially those of the exterior parts, Man names the *Sensitive Organs*; which Parts (in my opinion) have their perceptive actions, after the manner of patterning, or picturing the exterior Form, or Frame, of Foreign Objects: As for example, The present Object is a Candle; the Human Organ of Sight pictures the Flame, Light, Week, or Snuff, the Tallow, the Colour, and the dimension of the Candle; the Ear patterns out the sparkling noise; the Nose patterns out the scent of the Candle; and the Tongue may pattern out the tast of the Candle: but, so soon as the Object is removed, the figured of the Candle is altered into the present Object, or as much of one present Object, as is subject to Human Perception. Thus the several parts or properties, may be patterned out by the several Organs. Also, every altered action, of one and the same Organ, are altered Perceptions; so as there may be numbers of several pictures or Patterns made by the Sensitive Actions of one Organ; I will not say, by one act; yet there may be much variety in one action. But

1 That is, all of our organs sense and "touch" in distinct ways and produce different types of knowledge based on these varied experiences.

this is to be noted, That the Object is not the *cause* of Perception, but is only the *occasion*: for, the Sensitive Organs can make such like figurative actions, were there no Object present; which proves, that the Object is not the Cause of the Perception.[1] Also, when as the Sensitive parts of the Sensitive Organs, are Irregular, they will make false perceptions of present Objects; wherefore the Object is not the Cause. But one thing I desire, not to be mistaken in; for I do not say, that all the parts belonging to any of the particular Organs, move only in one sort or kind of perception; but I say, Some of the parts of the Organ, move to such, or such perception: for, all the actions of the Ears, are not only hearing; and all the actions of the Eye, seeing; and all the actions of the Nose, smelling; and all the actions of the Mouth, tasting; but, they have other sorts of actions:[2] yet, all the sorts of every Organ, are according to the property of their figurative Composition.

CHAP. X.

Of the Rational Parts of the Human Organs.

As for the Rational parts of the Human Organs, they move according to the Sensitive parts, which is, to move according to the Figures of Foreign Objects; and their actions are (if Regular) at the same point of time, with the Sensitive: but, though their Actions are alike, yet there is a difference in their Degree; for, the figure of an Object in the Mind, is far more pure than the figure in the Sense. But, to prove that the Rational (if Regular) moves with the Sense, is, That all the several Sensitive perceptions of the Sensitive Organs, (as all the several Sights, Sounds, Scents, Tasts, and Touches) are thoughts of the same.[3]

---

1 Perception, then, is a volitional act; sensitive organs choose to perceive, with external objects as the "occasion" rather than primary cause of that perception. In this, Cavendish clearly diverges from mechanical accounts of perception. For more on human perception in relation to external objects, see Part 1, Chapter IX (p. 68), and *Observations* 169–75. See also Appendix B (pp. 237–44).

2 Our various organs therefore do more than single, identifiable actions; e.g., eyes move and perceive in ways beyond just vision.

3 Rational matter operates along with the sensitive to "pattern" thoughts of sensory figures, and these thoughts are quicker and more agile than the slower acquisition of sensory data. We must remember, however, that all matter—sensitive and rational—can perceive and think, but in distinct ways.

CHAP. XI.

Of the difference between the Human Conception, and Perception.

There are some differences between Perception, and Conception: for, Perception doth properly belong to present Objects; whereas Conceptions have no such strict dependency: But, Conceptions are not proper to the Sensitive Organs, or parts of a Human Creature; wherefore, the Sensitive never move in the manner of Conception, but after an irregular manner; as when a Human Creature is in some violent Passion, Mad, Weak, or the like Distempers. But this is to be noted, That all sorts of Fancies, Imaginations, *&c.* whether Sensitive, or Rational, are after the manner of Conceptions, that is, do move by Rote, and not by Example. Also, it is to be noted, That the Rational parts can move in more various Figurative Actions than the Sensitive; which is the cause that a Human Creature hath more Conceptions than Perceptions; so that the Mind can please it self with more variety of Thoughts than the Sensitive with variety of Objects: for variety of Objects consists of Foreign Parts; whereas variety of Conceptions consists only of their own Parts:[1] Also, the Sensitive Parts are sooner satisfied with the perception of particular Objects, than the Mind with particular Remembrances.

CHAP. XII.

Of the Several Varieties of Actions of Human Creatures.

To speak of all the Several Actions of the Sensitive and Rational parts of one Creature, is not possible, being numberless: but, some of those that are most notable, I will mention, as, Respirations, Digestions, Nourishments, Appetites, Satiety, Aversions, Conceptions, Opinions, Fancies, Passions, Memory, Remembrance, Reasoning, Examining, Considering, Observing, Distinguishing, Contriving, Arguing, Approving, Disapproving, Discoveries, Arts, Sciences. The Exterior Actions are, Walking, Running, Dancing, Turning, Tumbling, Bearing, Carrying, Holding, Striking, Trembling, Sighing, Groaning, Weeping, Frowning, Laughing, Speaking, Singing and Whistling: As for Postures, they cannot be well described; only, Standing, Sitting, and Lying.

---

1 Conceptions are produced within the mind and do not depend on patterning external objects. Imagination is a kind of conception that works "by Rote," or by calling up images and ideas at will.

CHAP. XIII.

Of the manner of Information between the Rational and Sensitive Parts.

The manner of Information amongst the Self-moving Parts of a Human Creature, is after divers and several manners, or ways, amongst the several parts: but, the manner of Information between the Sensitive and Rational parts, is, for the most part, by Imitation; as, imitating each other's actions: As for example, The Rational parts invent some Sciences; the sensitive endeavour to put those Sciences into an Art. If the Rational perceive the Sensitive actions are not just, according to that Science, they inform the Sensitive; then the Sensitive Parts endeavour to work, according to the directions of the Rational: But, if there be some obstruction or hindrance, then the Rational and Sensitive agree to declare their Design, and to require assistance of other Associates, which are other Men; as also, other Creatures. As for the several Manners and Informations between Man and Man, they are so ordinary, I shall not need to mention them.

CHAP. XIV.

Of Irregularities and Regularities of the Self-moving Parts of Human Creatures.

Nature being poised, there must of necessity be Irregularities, as well as Regularities, both of the Rational and Sensitive parts; but when the Rational are Irregular, and the Sensitive Regular, the Sensitive endeavour to rectifie the Errors of the Rational. And if the Sensitive be Irregular, and the Rational Regular, the Rational do endeavour to rectifie the Errors of the Sensitive: for, the particular parts of a Society, are very much assistant to each other, as we may observe by the Exterior parts of Human Bodies; the Hands endeavour to assist any part in distress; the Leggs will run, the Eyes will watch, the Ears will listen, for any advantage to the Society; but when there is a general Irregularity, then the Society falls to ruine.

CHAP. XV.

Of the Agreeing, or Disagreeing, of the Sensitive and Rational Parts of Human Creatures.

There is, for the most part, a general agreement between the Rational and Sensitive Parts of Human Creatures; not only in their particular, but general actions; only the Rational are the Designing-parts; and the Sensitive, the Labouring parts: As for proof, The Mind designs to go to such, or such Foreign Parts, or Places; upon which design the Sensitive Parts will labour to execute the Mind's intention, so as the whole Sensitive Body labours to go to the designed place, without the Mind's further Concern: for, the Mind takes no notice of every action of the Sensitive parts; neither of those of the Eyes, Ears; or of the Leggs, or feet; nor of their perceptions: for, many times, the Mind is busied in some Conception, Imagination, Fancy, or the like; and yet the Sensitive Parts execute the Mind's Design exactly. But, for better proof, When as the Sensitive parts are sick, weak, or defective, through some irregularities, the Sensitive parts cannot execute the Mind's Design: also, when the Sensitive parts are careless, they oft mistake their way; or when they are irregularly opposed, or busied about some Appetite, they will not obey the Mind's desire; all which are different degrees of Parts. But, as it is amongst the particular parts of a Society; so, many times, between several Societies; for, sometimes, the Sensitive parts of two Men will take no notice of each other: As for example, When two men speak together, one man regards not what the other says; so many times, the Sensitive parts regard not the Propositions of the Rational; but then the Sensitive is not perfectly Regular.

CHAP. XVI.

Of the Power of the Rational; or rather, of the Indulgency of the Sensitive.

The Rational Corporeal Motions, being the purest, most free, and so most active, have great power over the Sensitive; as to perswade, or command them to obedience: As for example, When a man is studying about some Inventions of Poetical Fancies, or the like; though the Sensitive Corporeal Motions, in the Sensitive Organs, desire to desist from patterning of Objects, and would move towards sleep; yet the Rational will not suffer them, but cause them to work, *viz.* to write, or to read, or do some other Labour: Also, when the Rational Mind is merry, it will cause the Leggs to dance, the Organs of the Voice to sing, the Mouth to speak, to eat, to drink, and the like: If the Mind moves to sadness, it causes the Eyes to weep, the Lungs to sigh, the Mouth to speak words of Complaint. Thus the Rational Corporeal Motions of the Mind, will occasion the Senses to watch, to work, or to sport and play. But mistake me not; for I do not mean, the Senses are bound to obey the Rational Designs; for, the Sensitive Corporeal Motions, have as much freedom of Self-moving, as the Rational: for, the Command of the Rational, and the Obedience of the Sensitive, is rather an Agreement, than a Constraint: for, in many cases, the Sensitive will not agree, and so not obey:[1] also, in many cases, the Rational submits to the Sensitive: also, the Rational sometimes will be irregular; and, on the other side, sometimes the Sensitive will be irregular, and the Rational regular; and sometimes both irregular.

CHAP. XVII.

Of Human Appetites and Passions.

The Sensitive Appetites, and the Rational Passions do so resemble each other, as they would puzzle the most wise Philosopher to distinguish them; and there is not only a Resemblance, but, for the most part, a sympathetical Agreement between the Appetites, and the Passions; which strong conjunction, doth often occasion disturbances to the whole life of Man; with endless Desires, unsatiable Appetites, violent Passions, unquiet Humors, Grief, Pain, Sadness, Sickness, and the like; through which, Man seems to be more restless, than any other Creature: but, whether the cause be in the Manner, or Form of Man's Composition, or occasioned by some Irregularities; I will leave to those who are wiser than I, to judg. But this is to be noted, That the more Change and Alterations the Rational and Sensitive Motions make, the more variety of Passions and Appetites the Man hath: also, the quicker the Motions are, the sharper Appetite, and the quicker Wit, Man hath. But, as all the Human Senses are not bound to one Organ; so all Knowledges are not bound to one Sense, no more than all the Parts of Matter to the composition of one particular Creature: but, by some of the Rational and Sensitive actions, we may perceive the difference of some of the Sensitive and Rational actions; as, Sensitive Pain, Rational Grief; Sensitive Pleasure, Rational delight; Sensitive Appetite, Rational Desire; which are sympathetical actions of the Rational and Sensitive Parts: Also, through sympathy, Rational Passions will occasion Sensitive Appetites; and Appetites, the like Passions.

CHAP. XVIII.

Of the Rational Actions of the Head and Heart of Human Creatures.

As I formerly said, In every Figurative Part of a Human Creature, the Actions are different, according to the Property of their different Composers; so that the Motions of the Heart are different to the Motions of the Head, and of the other several Parts: but,

1 This "agreement" is crucial to Cavendish's philosophy: natural matter operates via volition and sympathy, not by force.

as for the Motions of the Head, they are (in my Opinion) more after the manner of Emboss'd Figures; and those of the Heart, more after the manner of Flat Figures; like Painting, Printing, Engraving, *&c.* For, if we observe, the Thoughts in our Heads are different from the Thoughts in our Hearts.[1] I only name these two Parts, by reason they seem to sympathize, or to agree, more particularly to each other's actions, than some of the other Parts of Human Creatures.

CHAP. XIX.

Of Passions and Imaginations.

Some sorts of Passions seem to be in the Heart; as, Love, Hate, Grief, Joy, Fear, and the like; and all Imaginations, Fancies, Opinions, Inventions, *&c.* in the Head. But, mistake me not, I do not say, that none of the other Parts of a Man have not Passions and Conceptions: but, I say, they are not after the same manner, or way, as in the Heart, or Head: as for example, Every Part of a Man's Body is sensible, yet not after one and the same manner: for, every Part of a Man's Body hath different perceptions, as I have formerly declared, and yet may agree in general actions: but, unless the several composed Parts of a Human Creature, had not several perceptive actions, it were impossible to make a general perception, either amongst the several Parts of their own Society, or of Foreign Objects. But, it is impossible for me to describe the different manners and ways of the particular Parts, or the different actions of any one Part: for, what Man can describe the different perceptive actions of that composed Part, the Eye, and so of the rest of the Parts.

CHAP. XX.

That Associations, Divisions, and Alterations, cause several Effects.

The Rational and Sensitive Corporeal Motions, are the perceptive Parts of Nature; and that which causes acquaintance amongst some parts, is their Uniting and Association: That which loses acquaintance of other Parts, is their Divisions and Alterations: for, as Self-compositions cause particular Knowledges, or Acquaintances: So Self-divisions cause particular Ignorances, or Forgetfulnesses: for, as all kinds and sorts of Creatures are produced, nourished, and encreased by the Association

1 Again, all parts know and think—not just the mind, or the rational parts—and these are embodied processes (as illustrated in these overtly material images of painting, embossing, and engraving).

of Parts; so are all kinds and sorts of Perceptions; and according as their Associations, or their Compositions do last, so doth their Acquaintance; which is the cause, that the Observations and Experiences of several and particular Creatures, such as Men, in several and particular Ages, joyned as into one Man or Age, causes strong and long-liv'd Opinions, subtile and ingenious Inventions, happy and profitable Advantages; as also, probable Conjectures, and many Truths, of many Causes and Effects: Whereas, the Divisions of particular Societies, causes what we name Death, Ignorance, Forgetfulness, Obscurity of particular Creatures, and of perceptive Knowledges; so that as particular perceptive Knowledges do alter and change, so do particular Creatures: for, though the Kinds and Sorts last, yet the Particulars do not.

CHAP. XXI.

Of the Differences between Self-Love, and Passionate Love.

Self-love, is like Self-knowledg, which is an innate Nature; and therefore is not that Love Man names *Passionate Love*: for, Passionate Love belongs to several Parts; so that the several parts of one Society, as one Creature, have both Passionate Love, and Self-love, as being sympathetically united in one Society: Also, not only the Parts of one and the same Society, may have Passionate Love to each other; but, between several Societies; and not only several Societies of one Sort, but of different Sorts.

THE SIXTH PART.

CHAP. I.

Of the Motions of some parts of the Mind; and of Forrein Objects.

Notions, Imaginations, Conceptions, and the like, are such Actions of the Mind, as concern not Forrein Objects: and some Notions, Imaginations, or Conceptions of one man, may be like to another man, or many men. Also, the Mind of one man may move in the like Figurative Actions, as the Sensitive Actions of other sorts of Creatures; and that, Man names *Understanding*: and if those Conceptions be afterwards produced, Man names them *Prudence*, or *Fore-sight*; but if those Parts move in such Inventions as are capable to be put into Arts, Man names that *Ingenuity*: but, if not capable to be put into the practice of Arts, Man names it, *Sciences*: if those Motions be so subtile, that the Sensitive cannot imitate them, Man names them, *Fancies*: but, when those Rational Parts move promiscuously, as partly after their own inventions, and partly after the manner of Forrein or outward Objects; Man names them, *Conjectures*, or *Probabilities*: and when there are very many several Figurative, Rational Motions, then Man says, *The Mind is full of Thoughts*: when those Rational Figurative Motions, are of many and different Objects, Man names them, *Experiences*, or *Learning*: but, when there are but few different sorts of such Figurative Motions, Man names them *Ignorances*.

CHAP. II.

Of the Motions of some Parts of the Mind.

When the Rational Figurative Corporeal Motions of an Human Creature, take no notice of Forrein Objects, Man nameth that, *Musing*, or *Contemplating*. And, when the Rational Parts repeat some former Actions, Man names that, *Remembrances*. But, when those Parts alter those Repetitions, Man names that, *Forgetfulness*. And, when those Rational Parts move, according to a present Object, Man names it, *Memory*. And when those Parts divide in divers sorts of Actions, Man names it, *Arguing*, or *Disputing in the Mind*. And when those divers sorts of Actions are at some strife, Man names it, A *contradicting of himself*. And if there be a weak strife, Man names it, *Consideration*. But, when those different Figurative Motions move of one accord, and sympathetically, this Man names, *Discretion*. But, when those different sorts of Actions move sympathetically, and continue in that manner of action, without any alteration, Man names it, *Belief*, *Faith*, or *Obstinacy*. And when those Parts make often changes, as altering their Motions, Man names it *Inconstancy*. When their Rational Parts move slowly, orderly, equally, and sympathetically, Man names it *Sobriety*. When all the Parts of the Mind move regularly, and sympathetically, Man names it, *Wisdom*. When some Parts move partly regularly, and partly irregularly, Man names that, *Foolishness*, and *Simplicity*. When they move generally irregularly, man names it *Madness*.

CHAP. III.

Of the Motions of Human Passions, and Appetites; as also, of the Motions of the Rational and Sensitive Parts, towards Forrein Objects.

When some of the Rational Parts move sympathetically, to some of the Sensitive Perceptions; and those Sensitive Parts sympathize to the Object, it is *Love*. If they move antipathetically to the Object, it is *Hate*. When those Rational and Sensitive Motions, make many and quick repetitions of those sympathetical actions, it is *Desire* and *Appetite*. When those Parts move variously, (as concerning the Object) but yet sympathetically (concerning their own Parts) it is *Inconstancy*. When those Motions move cross towards the Object, and are perturbed, it is *Anger*. But when those perturbed Motions are in confusion, it is *Fear*. When the Rational Motions are partly sympathetical, and partly antipathetical, it is *Hope*, and *Doubt*. And if there be more sympathetical Motions than antipathetical, there is more *Hope* than *Doubt*. If more antipathetical than sympathetical, then more *Doubt* than *Hope*. If those Rational Motions move after a dilating manner, it is *Joy*. If after a contracting manner, it is *Grief*. When those Parts move partly after a contracting, and partly after an attracting manner, as attracting from the Object, it is *Covetousness*. But, if those Motions are sympathetical to the Object, and move after a dilating manner towards the Object, it is *Generosity*. If those Motions are sympathetical to the Object, and move after the manner of a Contraction, it is *Pity* or *Compassion*. If those Motions move antipathetically towards the Object, yet after a dilating manner, it is *Pride*. When those Motions move sympathetically towards the Object, after a dilating manner, it is *Admiration*. If the dilating Action is not extream, it is only *Approving*. If those Motions are antipathetical towards the Object, and are after the manner of an extream contraction, it is *Horror*. But, if those Actions are not so extraordinary as to be extream, it is only *Disapproving*, *Despising*, *Rejecting*, or *Scorning*. If the Rational Parts move carelessly towards Forrein Object, as also partly antipathetically, Man nameth it, *Ill-nature*. But, if sympathetically and industriously, Man nameth it, *Good-nature*. But this is to be noted, That there are many sorts of Motions of one and the same kind; and many several particular Motions, of one sort or Motion; which causes some difference in the Effects: but, they are so nearly related, that it requires a more subtile Observation than I have, to distinguish them.

CHAP. IV.

Of the Repetitions of the Sensitive and Rational Actions.

Both the Rational and Sensitive Corporeal Motions, make often Repetitions of one and the same Actions: The Sensitive Repetitions, Man nameth, *Custom*. The Rational Repetitions, Man nameth, *Remembrances*: for, Repetitions cause a facility amongst the Sensitive Parts; but yet, in some Repeating Actions, the Senses seem to be tired, being naturally delighted in variety. Also, by the Rational Repetitions, the Mind is either delighted, or displeased; and sometimes, partly pleased, and partly displeased: for, the Mind is as much pleased, or displeased in the absence of an Object, as in the presence; only the Pleasure, and Displeasure of the Senses, is not joyned with the Rational: for, the Sense, if Regular, makes the most perfect Copies when the Object is present: but, the Rational can make as perfect Copies in the absence, as in the presence of the Object; which is the cause that the Mind is as much delighted, or grieved, in the absence of an Object, as with the presence: As for example, A Man is as much grieved when he knows his Friend is wounded, or dead, as if he had seen his Wounds, or had seen him dead: for, the Picture of the dead Friend, is in the mind of the living Friend; and if the dead Friend was before his Eyes, he could but have his Picture in his mind; which is the same for an absent Friend alive; only, as I said, there is wanting the Sensitive Perception of the absent Object: And certainly, the Parts of the Mind have greater advantage than the Sensitive Parts; for, the Mind can enjoy that which is not subject to the Sense; as those things Man names, *Castles in the Air*, or *Poetical Fancies*; which is the reason Man can enjoy Worlds of its own making, without the assistance of the Sensitive Parts; and can govern and command those Worlds;[1] as also, dissolve and compose several Worlds, as he pleases: but certainly, as the pleasures of the Rational Parts are beyond those of the Sensitive, so are their Troubles.

CHAP. V.

Of the Passionate Love, and Sympathetical Endeavours, amongst the Associate Parts of a Human Creature.

In every Regular Human Society, there is a Passionate Love amongst the Associated Parts, like fellow-Students of one Colledg, or fellow-Servants in one House, or Brethren in one Family, or Subjects in one Nation, or Communicants in one Church: So the Self-moving Parts of a Human Creature, being associated, love one another, and therefore do endeavour to keep their Society from dissolving. But perceiving, by

1 The suggestion that the imagination can produce what never existed before—and what was never experienced via the senses—is important, and diverges from the opinions of other contemporary thinkers like Hobbes. Here Cavendish may also refer to the autonomy of her own "Poetical Fancies" and specifically the "World" of her 1666 fiction, *Blazing World.*

the example of the lives of the same sort of Creatures, that the property of their Nature is such, that they must dissolve in a short time, this causes these Human sorts of Creatures, (being very ingenuous) to endeavour an after-life: but, perceiving again, that their after-life cannot be the same as the present life is, they endeavour (since they cannot keep their own Society from dissolving) that their Society may remain in remembrance amongst the particular and general Societies of the same sort of Creatures, which we name *Mankind*: And this Design causes all the Sensitive and Rational Parts, in one Society, to be industrious, to leave some Mark for a lasting Remembrance, amongst their fellow-Creatures: which general remembrance, Man calls *Fame*; for which *Fame*, the Rational Parts are industrious to design the manner and way, and the Sensitive Parts are industrious to put those Designs in execution; as, their Inventions, into Arts or Sciences; or to cause their Heroick or Prudent, Generous or Pious Actions; their Learning, or witty Fancies, or subtile Conceptions, or their industrious Observations, or their ingenious Inventions, to be set in Print; or their Exterior Effigies to be cast, cut, or engraven in Brass, or Stone, or to be painted; or they endeavour to build Houses, or cut Rivers, to bear their Names; and millions of other Marks, for remembrance, they are industrious to leave to the perception of after-Ages: And many men are so desirous of this after-life, that they would willingly quit their present life, by reason of its shortness, to gain this after-life, because of the probability of a long continuance; and not only to live so in many several Ages, but in many several Nations. And amongst the number of those that prefer a long after-life, before a short present life, I am one.[1] But, some men dispute against these Desires, saying, That *it doth a man no good to be remembred when he is dead*. I answer: it is very pleasing, whilst a man lives, to have in his Mind, or in his Sense, the Effigies of the Person, and of the good Actions of his Friend, although he cannot have his present company. Also, it is very pleasant to any body to believe, that the Effigies either of his own Person, or Actions, or both, are in the Mind of his Friend, when he is absent from him; and, in this case, Absence and Death are

---

1 Cavendish often discusses her desire to achieve immortality through her work. E.g., see the prefatory epistle to this text (pp. 53–54), as well as the prefatory letters to *PPO* (1665) and *Blazing World*.

much alike. But, in short, God lives no other ways amongst his Creatures, but in their Rational Thoughts, and Sensitive Worship.

CHAP. VI.
Of ACQUAINTANCE.

As there are Perceptive Acquaintances amongst the Parts of a Human Creature; so there is a Perceptive Acquaintance between, or amongst the Human sorts of Creatures. But, mistake me not; for I do not say, Men only are acquainted with each other; for, there is not only an Acquaintance amongst every particular sort, as between one and the same sort of Creatures, but there are some Acquaintances between some sorts of different kinds: as for example, between some sorts of Beasts, and Men; as also, some sorts of Birds, and Men, which understand each other, I will not say, so well as Man and Man; but so well, as to understand each other's Passions: but certainly, every particular sort of Creatures, of one and the same kind, understand each other, as well as Men understand one another; and yet, for all that, they may be unacquainted: for, Acquaintance proceeds from Association; so that, some Men, and some Beasts, by Association, may be acquainted with each other; when as some Men, not associating, are meer strangers. The truth is, Acquaintance belongs rather to Particularities, than Generalities.

CHAP. VII.
Of the Effects of Forrein Objects of the Sensitive Body; and of the Rational Mind of a Human Creature.

According as the Rational Parts are affected, or disaffected with Forrein Objects, the Sensitive is apt to express the like affections, or disaffections: for, most Forrein Objects occasion either pleasure and delight, or displeasure and dislike: but, the effects of Forrein Objects are very many, and, many times very different; as, some Objects of Devotion, occasion a Fear, or Superstition, and Repentance in the Mind; and the Mind occasions the Sensitive Parts to several actions, as, Praying, Acknowledging Faults, Begging pardon, making Vows, imploring Mercy, and the like, in words: also, the Body bows, the Knees bend, the Eyes weep, the hands hold up, and many the like devout actions. Other sorts of Objects occasion pity and compassion in the Mind, which occasions the Sensitive Parts to attend the sick, relieve the poor, help the distressed, and many more actions of Compassion. Other sorts of Forrein Objects, occasion the Rational Mind to be dull and melancholy; and then the Sensitive Parts are dull, making no variety of Appetites, or regard Forrein Objects. Other sorts of Objects occasion the Mind to be vain and ambitious, and often to be proud; and those occasion the Sensitive Actions to be adventurous and bold; the Countenance of the face, scornful; the Garb of the Body, stately; the Words, vaunting, boasting, or bragging. Other Objects occasion the Mind to be furious; and then the Sensitive Actions are, Cursing Words, Frowning Countenances, the Leggs stamping, the Hands and Arms fighting, and the whole Body in a furious posture. Other sorts of Objects occasion the Mind to a passionate Love; and then the Sensitive Actions are, Flattering, Professing, Protesting in words, the Countenance smiling, the Eyes glancing; also, the Body bows, the Leggs scrape, the Mouth kisses: also, the Hands mend their Garments, and do many of the like amorous actions. Other Objects occasion the Mind to Valour; and then the Sensitive Actions are, Daring, Encouraging, or Animating. Other Objects occasion the Mind to Mirth, or Cheerfulness; and they occasion the Sensitive Actions of the Voice, to Sing, or Laugh; the Words to be jesting, the Hands to be toying, the Leggs to be dancing. Other sorts of Objects occasion the Mind to be Prudent; and then the Sensitive Actions, are Sparing or Frugal. Other sorts of Objects occasion the Mind to be Envious, or Malicious; and then the Sensitive Actions are Mischievous. There are great numbers of Occasional Actions, but these are sufficient to prove, *That Sense and Reason understand each other's Actions or Designs.*

CHAP. VIII.

Of the Advantage and Disadvantage of the Encounters of several Creatures.

There is a strong Sympathy between the Rational and Sensitive Parts, in one and the same Society, or Creature: not only for their Consistency, Subsistency, Use, Ease, Pleasure, and Delight; but, for their Safety, Guard, and Defence: as for example, When one Creature assaults another, then all the Powers, Faculties, Properties, Ingenuities, Agilities, Proportions, and Shape, of the Parts of the Assaulted, unite against the Assaulter, in the defence of every particular Part of their whole Society; in which Encounter, the Rational advises, and the Sensitive labours. But this is to be noted concerning advantage and disadvantage in such Encounters, That some sorts of Creatures have their advantage in the Exterior Shape, others meerly in the Number of Parts; others in the agility of their Parts, and some by the ingenuity of their parts:

but, for the most part, the greater Number have advantage over the less, if the greater number of Parts be as regular, and as ingenious as the less number: but, if the less number be more regular, and more ingenious than the greater, then 'tis a hundred to one but the less number of Parts have the advantage.

CHAP. IX.

That All Human Creatures have the like Kinds and Sorts of Properties.

All Human Creatures have the like Kinds and Sorts of Properties, Faculties, Respirations, and Perceptions; unless some Irregularities in the Production, occasion some Imperfections, or some Misfortunes, in some time of his Age: yet, no Man knows what another Man perceives, but by guess, or information of the Party: but, as I said, if they have no Imperfections, all Human Creatures have like Properties, Faculties, and Perceptions: As for example, All Human Eyes may see one and the same Object alike; or hear the same Tune, or Sound; and so of the rest of the Senses. They have also the like Respirations, Digestions, Appetites; and the like may be said of all the Properties belonging to a Human Creature. But, as one Human Creature doth not know what another Human Creature knows, but by Confederacy; so, no Part of the Body, or Mind of a Man, knows each Part's perceptive knowledg, but by Confederacy: so that, there is as much Ignorance amongst the Parts of Nature, as Knowledg. But this is to be noted, That there are several manners and ways of Intelligences, not only between several sorts of Creatures, or amongst particulars of one sort of Creatures; but, amongst the several Parts of one and the same Creature.[1]

CHAP. X.

Of the Irregularity of the Sensitive, and of the Rational Corporeal Motions.

As I have often mentioned, and do here again repeat, That the Rational and Sensitive Parts of one Society, or Creature, do understand, as perceiving each other's Self-moving Parts; and the proof is, That, sometimes, the Human Sense is regular, and the Human Reason irregular; and sometimes that Reason regular, and the Sense irregular: but, in these differences, the Regular Parts endeavour to reform the Irregular; which causes,

---

1 This chapter is an important expression of Cavendish's panpsychism: all parts of nature are conscious and possess knowledge, which is variously transmitted and understood by other parts.

many times, repetitions of one and the same Actions, and Examinations; as, sometimes the Reason examines the Sense; and sometimes the Sense, the Reason: and sometimes the Sense and Reason do examine the Object; for, sometimes an Object will delude both the Sense and Reason; and sometimes the Sense and Reason are but partly mistaken: As for example, A fired end of a Stick, by a swift exterior Circular Motion, appears a Circle of fire, in which they are not deceived: for, by the Exterior Motion, the fired end is a Circle; but they are mistaken, to conceive the Exterior Figurative Action to be the proper natural Figure: but when one man mistakes another, that is some small Error, both of the Sense and Reason. Also, when one man cannot readily remember another man, with whom he had formerly been acquainted, it is an Error; and such small Errors, the Sense and Reason do soon rectifie: but in causes of high Irregularities, as in Madness, Sickness, and the like, there is a great Bustle amongst the Parts of a Human Creature; so as those Disturbances cause unnecessary Fears, Grief, Anger, and strange Imaginations.

CHAP. XI.

Of the Knowledg between the Sensitive Organs of a Human Creature.

The Sensitive Organs are only ignorant of each other, as they are of Forrein Objects: for, as all the Parts of Forrein Objects, are not subject to one Sensitive Organ; so all the Sensitive Organs are not subject to each Sensitive Organ of a Human Creature: yet, in the perceptive Actions of Forrein Objects, they do so agree, that they make an united Knowledg: Thus we may be particularly ignorant one way, and yet have a general Knowledg another way.

CHAP. XII.

Of Human Perception, or Defects of a Human Creature.

It is not the great quantity of Brain, that makes a Man wise; nor a little quantity, that makes a Man foolish: but, the irregular, or regular Rational Corporeal Motions of the Head, Heart, and the rest of the Parts, that causes dull Understandings, short Memories, weak Judgments, violent Passions, extravagant Imaginations, wild Fancies, and the like. The same must be said of the Sensitive Irregular Corporeal Motions, which make Weakness, Pain, Sickness, disordered Appetites, and perturbed Perceptions, and the like: for, Nature poysing her Actions by Opposites, there must needs be Irregularities, as well as Regularities; which is the cause that seldom any Creature is so exact, but there is some Exception. But, when the Sensitive and Rational Corporeal Motions are

Regular, and move sympathetically, then the Body is healthful and strong, the Mind in peace and quiet, understands well, and is judicious: and, in short, there are perfect Perceptions, proper Digestions, easie Respirations, regular Passions, temperate Appetites. But when the Rational Corporeal Motions are curious in their change of Actions, there are subtile Conceptions, and elevated Fancies: and when the Sensitive Corporeal Motions move with curiosity, (as I may say) then there are perfect Senses, exact Proportions, equal Temperaments; and that, Man calls *Beauty*.

CHAP. XIII.
Of Natural FOOLS.

There is a great difference between a Natural Fool, and a Mad Man: for, Madness is a Disease, but a Natural Fool is a Defect;[1] which Defect was some Error in his Production, that is, in the form and frame either of the Mind, or Sense, or both; for, the Sense may be a Natural Fool as well as the Reason; as we may observe in those sorts of Fools whom we name *Changelings*,[2] whose Body is not only deformed, but all the Postures of the Body are defective, and appear as so many fools: but sometimes, only some Parts are fools; as for example, If a Man be born Blind, then only his Eyes are Fools; if Deaf, then only his Ears are Fools, which occasions his dumbness; Ears being the informing Parts, to speak; and wanting those informations, he cannot speak a Language. Also, if a Man is born lame, his Leggs are Fools; that is, those Parts have no knowledg of such Properties that belong to such Parts; but the Sensitive Parts may be wise, as being knowing; and the Rational Parts may be defective; which Defects, Man names *Irrational*. But this is to be noted, That there may be Natural and Accidental Fools, by some extraordinary Frights, or by extraordinary Sickness, or through the defects of Old Age. As for the Errors of Production, they are incurable; as also, those of Old Age; the First being an Error in the very Foundation, and the other a Decay of the whole Frame of the Building: for, after a Human Creature is brought to that perfection, as to be,

1 The etiology of madness preoccupied many thinkers of Cavendish's era, including Hobbes, Thomas Sydenham (1624–89), and van Helmont.

2 In traditional folklore, a "changeling" was a deformed child left by fairies in place of a healthy child. The term was also used more generally to refer to physical and/or mental irregularities.

as we may say, at full growth and strength, at the prime of his age; the Human Motions, and the very Nature of Man, after that time, begins to decay; for then the Human Motions begin to move rather to the dissolution, than to the continuance; although some Men last to very old Age, by reason the unity of their Society is regular and orderly, and moves so Sympathetically as to commit few or no Disorders, or Irregularities; and such old Men are, for the most part, Healthful, and very wise, through long Experience; and their Society having got a habit of Regularity, is not apt to be disturbed by Forrein Parts. But this is to be noted, That sometimes the Sensitive Body decays, before the Rational Mind; and sometimes the Rational Mind, before the Sensitive Body. Also, this is to be noted, That when the Body is defective, but not the Mind; then the Mind is very industrious to find out Inventions of Art, to help the Defects that are natural. But pray mistake me not; for I do not say, That *all* Deformities, or Defects, but only *some* particular sorts of Deformity, or Defects, are Foolish.

THE SEVENTH PART.

CHAP. I.

Of the Sensitive Actions of Sleeping and Waking.

The Sensitive and Rational Corporeal Figurative Motions, are the cause of infinite varieties: for, though Repetitions make no varieties; yet, every altered action is a variety: Also, different Actions, make different Effects; opposite Actions, opposite Effects; not only of the actions of the several Self-moving Parts, or Corporeal Motions, but of the same Parts: As for example, The same Parts, or Corporeal Motions, may move from that, Man names *Life*, to that which Man names *Death*; or, from Health to Sickness, from Ease to Pain, from Memory to Forgetfulness, from Forgetfulness to Remembrance, from Love to Hate, from Grief to Joy, from Irregularity to Regularity; or, from Regularity to Irregularity, and the like; and from one Perception to another: for, though all actions are perceptive, yet there are several kinds, several sorts, and several particular perceptions: But, amongst the several Corporeal Motions of Animal, or Human kind, there are the opposite Motions of what we name *Waking*, and *Sleeping*; the difference is, That Waking-actions are, most commonly, actions of Imitation, especially of the Sensitive Parts; and are more the Exterior, than the Interior actions of a Human Creature. But, the actions of Sleep, are the alterations of the Exterior Corporeal Motions, moving more interiorly, as it were inwardly, and voluntarily: As for example, The Optick Corporeal Motions, in Waking-actions, work, or move, according to the outward Object: but, in Sleeping-actions, they move by rote, or without Examples; also, as I said, they move, as it were, inwardly; like as a Man should turn himself inward, or outward, of a door, without removing from the door, or out of the place he stood in.[1]

CHAP. II.
Of SLEEPING.

Although the Rational and Sensitive Corporeal Motions, can never be tired, or weary of moving or acting, by reason it is their nature to be a perpetual Corporeal Motion; yet they may be weary, or tired with particular actions. Also, it is easier and more delightful, to move by Rote, than to take Copies, or Patterns; which is the reason that Sleep is easie and gentle, if the Corporeal Motions be regular; but if they be irregular, Sleep is perturbed. But this is to be noted, That the Corporeal Motions delight in varieties so well, that, many times, many and various Objects will cause the Sensitive and Rational Corporeal Motions in a Man, to retard their actions of Sleep; and, oft-times, want of variety of Forrein or outward Objects, will occasion the action of Sleep; or else Musing and Contemplating actions. Also, it is to be noted, That if some Parts of the Body, or Mind, be distempered with Irregularities, it occasions such disturbances to the Whole, as hinders that repose; but if the Regular Parts endeavour not to be disturbed with the Irregular; and the Irregulars do disturb the Regular; then it occasions that which Man names, *Half-sleeps*, or *Slumbers*, or *Drowsiness*. And if the Regular Corporeal Motions get the better, (as many times they do) then we say, Sleep hath been the occasion of the Cure; and it oft proves so. And it is a common saying, *That a good Sleep will settle the Spirits, or ease the Pains*; that is, when the Regular Corporeal Motions have had the better of the Irregular.

---

1 This account of dreaming as rational thought working "without Examples," or without perception, stands in stark contrast to that of Hobbes, who claims that dreams and imaginations are the remnants of "decaying sense." See *Leviathan* 42.

CHAP. III.

Of Human DREAMS.[1]

There are several kinds, sorts, and particulars of Corporeal Irregularities, as well as of Regularities; and amongst the infinite kinds, sorts, and particulars, there is that of Human Dreams; for, the Exterior Corporeal Motions in Waking-actions, do copy or pattern outward Objects; whereas, in actions of Sleep, they act by rote, which, for the most part, is erroneous, making mixt Figures of several Objects; as, partly like a Beast; and partly, like a Bird, or Fish; nay, sometimes, partly like an Animal, and partly like a Vegetable; and millions of the like Extravagancies; yet, many times, Dreams will be as exact as if a Man was awake, and the Objects before him; but, those actions by rote, are more often false than true: but, if the Self-moving Parts move after their own inventions, and not after the manner of Copying; or, if they move not after the manner of Human Perception, then a Man is as ignorant of his Dreams, or any Human Perception, as if he was in a Swound;[2] and then he says, he did not dream; and, that such Sleeps are like Death.

CHAP. IV.

Of the Actions of DREAMS.

When the Figures of those Friends and Acquaintants that have been dead a long time, are made in our Sleep, we never, or seldom question the truth of their being alive, though we often question them how they came to be alive: And the reason that we make no doubt of their being alive, is, That those Corporeal Motions of Sleep, make the same pattern of that Object in Sleep, as when that Object was present, and patterned awake; so as the Picture in Sleep seems to be the Original awake: and until such times that the Corporeal Motions alter their Sleeping-Actions to Waking-Actions, the truth is not known. Though Sleeping and Dreaming, is somewhat after the manner of Forgetfulness and Remembrance; yet, perfect Dreams are as perceptive as Waking-patterns of present Objects; which proves, That both the Sensitive and Rational Motions, have Sleeping Actions;[3] but both

---

1 Again in the case of dreaming, Hobbes is a key source for Cavendish; see especially *Leviathan* 43–45.

2 A swoon or faint.

3 When we sleep, in other words, our minds engage in "Sleeping" versions of perception, imagination, and cognition, which are material processes that ignite material passions and thoughts.

the Sensitive and Rational Corporeal Actions in Sleep, moving partly by rote, and partly voluntarily, or by invention, make Walking-Woods, or Woodden Men; or make Warrs and Battels, where some Figures of Men are kill'd, or wounded, others have victory: They also make Thieves, Murderers, falling Houses, great Fires, Floods, Tempests, high Mountains, great Precipices; and sometimes pleasant Dreams of Lovers, Marriage, Dancing, Banquetting, and the like: And the Passions in Dreams are as real, as in waking actions.

CHAP. V.

Whether the Interior Parts of a Human Creature, do sleep.

The Parts of my Mind were in dispute, Whether the Interior Parts of a Human Creature, had sleeping and waking actions? The Major Part was of opinion, That Sleep was not proper to those Human Parts, because the Interior Motions were not like the Exterior. The Opinion of the Minor Part was, That change of Action, is like Ease after Labour; and therefore it was probable, the Interior Parts had sleeping and waking actions. The Opinion of the Major Parts, was, That if those Parts, as also the Food received into the Body, has sleeping actions, the Body could not be nourished; for, the Meat would not be digested into the like Parts of the Body, by reason sleeping actions were not such sorts of actions. The Opinion of the Minor Parts was, That the sleeping actions were nourishing actions, and therefore were most proper for the Interior Parts; and, for proof, the whole Human Body becomes faint and weak, when they are hindred, either by some Interior Irregularity, or through some Exterior Occasion, from their sleeping actions. The Opinion of the Major Part, was, That sleeping actions are actions of rote, and not such altering actions as digesting actions, and nourishing actions, which are uniting actions. Besides, that the reason why the Interior actions are not sleeping actions, was, That when the Exterior Parts move in the actions of Sleep, the Interior Parts move when the Exterior are awake; as may be observed by the Human Pulse, and Human Respiration; and by many other Observations which may be brought.

CHAP. VI.

Whether all the Creatures in Nature, have Sleeping and Waking Actions.

Some may ask this Question, *Whether all Creatures have sleeping Actions?* I answer, That though sleeping actions are proper to Human Creatures, as also, to most Animal Creatures; yet, such actions may not any ways be proper to other kinds and sorts of Creatures: and if (as in all probability it is) that the Interior[1] Parts of a Human Creature have no such sleeping actions, it is probable that other kinds and sorts of Creatures move not at any time, in such sorts of actions. But some may say, *That if Nature is poysed, all Creatures must have sleeping actions, as well as waking actions.* I answer, That though Nature's actions are poysed, yet that doth not hinder the variety of Nature's actions, so as to tye Nature to particular actions: As for example, The Exterior Parts of Animals have both sleeping and waking actions; yet that doth not prove, that therefore all the Parts or Creatures in Nature, must have sleeping and waking actions. The same may be said of all the actions of an Animal Creature, or of a Human Creature; nay, of all the Creatures of the World: for, several kinds and sorts of Creatures, have several kinds and sorts of Properties: Wherefore, if there be other kinds and sorts of Worlds besides this, 'tis probable that those Worlds, and all the Parts, or several kinds and sorts of Creatures there, have different properties and actions, from those of this World;[2] so that though Nature's actions are poysed and balanced, yet they are poysed and balanced after different manners and ways.

CHAP. VII.

Of Human Death.

Death is not only a general Alteration of the Sensitive and Rational Motions, but a general Dissolution of their Society. And as there are degrees of Time in Productions, so in Dissolutions. And as there are degrees to Perfection, as from Infancy to Manhood; so there are degrees from Manhood to Old Age. But, as I said, *Death* is a general Dissolution, which makes a Human Creature to be no more: yet, some Parts do not dissolve so soon as others; as for example, Human Bones; but, though the Form or Frame of Bones is not dissolved; yet the Properties of those Bones are altered. The same when a Human Creature is kept by Art from dissolving, so as the Form, or Frame, or Shape may continue; but

1 In the corrected text, Cavendish changed this word to read "Interior" rather than "Exterior."

2 The possibility of other worlds that might or might not be perceivable to humans fascinated Cavendish; she goes on to discuss this at length in Part 13, Chapter 14 (p. 184), and in the Appendix (pp. 193–211).

all the Properties are quite altered; though the Exterior Shape of such Bodies doth appear somewhat like a Man, yet that Shape is not a Man.

CHAP. VIII.

Of the Heat of Human Life, and the Cold of Human Death.

There are not only several sorts of Properties belonging to several sorts of Creatures, but several sorts of Properties belonging to one and the same sort of Creature; and amongst the several sorts of Human Properties, Human Heat is one, which Man names *Natural Heat*: but, when there is a general alteration of the Human Properties, there is that alteration of the Property as well of his Natural, as Human Heat: but, Natural Heat is not the cause of Human Life, though Human Life is the cause of that Natural Heat: so that, when Human Life is altered or dissolved, Human Heat is altered or dissolved: And as Death is opposite Actions to that Man names *Life*; so Cold is opposite Actions to that Man names *Heat*.

CHAP. IX.

Of the Last Act of Human Life.

The reason some Human Creatures dye in more pain than others, is, That the Motions of some Human Creatures are in strife, because some would continue their accustomed Actions, others would alter their accustomed Actions; which Strife causes Irregularities, and those Irregularities cause Differences, or Difficulties, which causes Pain: but certainly, the last Act of Human Life is easie; not only that the Expulsive Actions of Human Respirations, are more easie than the Attracting Actions; but, that in the last act of Human Life, all the Motions do generally agree in one Action.

CHAP. X.

Whether a Human Creature hath Knowledg in Death, or not?

Some may ask the Question, *Whether a dead Man hath any Knowledg or Perception*? I answer, That a dead Man hath not a Human Knowledg or Perception; yet all, and every Part, hath Knowledg and Perception: But, by reason there is a general alteration of the actions of the Parts of a Human Creature, there cannot possibly be a Human Knowledg or Perception. But some may say, That a Man in a Swound hath a general alteration of Human actions; and yet those Parts of a Human Creature do often repeat those former actions, and then a Man is as he was before he was in that Swound. I answer,

That the reason why a Man in a Swound hath not the same Knowledg as when he is not in a Swound, is, that the Human Motions are not generally altered, but only are generally irregular; which makes such a disturbance, that no Part can move so regularly, as to make proper Perceptions; as in some sorts of Distempers, a Man may be like a Natural Fool; in others, he may be Mad; and is subject to many several Distempers, which cause several Effects: but a Human Swound is somewhat like Sleeping without Dreaming; that is, the Exterior Senses do not move to Human Exterior Perception.

CHAP. XI.

Whether a Creature may be new Formed, after a general Dissolution.

Some may ask the Question, *Whether a Human Creature, or any other Creature, after their Natural Properties are quite altered, can be repeated, and rechanged, to those Properties that formerly were?*

I answer, Yes, in case none of the Fundamental Figurative Parts be dissolved.

But some may ask, *That if those dissolved Parts were so inclosed in other Bodies, that none of them could easily disperse or wander; whether they might not joyn into the same Form and Figure again, and have the same Properties?*

I answer, I cannot tell well how to judg; but I am of the opinion, they cannot: for, it is the property of all such Productions, to be performed by degrees, and that there should be a dividing and uniting of Parts, as an intercourse of Home and Forrein Parts; and so there is requir'd all the same Parts, and every Part of the same Society, or that had any adjoining actions with that particular Creature; as all those Parts, or Corporeal Motions, that had been from the first time of Production, to the last of the Dissolving; and that could not be done without a Confusion in Nature.

But some may say, *That although the same Creature could not be produced after the same manner, nor return to the degree of his Infancy, and pass the degrees from his Infancy, to some degree of Age; yet, those parts that are together, might so joyn, and move, in the same manner, as to be the same Creature it was before its dissolution?*

I answer, It may not be impossible: but yet, It is very improbable, that such numerous sorts of Motions, after so general an Alteration, should so generally agree in an unnatural action.[1]

---

1 Cavendish finds the restoration of human life unlikely, due to the complexity of "numerous sorts of Motions" acting in concert, but she goes on to explore this idea further in Part 8 (p. 118), and, more substantially, in Part 5 of the Appendix (pp. 212–21).

CHAP. XII.
Of FOREKNOWLEDG.

I have had some Disputes amongst the Parts of my Mind, *Whether Nature hath Foreknowledg?* The Opinion of the Minor Parts was, That Nature had Foreknowledg, by reason all that was Material, was part of her self; and those Self-parts having Self-motion, she might foreknow what she would act, and so what they should know. The Opinion of the Major Parts was, That by reason every Part had Self-motion, and natural Free-will, Nature could not foreknow how they would move, although she might know how they have moved, or how they do move.

After this Dispute was ended, then there was a Dispute, *Whether the particular Parts had a Foreknowledg of Self-knowledg?* The Opinion of the Minor Parts was, That since every Part in Nature had Self-motion, and natural Free-will, every Part could know how they should move, and so what they should know. The Opinion of the Major Parts was, That first, the Self-knowledg did alter according to Self-action, amongst the Self-moving Parts: but, the Self-knowledg of the Inanimate Parts, did alter according to the actions of the Sensitive Self-moving Parts; and the Perceptive actions of the Self-moving Parts, were according to the form and actions of the Objects: so that Foreknowledg of Forein Parts, or Creatures, could not be: And for Foreknowledg of Self-knowledg of the Self-moving Parts, there were so many occasional actions, that it was impossible the Self-moving Parts could know how they should move, by reason that no Part had an Absolute Power, although they were Self-moving, and had a natural Free-will: which proves, That Prophesies are somewhat of the nature of Dreams, whereof some may prove true by chance; but, for the most part, they are false.

THE EIGHTH PART.

CHAP. I.
Of the Irregularity of Nature's Parts.

Some may make this Question, that, *If Nature were Self-moving, and had Free-will, it is probable that she would never move her Parts so irregularly, as to put her self to pain.*

I answer, first, That Nature's Parts move themselves, and are not moved by any Agent. Secondly, Though Nature's Parts are Self-moving, and Self-knowing, yet they have not an infinite or uncontrollable Power; for, several Parts, and Parties, oppose, and oft-times obstruct each other; so that many times they are forced to move, and they may not when they would. Thirdly, Some Parts may occasion other Parts to be irregular, and keep themselves in a regular posture. Lastly, Nature's Fundamental actions are so poysed, that Irregular actions are as natural as Regular.

CHAP. II.

Of the Human Parts of a Human Creature.

The Form of Man's Exterior and Interior Parts, are so different, and so numerous; that I cannot describe them, by reason I am not so learned to know them: But, some Parts of a Human Creature, Man names *Vital*; because, the least disturbance of any of those Parts, endangers the Human Life: and if any of those Vital Parts are diminished, I doubt whether they can be restored; but if some of those Parts can be restored, I doubt all cannot. The Vital Parts are, the Heart, Liver, Lungs, Stomack, Kidneys, Bladder, Gaul, Guts, Brains, Radical Humours, or Vital Spirits; and others which I know not of. But this is to be noted, That Man is composed of Rare and Solid Parts, of which there are more and less Solid, more and less Rare; as also, different sorts of Solid, and different sorts of Rare: also, different sorts of Soft and Hard Parts; likewise, of Fixt and Loose Parts; also, of Swift and Slow Parts. I mean by Fixt, those that are more firmly united.

CHAP. III.

Of Human Humours.

Humours are such Parts, that some of them may be divided from the whole Body, without danger to the whole Body; so that they are somewhat like Excremental parts, which Excremental parts, are the superfluous parts: for, though the Humours be so necessary, that the Body could not well subsist without them; yet, a Superfluity of them is as dangerous, (if not more) as a Scarcity. But there are many sorts of Humours belonging to a Human Creature, although Man names but Four, according to the Four Elements, *viz. Flegm*, *Choler*, *Melancholy*, and *Blood*: but, in my opinion, there are not only several sorts of *Choler*, *Flegm*, *Melancholy*, and *Blood*; but other sorts that are none of these Four.[1]

1 Cavendish adopts the Galenic system of humors—phlegm, blood, yellow bile (choler), and black bile (melancholy)—but also suggests that there are many more humors than are commonly assumed.

CHAP. IV.

Of BLOOD.

I have heard, that the Opinions of the most Learned Men, are, That all Animal Creatures have Blood, or at least, such Juyces that are in lieu of Blood; which Blood, or Juyces, move circularly:[1] for my part, I am too ignorant to dispute with Learned Men; but yet I am confident, a *Moth* (which is a sort of Worm, of Fly, that eats Cloth) hath no Blood, no, nor any Juyce; for, so soon as it is touched, it dissolves straight to a dry dust, or like ashes. And there are many other Animals, or Insects, that have no appearance of Blood; therefore the life of an Animal doth not consist of Blood: And as for the Circulation of Blood, there are many Animal Creatures that have not proper Vessels, as Veins and Arteries, or any such Gutters, for their Blood, or Juyce, to circulate through. But, say the Blood of Man, or of such like Animal, doth circulate; then it is to be studied, Whether the several parts of the Blood do intermix with each other, as it flows; or, whether it flows as Water seems to do; where the following parts may be as great strangers to the Leading parts, as in a Crowd of People, where some of those behind, do not know those that are before: but, if the Blood doth not intermix as it flows, then it will be very difficult for a Chyrurgion,[2] or Physician, to find where the ill Blood runs: besides, if the Blood be continually flowing, when a sick Man is to be let blood, before the Vein is opened, the bad Blood may be past that Part, or Vein, and so only the good Blood will be let out; and then the Man may become worse than if he had not been let blood.[3]

CHAP. V.

Of the Radical Humours, or Parts.

There are many Parts in a Human Body, that are as the Foundation of a House; and being the Foundation, if any of those Parts be removed or decayed, the House immediately falls to ruine. These Fundamental Parts, are those we name the *Vital Parts*; amongst which are those Parts we name the *Vital* and *Radical Spirits*, which are the Oyl and Flame of a Human Creature, causing the Body to have that we name a *Natural Heat*, and a *Radical*

---

1 The circulation of blood had only been discovered in 1628 by William Harvey. Whether all animal creatures had blood was an actively debated question at this time.

2 Surgeon.

3 Blood-letting was a common medical practice that was thought to treat a wide range of physical and mental illnesses.

Moisture.[1] But it is to be noted, That these Parts, or Corporeal Motions, are not like gross Oyl, or Flame: for, I believe, there are more differences between those Flames, and ordinary Flames, than between the Light of the Sun, and the Flame of a Tallow Candle; and as such difference between this Oyl, and the greasie Oyl, as between the purest Essence, and Lamp-Oyl. But, these Vital Parts are as necessary to the Human Life, as the solid Vital Parts, *viz.* the Heart, Liver, Lungs, Brains, and the like.

CHAP. VI.

Of Expelling Malignant Disorders in a Human Creature.

Expelling of Poyson, or any Malignity in the Body, is, when that Malignity hath not got, or is not settled into the Vital Parts; so that the Regular Motions of the Vital Parts, and other Parts of the Body, endeavour to defend themselves from the Forrein Malignancies; which if they do, then the Malignant Motions do dilate to the Exterior Parts, and issue out of those Exterior Passages, at least, through some; as, either by the way of Purging, Vomiting, Sweating, or Transpiration, which is a breathing through the Pores, or other passages. After the same manner is the expelling of Surfeits, or Superfluities of Natural Humours: but, if the Malignity or Surfeit, Superfluity or superfluous Humours, have the better, (as I may say) then those Irregular Motions, by their Disturbances, cause the Regular Motions to be Irregular, and to follow the Mode; which is, to imitate Strangers, or the most Powerful; the most Fantastical, or the most debauch'd: for it is, many times, amongst the Interior Motions of the Body, as with the Exterior Actions of Men.

CHAP. VII.

Of Human Digestions and Evacuations.

To treat of the several particular Digestive Actions of a Human Creature, is impossible: for, not only every part of Food hath a several manner of Digestive Action; but, every action in Transpiration, is a sort of Digestion and Evacuation: so that, though every sort of Digestion and Evacuation, may be ghest at; yet, every Particular is not so known, that it can be described. But this is to be noted, That there is no Creature that hath Digestive Motions, but hath Evacuating Motions; which Actions, although they are but Dividing, and Uniting; yet they are such different manners and ways of uniting and dividing, that the

1 Heat and moisture were associated with the "sanguine" humor, or blood.

most observing Man cannot particularly know them, and so not express them: but, the Uniting actions, if regular, are the Nourishing actions; the Dividing actions, if regular, are the Cleansing actions: but if irregular, the Uniting actions are the Obstructive actions; and the Dividing actions, the Destructive actions.

CHAP. VIII.

Of DISEASES in general.

There are many sorts of Human Diseases; yet, all sorts of Diseases are Irregular Corporeal Motions; but, every sort of Motion is of a different Figure: so that, several Diseases are different Irregular Figurative Motions; and according as the Figurative Motions vary, so do the Diseases:[1] but, as there are Human Diseases, so there are Human Defects; which Defects (if they be those which Man names *Natural*) cannot be rectified by any Human Means. Also, there are Human Decays, and Old Age; which, although they cannot be prevented, or avoided; yet, they may, by good Order, and wise Observations, be retarded: but there are not only numerous sorts of Diseases, but every particular it self, and every particular sort, are more or less different; insomuch, that seldom a Disease of one and the same sort, is just alike, but there are some differences; as in Men, who though they be all of one sort of Animal-kind, yet seldom any two Men are just alike: and the same may be said of Diseases both of Body and Mind; as for example, concerning Irregular Minds, as in Mad-Men; Although all Mad-Men are mad, yet not mad alike; though they all have the Disease either of Sensitive or Rational Madness, or are both Sensitively and Rationally mad. Also, this is to be noted, That as several Diseases may be produced from several Causes, so several Diseases from one Cause, and one Disease from several Causes; which is the cause that a Physician ought to be a long and subtile Observer and Practiser, before he can arrive to that Experience which belongs to a good Physician.

CHAP. IX.

Of the Fundamental Diseases.

There are numerous sorts of Diseases, to which Human Creatures are subject; and yet there are but few Fundamental Maladies;

---

1 This concept of disease as a material entity shares some similarities with van Helmont's description of disease in *Oriatrike* (1662); in general, however, Cavendish rejects van Helmont's medical outlook. See also Appendix C2.

which are these as follow; Pain, Sickness, Weakness, Dizziness, Numbness, Deadness, Madness, Fainting and Swounding; of which one is particular, the rest are general: The particular is Sickness, to which no parts of the Body are subject, but the Stomack: for, though any parts of the Body may have Pain, Numbness, Dizziness, Weakness, or Madness; yet in no part can be that which is name Sickness, but the Stomack. As for Dizziness, the Effects are general, as may be observed in some drunken Men: for, many times, the Head will be in good Temper, when the Leggs (I cannot say, are dizzie, yet) will be so drunk, as neither to go or stand; and many times the Tongue will be so drunk, as not to speak plain, when all the rest of the body is well temper'd; at least so well, as not to be any ways perceived, but by the tripping of their Speech: but, as I said, no Part is subject to be sick, but the Stomack: And though there are numerous sorts of Pains to which every Part is subject, and every several Part hath a several Pain; yet they are still Pain. But some may say, *That there are also several sorts of Sicknesses.* I grant it; but yet those several sorts of Sicknesses, belong only to the Stomack, and to no other Part of the Body.

THE NINTH PART.

CHAP. I.

Of SICKNESS.

To go on as orderly as I can, I will treat of the Fundamental Diseases, and first of *Sickness*, by reason it is the most particular Disease: for though, as I have said, no part of a Human Creature is subject to that Disease, (namely, Sickness) but the Stomack; yet, there are different sorts of Sicknesses of the Stomack; as for example, Some sorts of Sickness is like the flowing and ebbing of the Sea: for, the Humours of the Stomack agitate in that manner, as, if the flowing motions flow upwards, it occasions Vomiting; if downwards, Purging: if the Humours divide, as, partly to flow upwards, and partly downwards, it occasions both Vomiting and Purging.

But the Question is, *Whether it is the motion of the Humours, that occasions the Stomack to be sick; or the sickness of the Stomack, that occasions the Humours to flow?*

I answer: That 'tis probable, that sometimes the flowing of the Humours causes the Stomack to be sick; and sometimes the sickness of the Stomack occasions the Humours to flow; and sometimes the Stomack will be sick without the flowing of Humours, as when the Stomack is empty; and sometimes the

Humours will flow, without any disturbance to the Stomack; and sometimes both the Humours and the Stomack do jointly agree in Irregularities: but, as I said, there are several sorts of sicknesses of the Stomack, or at least, that sickness doth produce several sorts of Effects; as, for example, some sorts of sickness will occasion faint and cold Sweats; which sick Motion is not flowing up or down of the Humours; but it is a cold dilation, or rarifying, after a breathing manner; also expelling of those rarified parts through the pores: Other sorts of Motions of the Humours, are like Boyling motions, *viz.* Bubling motions; which occasion steaming or watry vapours, to ascend to the Head; which vapours are apt to cloud to perception of Sight.[1] Other sorts of sick Motions, are Circular, and those cause a swimming, or a dizzie motion in the Head, and sometimes a staggering motion in the Leggs. Other sorts of sick Motions are occasioned through tough and clammy Humours, the motion of which Humours, is a winding or turning in such a manner, that it removes not from its Center; and until such time as that Turning or Winding Motions alter, or the Humour is cast out of the Stomack, the Patient finds little or no ease.

CHAP. II.
Of PAIN.

As I said, No Part is subject to be sick, but the Stomack; but every several Part of a Human Creature, is subject to *Pain*; and not only so, but every particular Part is subject to several sorts of Pain; and every several sort of Pain, hath a several Figurative Motion: but to know the different Figurative Motions, will require a subtile Observation: for, though those painful Parts, know their own Figurative Motions; yet, the whole Creature (suppose *Man*) doth not know them. But it may be observed, Whether they are caused by Irregular Contractions or Attractions, Dilations or Retentions, Expulsions or Irregular Pressures and Re-actions, or Irregular Transformations, or the like; and by those Observations, one may apply, or endeavour to apply proper Remedies; but all Pain proceeds from Irregular and perturbed Motions.

---

1 "Vapors," or internal emanations, were an oft-discussed cause of illness in the early modern era and were thought to stem from the gut or bowels. Some also believed they arose from the womb and were therefore more prevalent in women.

CHAP. III.

Of DIZZINESS.

I Cannot say, *Dizziness* belongs only to the Head of an Animal Creature, because we may observe, by irregular Drinkers, that sometimes the Leggs will seem more drunk than their Heads; and sometimes all Parts of their Body will seem to be temperate, as being Regular, but only the Tongue seems to be drunk: for, staggering of the Leggs, and a staggering of the Tongue, or the like, in a drunken Distemper, is a sort of Dizziness, although not such a sort as that which belongs to the Head; so that, when a man is dead-drunk, we may say, that every part of that Body is *Dizzily drunk*. But mistake me not; for I do not mean, that all sorts of dizzinesses proceed from drinking; I only bring Drunkenness for an Example: but, the Effects of dizziness of the Head, and other parts of the Body, proceed from different Causes; for, some proceed from Wind, not Wine; others from Vapour; some from the perception of some Forrein Object; and numbers of the like Examples may be found. But this is to be noted, That all such sorts of Swimming and Dizziness in the Head, are produced from Circular Figurative Motions. Also it is to be noted, That many times the Rational Corporeal Motions are Irregular with the Sensitive, but not always: for, sometimes in these and the like Distempers, the Sensitive will be Irregular, and the Rational Regular; but, for the most part, the Rational is so compliant with the Sensitive, as to be Regular, or Irregular, as the Sensitive is.

CHAP. IV.

Of the Brain seeming to turn round in the Head.

When the Human Brain seems to turn round, the cause is, that some Vapours do move in a Circular Figure, which causes the Head to be dizzy; as when a man turns round, not only his Head will be dizzy, but all the Exterior Parts of his Body; insomuch that some, by often turning round, will fall down; but if, before they fall, they turn the contrary way, they will be free from that dizziness: The reason of which is, That, by turning the contrary way, the Body is brought to the same posture it was before; as, when a man hath travell'd some way, and returns the same way back, he returns to the place where first he began his Journey.

CHAP. V.

Of WEAKNESS.

There are many sorts of *Weakness*; some Weakness proceeds from Age; others, through want of Food; others are occasioned by

Oppression; others by, by Disorders and Irregularities; and so many other sorts, that it would be too tedious to repeat them, could I know them: But, such sorts of Weakness, as Human Creatures are subject to, after some Disease or Sickness, are somewhat like Weariness after a Laborious or over-hard Action; as, when a Man hath run fast, or labored hard, he fetches his breath short and thick; and as most of the Sensitive Actions are by degrees, so is a Returning to Health after Sickness: but, all Irregularities are Laborious.

CHAP. VI.
Of SWOUNDING.

The cause why a Man in *Swound*, is, for a time, as if he were dead; is, an Irregularity amongst some of the Interior Corporeal Motions, which causes an Irregularity of the Exterior Corporeal Motions, and so a general Irregularity; which is the cause that a Man appears as if he were dead.

But some may say, *A Man in a Swound is void of all Motion.*

I answer: That cannot be: for, if the Man was really dead, yet his Parts are moving, though they move not according to the property or nature of a living Man: but, if the Body had not consistent Motions, and the Parts did not hold together, it would be dissolved in a moment; and when the Parts do divide, they must divide by Self-motion: but, in a Man in a Swound, some of his Corporeal Motions are only altered from the property and nature of a living Man; I say, some of his Corporeal Motions, not all: Neither do those Motions quite alter from the nature of a living Man, so as the alterations of the Fundamental Motions do: but they are so alter'd, as Language may be alter'd, *viz.* From *Hebrew* to *Greek, Latin, French, Spanish, English*, and many others; and although they are all but Languages, yet they are several Languages or Speeches; so the alteration of the Corporeal Motions of a Man in a Swound, is but as the altering of one sort of Language to another; as put the case, *English* were the Natural Language or Speech, then all other Languages were unknown to him that knows no other than his Natural: So a Man in a Swound is ignorant of those Motions in the Swound: but, when those Motions return to the Nature of a living Man, he hath the same knowledg he had before. Thus Human Ignorance, and Human Knowledg, may be occasioned by the alterations of the Corporeal Motions. The truth is, that Swounding and Reviving, is like Forgetfulness and Remembrance, that is, Alteration and Repetition, or Exchange of the same Actions.

CHAP. VII.

Of Numb and Dead Palsies, or Gangren's.

As for *Numb* and *Dead Palsies*,[1] they proceed not only from disordered and Irregular Motions, but from such Figurative Motions as are quite different from the nature of the Creature: for, though it be natural for a Man to dye; yet the Figurative Motions of Death are quite different from the Figurative Motions of Life; so in respect to that which Man names *Life*, that which Man names *Death*, is unnatural: but, as there are several sorts of that Man names *Life*, or *Lives*; so there are several sorts of those Corporeal Motions, Man names *Death*: but, *Dead Palsies* of some Parts of a Man's Body, are not like those of a Man when he is, as we say, *quite dead*; for, those are not only such sorts of Motions that are quite, or absolutely different from the life of the Man, or such like Creature; but such as dissolve the whole Frame, or Figure of the Creature: But, the Motions of a *Dead Palsie*, are not dissolving Motions, although they are different from the natural living Motions of a Man. The same, in some manner, are *Numb Palsies*; only the Motions of *Numb Palsies* are not so absolutely different from the natural living Motions; but have more Irregularities, than perfect Alterations. As for that sort of Numbness we name *Sleepy Numbness*, it is occasioned though some obstruction that hinders and stops the Exterior Sensitive Perception. As, when the Eyes are shut, or blinded, or the Ears stopt, or the Nostrils; the Sensitive Figurative Motions of those Sensitive Organs, cannot make Perceptions of Forrein Objects: so, when the Pores of the Flesh, which are the perceptive Organs of Forrein Touches, are stopt, either by too heavy burthens of pressings, or tying some Parts so hard, as to close the Exterior Organs, (*viz.* the Pores) they cannot make such Perceptions as belong to Touch: but, when those hinderances are removed, then the Sensitive Perception of Touch, is, in a short time, as perfect as before.

As for *Gangren's*,[2] although they are somewhat like *Dead Palsies*, yet they are more like those sorts of dead Corporeal Motions, that dissolve the Frame and Form of a Creature: for, *Gangren's* dissolve the Frame and Form of the Diseased Part; and the like do all those Corporeal Motions that cause Rottenness, or Parts to divide and separate after a rotten manner.

---

1 The loss of sensation in various parts of the body.

2 I.e., gangrene, or the death of body tissue.

CHAP. VIII.
Of MADNESS.

There are several sorts of that Distemper named *Madness*; but they all proceed through the Irregularities, either of the Rational, or the Sensitive Parts; and sometimes from the Irregularities both of Sense and Reason: but these Irregularities are not such as are quite different from the Nature or Property of a Human Creature, but are only such Irregularities as make false Perceptions of Forrein Objects, or else make strange Conceptions; or move after the manner of Dreams in waking-actions; which is not according to the Perception of the present Objects: As for example, The Sensitive Motion of the Exterior Parts, make several Pictures on the outside of the Organs; when as no such Object is present; and that is the reason Mad-men see strange and unusual Sights, hear strange and unusual Sounds, have strange and unusual Tasts and Touch: but, when the Irregularities are only amongst the Rational Parts, then those that are so diseased, have violent Passions, strange Conceptions, wild Fancies, various Opinions, dangerous Designs, strong Resolutions, broken Memories, imperfect Remembrances, and the like. But, when both the Sensitive and Rational are sympathetically disorderly; then the Mad-men will talk extravagantly, or laugh, sing, sigh, weep, tremble, complain, *&c.* without cause.

CHAP. IX.
The Sensitive and Rational Parts may be distinctly Mad.[1]

The Senses may be irregularly mad, and not the Reason; and the Reason may be irregularly mad, and not the Sense; and, both Sense and Reason may be both sympathetically mad: And, an evident proof that there is a Rational and Sensitive Madness, is, That those whose Rational Parts are Regular, and only some of the Sensitive Irregular, will speak soberly, and declare to their Friends, how some of their Senses are distemper'd, and how they see strange and unusual Sights, hear unusual Sounds, smell unusual Sents, feel unusual Touches, and desire some Remedy for their Distempers. Also, it may be observed, That sometimes the Rational Parts are madly distemper'd, and not the Sensitive; as when the Sensitive Parts make no false Perceptions, but only the Rational; and then only the Mind is out of order, and is extravagant, and not the

1 Because all of nature is sentient and self-moving, Cavendish must acknowledge that all things—and all types of matter—can go mad.

Senses: but, when the Sense and Reason are madly Irregular, then the diseased Man is that we name, *Outragiously Mad.*

CHAP. X.

The Parts of the Head are not only subject to Madness, but also the other Parts of the Body.

Madness is not only in the Head, but in other Parts of the Body: As for example, Some will feel unusual Touches in their Hands, and several other parts of their Body. We may also observe by the several and strange Postures of Mad-men, that the several Parts of the Body are madly distemper'd. And it is to be noted, That sometimes some Parts of the Body are mad, and not the other; as, sometimes only the Eyes, sometimes only the Ears; and so of the rest of the Organs, and of the rest of the Parts of the Body; one Part only being mad, and the rest in good order. Moreover, it is to be noted, That some are not continually mad, but only mad by fits, or at certain times; and those fits, or certain times of disorders, proceed from a custom or habit of the Rational or Sensitive Motions, to move Irregularly at such times; and a proof that all the Parts are subject to the Distemper of *Madness*, is, That every part of the Body of those sorts of Mad-men that believe their Bodies to be Glass, moves in a careful and wary motion, for fear of breaking in pieces.[1] Neither are the Exterior Parts only subject to the Distemper of Madness, but the Interior Parts, as may be observed, when the whole Body will tremble through a mad fear, and the Heart will beat disorderly, and the Stomack will many times be sick.

CHAP. XI.

The Rational and Sensitive Parts of a Human Creature, are apt to disturb each other.

Although the Rational and Sensitive Corporeal Motions, may, and do sometimes, disagree; yet, for the most part, there is such a sympathetical Agreement between the Sensitive and Rational Corporeal Motions of one Society, (*viz.* of one Creature) as they often disturb each other: As for example, If the Rational Motions are so irregular, as to make imaginary Fears, or fearful Imaginations, these fearful Imaginations cause the Sensitive Corporeal

1 The "glass delusion" was commonly discussed during the period, as evident in the work of Robert Burton (1577–1640), Miguel de Cervantes (1547–1616), Descartes, Constantijn Huygens (1596–1687), and John Locke (1632–1704).

motions, to move according to the Irregularities of the Rational; which is the cause, in such fears, that a man seems to see strange and unusual Objects, to hear strange and unusual Sounds, to smell unusual Sents, to feel unusual Touches, and to be carried to unusual Places; not that there are such Objects, but the Irregular Senses make such Pictures in the Sensitive Organs; and the whole Body may, through the strength of the Irregular motions, move strangely to unusual places: As for example, A Mad-man, in a strong mad fit, will be as strong as Ten men; whereas, when the mad Fit is over, he seems weaker than usually, or regularly, he used to be; not that the Self-moving Parts of Nature are capable of being weaker, or stronger, than naturally they are: but having liberty to move as they will, they may move stronger, or weaker, swifter or slower, regularly or irregularly, as they please; nor doth Nature commonly use Force. But this is to be noted, That there being a general Agreement amongst the particular Parts, they are more forcible than when those Parts are divided into Factions and Parties: so that in a general Irregular Commotion or Action, all the Sensitive Parts of the Body of a man, agree to move with an extraordinary force, after an unusual manner; provided it be not different from the property and nature of their Compositions; that is, not different from the Property and Nature of a Man. But this is likewise to be noted, That in a general Agreement, man may have other Properties, than when the whole Body is governed by Parts, as it is usual when the Body is Regular, and that every Part moves in his proper Sphere, as I may say, (for example) the Head, Heart, Lungs, Stomack, Liver, and so the rest, where each Part doth move in several sorts of Actions. The like may also be said of the Parts of the Leggs and Hands, which are different sorts of Actions; yet all move to the use and benefit of the whole Body: but, if the Corporeal motions in the Hands, and so in the Leggs, be irregular, they will not help the rest of the Parts; and so, in short, the same happens in all the Parts of the Body, whereof some Parts may be Regular, and others Irregular; and sometimes all may be Irregular. But, to conclude this Chapter, the Body may have unusual Force and Properties; as when a man says, He was carried and flung into a Ditch, or some place distant; and that he was pinch't, and did see strange sights, heard strange sounds, smelt strange scents; all which may very well be caused by the Irregular motions, either by a general Irregularity, or by some particular Irregularity; and the truth is, The particular Corporeal motions, know not the power of the general, until they unite by a general Agreement; and sometimes there may be such Commotions in the Body of a Man, as in a Common-wealth, where many times there is a general Uproar and Confusion, and none know the Cause, or who began it. But this is to be noted, That if the Sensitive motions begin the Disorder, then they cause the Rational to be so disordered, as they can neither advise wisely, or direct orderly, or perswade effectually.

CHAP. XII.

Of Diseases produced by Conceit.

As there are numerous sorts of *Diseases*, so there are numerous manners or ways of the production of Diseases; and those Diseases that are produced by *Conceit*, are first occasioned by the Rational Corporeal Figurative Motions:[1] for, though every several Conceit, or Imagination, is a several Rational Corporeal Figurative Motion; yet, every Conceit or Imagination doth not produce a Sensitive Effect: but in those that do produce a Sensitive Effect, it is the Conceit or Imagination of some sorts of Diseases; but in most of those sorts that are dangerous to Life, or causes Deformity: The reason is, That as all the Parts of Nature are Self-knowing, so they are Self-loving: Also, Regular Societies beget an united Love, by Regular Agreements, which cause a Rational Fear of a disuniting, or dissolving; and that is the reason, that upon the perception of such a Disease, the Rational, through some disorder, figures that Disease; and the Sensitive Corporeal Motions, take a pattern from the Rational, and so the Disease is produced.

THE TENTH PART.

CHAP. I.

Of FEVERS.

Some are of opinion, That all, or, at least, most Diseases, are accompanied, more or less, with a *Feverous Distemper*: If so, then we may say, A *Fever* is the *Fundamental Disease*: but, whether that Opinion is true, or no, I know not; but I observe, there are many sorts of Fevers, and so there are of all other Diseases or Distempers: for, every alteration, or difference, of one and the same kind of Disease, is a several sort. As for Fevers, I have observed, there are Fevers in the Blood, or Humours, and not in any of the Vital Parts; and those are ordinary Burning-Fevers: and there

1 I.e., diseases that stem from thoughts or imaginations.

are other sorts of Fevers that are in the Vital Parts, and all other Parts of the Body, and those are *Malignant Fevers*; and there are some sorts of Fevers which are in the Radical Humours, and those are *Hectick Fevers*; and there are other sorts of Fevers that are in those Parts, which we name the *Spiritous Parts*. Also, all *Consumptions* are accompanied with a Feverish Distemper: but, what the several Figurative Motions are of these several sorts of Fevers, I cannot tell.

CHAP. II.
Of the PLAGUE.

There are Two visible sorts of the Disease named the *Plague*: The weaker sort is that which produces Swellings, or inflamed or corrupted Sores, which are accompanied with a Fever.[1] The other sort is that which is named the *Spotted Plague*.[2] The First sort is sometimes Curable; but the Second is Incurable; at least, no Remedy as yet hath been found. The truth is, the *Spotted Plague* is a *Gangrene*, but is somewhat different from other sorts of *Gangren's*; for this begins amongst the Vital Parts, and, by an Infection, spreads to the Extream Parts; and not only so, but to Forrein Parts; which makes not only a general Infection amongst all the several Parts of the Body, but the Infection spreads it self to other Bodies. And whereas other sorts of *Gangren's* begin outwardly, and pierce inwardly; the *Plaguy Gangrene* begins inwardly, and pierces outwardly: so as the difference (as I said) is, That the ordinary sort of *Gangren's* infect the next adjoining Parts of the Body, by moderate degrees; whereas the *Plaguy Gangrene* infects not only the adjoining Parts of the same Body, and that suddenly, but infects Forreign Bodies. Also, the ordinary *Gangren's* may be stopped from their Infection, by taking off the Parts infected, or diseased. But the *Plaguy Gangrene* can no ways be stopped, because the Vital Parts cannot be separated from the rest of the Parts, without a total ruine: besides, it pierces and spreads more suddenly, than Remedies can be applyed. But, whether there are Applications of Preventions, I know not; for, those Studies belong more to the *Physicians*, than to a *Natural*

1 The mention of sores or swellings indicates that Cavendish is referring to the bubonic plague, which erupted in London in 1665–66.

2 Cavendish probably refers to typhus, although "spotted plague" was also used more loosely to refer to any kind of fever accompanied by eruptions or spots on the skin.

Philosopher. As for the Diseases we name the *Purples*, and the *Spotted Fever*, they are of the same Kind, or Kindred, although not of the same sort, as *Measles*, and the *Small-Pox*.[1] But this is to be noted, That Infection is an act of Imitation: for, one Part cannot give another Part a Disease, but only that some imitate the same sorts of Irregular Actions of other Parts; of which some are near adjoining Imitators, and some occasion a general Mode.

CHAP. III.

Of the Small-Pox, and Measles.

The *Small-Pox* is somewhat like the *Sore-Plague*,[2] not only by being Infectious, as both sorts of Plagues are; but, by being of a corrupt Nature, as the *Sore-Plague* is; only the *Small-Pox* is innumerable, or very many small Sores; whereas the *Sore-Plague* is but one or two great Sores. Also, the *Small-Pox* and *Sore-Plague*, are alike in this, That if they rise and break, or if they fall not flat, but remain until they be dry and scabbed, the Patient lives: but, if they fall flat, and neither break, nor are scabbed, the Patient is in danger to dye. Also, it is to be noted, That this Disease is sometimes accompanied with a Feverish Distemper; I say, Sometimes, not Always; and that is the cause that many dye, either with too hot, or too cooling Applications: for, in a Feverish Distemper, hot Cordials are Poyson; and when there is no Fever, Cooling Remedies are *Opium*: The like for letting Blood; for if the Disease be accompanied with a Fever, and the Fever be not abated by letting Blood, 'tis probable the Fever, joyned with the Pox, will destroy the Patient: and if no Fever, and yet loose Blood, the Pox hath not sufficient Moisture to dilate, nor a sufficient natural Vapour to breathe, or respirate; so as the Life of the Patient is choaked or stifled with the contracted Corruptions. As for *Measles*, though they are of the same kind, yet not of the same sort; for they are rather Small Risings, than Corrupted Sores, and so are less dangerous.

---

1 As Cavendish illustrates, there is much overlap in discussions of febrile illnesses like measles, typhus, spotted fever (tick-borne or otherwise), smallpox, plague, and general "agues" or fevers, so it is difficult to pinpoint the modern equivalent of "spotted fever."

2 Bubonic plague.

CHAP. IV.

Of the Intermission of Fevers or Agues.

AGUES[1] have several sorts of Distempers, and those quite opposite to each other, as Cold and Shaking, Hot and Burning, besides Sweating: Also, there are several times of Intermissions; as some are Every-day Agues, some Third-day Agues, and some *Quartan Agues*; and some Patient may be thus distempered, many times, in the compass of Four and twenty hours: but those are rather of the Nature of Intermitting Fevers, than of perfect Agues. Also, in Agues, there is many times a difference of the Hot and Cold fits: for sometimes the Cold Fits will be long, and the Hot short; other times, the Hot Fits will be long, and the Cold Fits short; other times, much of an equal degree: but, most Intermitting Fevers and Agues, proceed either from ill-digestive Motions, or from a superfluity of Cold and Hot Motions, or an Irregularity of the Cold, Hot, Dry, or Moist Motions, where each sort strives and struggles with each other. But, to make a comparison, Agues are somewhat like several sorts of Weather, as Freezing and Thawing, Cloudy or Rainy, or Fair and Sun-shining days: or like the Four Seasons of the Year, where the Cold Fits are like *Winter*, cold and windy; the Hot Fits are like *Summer*, hot and dry; and the Sweating Fits like *Autumn*, warm and moist; and, when the Fit is past, like the *Spring*. But, to conclude, the chief Cause of Agues, is, Irregular Digestions, that make half-concocted Humours;[2] and according as these half-concocted Humours digest, the Patient hath his Aguish Distempers, where some are every day, others every second day, some every third day, and some *Quartans*: but, by reason those half-concocted Humours, are of several sorts of Humors, some Cold, some Hot, some Cold and Dry, some Hot and Dry, or Hot and Moist; and those different sorts, raw, or but half-concocted Humours; they occasion such disorder, not only by an unnatural manner of Digestion, as not to be either timely, or regular, by degrees; but, those several sorts of Raw Humours, strive and struggle with each other for Power or Supremacy: but, according as those different Raw Humours concoct, the Fits are longer or shorter: also, according to the quantity of those Raw Humours, and according as those Humours are a gathering, or breeding, so are the times of those Fits and Intermissions. But here is to be noted, That some Agues may be occasioned from

---

1 Fevers.

2 By "half-concocted," Cavendish likely means humors that are irregular, or that appear or are combined in irregular ways.

some Particular Irregular Digestions; others from a General Irregular Digestion, some from some obscure Parts, others from ordinary Humours.

CHAP. V.
Of CONSUMPTIONS.

There are many sorts of *Consumptions*;[1] as, some are Consumptions of the Vital Parts, as the Liver, Lungs, Kidneys, or the like Parts: Others, a Consumption of the Radical Parts: Others a Consumption of the Spiritous Parts: Other Consumptions are only of the Flesh; which, in my opinion, is the only Curable Consumption. But, all Consumptions, are not only an Alteration, but a Wasting and Dis-uniting of the Fundamental Parts; only those Consuming Parts do, as it were, steal away by degrees; and so, by degrees, the Society of a Human Creature is dissolved.

CHAP. VI.
Of DROPSIES.

Dropsies[2] proceed from several Causes; as, some from a decay of some of the Vital Parts; others through a superfluity of indigested Humours; some from a supernatural Driness of some Parts; others through a superfluity of Nourishing Motions; some, through some Obstructions; others, through an excess of Moist Dyet: but, all Dropsies proceed not only from Irregular Motions, but from such a particular Irregularity, as all the Motions endeavour to be of one Mode, (as I may say) that is, To move after the manner of those sorts of Motions which are the innate Nature of Water, and are some sorts of Circular Dilations: but, by these actions, the Human Society endeavours to make a Deluge, and to turn from the Nature of Blood and Flesh, to the nature of Water.

CHAP. VII.
Of SWEATING.

All *Sweating-Diseases* are somewhat of the nature of Dropsies; but they are (at least, seem to be) more Exterior, than Interior Dropsies: but, though there be Sweating-Diseases which are Irregular; yet, Regular Sweating is as proper as Regular Breathing; and so healthful, that Sweating extraordinary, in some Diseases,

---

1 Consumption usually refers to a "wasting" disease, like pulmonary tuberculosis.

2 A prominent swelling of the limbs or abdomen; in modern terminology, edema.

occasions a Cure: for, Sweating is a sort of Purging; so that the evacuation of Sweat, through the Pores, is as necessary as other sorts of evacuation, as Breathing, Urine, Siege,[1] Spitting, Purging through the Nose, and the like. But, Excess of Sweating, is like other sorts of Fluxes,[2] of which, some will scowr[3] to death; others vomit to death; and others the like Fluxes will occasion death; the like is of Sweating: so that the *Sweating-Sickness* is but like a *Fluxive-Sickness*. But, as I said, Regular Sweating is as necessary as other ordinary Evacuations: and as some are apt to be restringent,[4] others laxative; and sometimes one and the same Man will be laxative, other times, costive; so are Men concerning Sweating: and as some Men take Medicines to purge by Stool, or Vomits, or Urine; so they take Medicines to purge by Sweating. And, as Man hath several sorts of Excremental Humours, so, several sorts of Sweats; as, Clammy Sweats, Cold Sweats, Hot Sweats, and Faint Sweats: and, as all Excess of other sorts of Purgings, causes a Man to be weak and faint; so doth Sweating.

CHAP. VIII.
Of COUGHS.

There are many several sorts of *Coughs*, proceeding from several Causes; as, some Coughs proceed from a Superfluity of Moisture; others from an Unnatural Heat; others from a Corruption of Humors; others from a Decay of the Vital Parts; others from sudden Colds upon Hot Distempers: Some are caused by an Interior Wind; some Coughs proceed from Salt Humors, Bitter, Sharp, and Sweet: some Coughs proceed from Flegm, which Flegm ariseth like a Scum in a Pot, when Meat is boiling on a Fire: for when the Stomack is distemperedly hot, the Humors in the Stomack boyl as Liquid Substances on the Fire; those boiling Motions bearing up the gross Humors beyond the Mouth of the Stomack, and, causing a Dispute between the Breath and Humors, produce the Effect of Straining, or Reaching upwards towards the Mouth, much like the Nature and Motions of Vomiting: but, by reason those Motions are not so strong in Coughing, as in Vomiting, the Coughing Motions bring up only pieces of parts of superfluous Flegm, or gross Spittle. The like for corrupt Humors. Other Coughs proceed from

1 I.e., excrement.

2 "Flux" usually refers to dysentery, but here it seems to refer to a range of evacuative disorders.

3 I.e., have diarrhea.

4 Binding or astringent.

Unnatural or Distempered Heats; which Heats cause Unnecessary Vapours, and those Vapours ascending up from the Bowels, or Stomack, to the Head, and finding a Depression, are converted or changed into a Watry Substance; which Watry Substance falls down, like mizling or small Rain, or in bigger drops, through the passage of the Throat and Wind-pipe: which being opprest, and the Breath hindered, causes a Strife; which Striving, is a Straining; like as when Crumbs of Bread, or Drops of Drink, go not rightly through the Throat, but trouble and obstruct the Wind-pipe, or when any such Matter sticks in the passage of the Throat: for, when any Part of the Body is obstructed, it endeavours to release it self from those Obstructions: Also, when the Vapour that arises, arises in very Thin and Rarified Vapour, that rarified Vapour thickens or condenses not so suddenly, being farther from the degree of Water; but when condensed into Water, it falls down by drops; which drops trickling down the Throat, (like as Tears from the Eyes trickle down the Cheeks of the Face) the Cough is not so violent, but more frequent: but if the Rheum be salt or sharp, that trickles down the Throat, it causes a gentle or soft smart, which is much like the touch of Tickling or Itching, which provokes a faint or weak Strain or Cough. Also, Wind will provoke to Strain or Cough: The Motion of Wind is like as if Hair should tickle the Nose. Or, Wind will cause a tickling in the Nose, which causes the Effect of Sneezing: for, Sneezing is nothing but a Cough through the Nose; I may say, It is a *Nose-Cough*. And Hickops are but Stomach-Coughs, Wind causing the Stomack to strain. Also, the Guts have Coughs, which are caused by the Wind, which makes a strife in the Guts and Bowels. Other Coughs are produced from Decayed Parts: for, when any Part is corrupted, it becomes less Solid than naturally it should be: As for example, The Flesh of the Body, when corrupted, becomes from Dense Flesh, to a Slimy Substance; thence, into a Watry Substance, which falls into Parts, or changes from Flesh, into a Mixt Corrupted Matter, which falls into Parts. The several Mixtures, or Distempered Substances, and Irregular Motions, causes Division of the composed Parts; but in the time of dissolving, and divisions of any Part, there is a strife which causes Pain: and if the strife be in the Lungs, it causes Coughs, by obstructing the Breath: but, some Coughs proceed from Vapours and Winds, arising from the decayed Interior Parts, sending up Vapours from the Dissolving Substance, which causeth Coughs; and some Coughs cause Decays of the Prime Interior Parts: for, when there falls from the Head a constant Distillation, this Distillation is like dropping Water, which will penetrate or divide Stone; and more easily will dropping or drilling Water do it, as Rheum,[1] will corrupt Spongy Matter as Flesh is: but, according as the Rheum is Fresh, Salt, or Sharp, the Parts are a longer or shorter time decaying: for, Salt and Sharp is Corroding; and, by the Corroding Motions, Ulcerates those Parts the Salt Rheums fall on, which destroys them soon. As for *Chin-Cough*,[2] 'tis a Wind or Vapour arising from the Lungs, through the Windpipe; and as long as the Wind or Vapour ascends, the Patient cannot draw in Reviving Air or Breath, but Coughs violently and incessantly, until it faint away, or have no Strength left; and with straining, will be as if it were choaked or strangled, and become black in the face, and, after the Cough is past, recover again; but some dye of these sorts of Coughs.

CHAP. IX.

Of GANGREN'S.

Gangren's are of the Nature of the *Plague*; and they are of Two sorts, as the *Plague* is; the one more sudden and deadly than the other: The only difference of their Infecting Qualities, is, That *Gangren's* spread by infecting still the next, or Neighbouring Parts; whereas Plagues infect Forrein, as much as Home-Parts. Also, the deadly sort of *Gangren's*, infect (as I may say) from the Circumference towards the Center: when as the deadly sorts of Plague, infect from the Center, towards the Circumference. But, that sort of *Gangrene* that is the weaker sort, infects only the next adjoining Parts, by degrees, and after a spreading manner, rather than after a piercing manner.

But some may object, That *Plagues* and *Gangren's* are produced from different Causes; as for example, Extream Cold will cause *Gangren's*; and Extream Heat causes *Plagues*.

I answer, That Two opposite Causes may produce like Effects, for which may be brought numerous Examples.

CHAP. X.

Of Cancers and Fistula's.

Cancers and *Fistula's*[3] are somewhat alike, in that they are both produced from Salt, or sharp corroding Motions: but in this they

---

1 Often choler or yellow bile; here Cavendish refers to a runny nose.

2 Whooping cough.

3 A fistula is an abnormal passage between any tubular or hollow organ and the surface of the body, or two tubular organs. King Louis XIV (r. 1643–1715) famously suffered from an anal fistula.

differ, that *Cancers* keep their Center, and spread in streams; whereas *Fistula's* will run from place to place: for if it be stopt in one place, it is apt to remove and break out in another. Yet *Cancers* are somewhat like *Gangren's*, in infecting adjoining Parts; so that unless a *Cancer* be in such a place as can be divided from the Sound Parts, it destroys the Human Life, by eating (as I may say) the Sound Parts of the Body, as all Corroding, and Sharp or Salt Diseases do.

CHAP. XI.
Of the GOUT.

As for the Disease named the *Gout*,[1] I never heard but of Two sorts; the *Fixt*, and the *Running Gout*: but, mistake me not, I mean *Fixt* for *Place*, not *Time*. The *Fixt* proceeds from Hot, Sharp, or Salt Motions: The *Running Gout* from Cold, Sharp Motions; but, both sorts are Intermitting Diseases, and very painful; and I have heard those that have had the *Fixt Gout*, say, That the pain of the *Fixt Gout*, is somewhat like the *Tooth-ach*: but, all *Gouts* are occasioned by Irregular Pressures and Re-actions. As for that sort that is named the *Windy Gout*, it is rather a *Sciatica*, than a *Gout*.

CHAP. XII.
Of the STONE.

Of the Disease of the *Stone* in Human Creatures, there are many sorts: for, though the *Stone* of the *Bladder*, of the *Kidneys*, and in the *Gaul*, be all of one kind of Disease called the *Stone*, yet they are of different sorts: but, whether the Disease of the *Stone* be produced of Hot or Cold Motions, I cannot judg: but 'tis probable, some are produced of Hot Motions, others of Cold; and perchance, others of such sorts of Motions as are neither perfectly Hot, nor Cold: for, the *Stone* is produced, as all other Creatures, by such or such sorts of Figurative Motions. Here is to be noted, That some of the Humours of the Body may alter their Motion, and turn from being Flegm, Choler, or the like, to be *Stone*; and so from being a Rare, Moist, or Loose Body, to be a Dry, Densed, Hard, or Fixt Body. But certainly, the *Stone* of the *Bladder*, *Kidneys* and

1 A metabolic disorder that causes uric-acid build-up and arthritis in the joints, especially the small bones of the feet. Here Cavendish seems to discuss both gout and arthritis more generally (or "running gout").

Gaul, are of several sorts, as being produced by several sorts of Figurative Motions; as also, according to the Properties and Forms of those several Parts of the Body they are produced in: for, as several sorts of Soyls, or Parts of the Earth, produce several sorts of Minerals; so several Parts of the Body, several sorts of the Disease of the *Stone*: And, as there are several sorts of Stones in the several Parts of the Earth; so, no doubt, there may not only be several sorts of Stone in several Parts, but several sorts in one and the same Part; at least, in the like Parts of several Men.[1]

CHAP. XIII.

Of Apoplexies, and Lethargies.

Apoplexies, Lethargies, and the like Diseases, are produced by some decay of the Vital Spirits, or by Obstructions, as being obstructed by some Superfluities, or through the Irregularities of some sorts of Motions, which occasion some Passages to close, that should be open. But mistake me not, I do not mean empty Passages; for there is no such thing (in my opinion) in Nature: but, I mean an open passage for a frequent Course and Recourse of Parts. But an *Apoplexy*[2] is somewhat of the Nature of a *Dead-Palsie*; and a *Lethargy*, of a *Numb-Palsie*; but I have heard, that the Opinion of Learned Men is, That some sorts of Vaporous Pains are the Fore-runners of *Apoplexies* and *Palsies*: but, in my opinion, though a Man may have two Diseases at once; yet surely, where Vapour can pass, there cannot be an absolute Stoppage.

CHAP. XIV.

Of EPILEPSIES.

Epilepsies, or that we name the *Falling-Sickness*, is of the nature of Swounding or Fainting Fits: but there are two visible sorts; the one is, that only the Head is affected, and not the other Parts of the Body; and for proof, Those that are thus distempered only in the Head, all the other Parts will struggle and

1 Bladder-, gall-, and kidney-stones were often attributed to the humors, although here Cavendish combines that assumption with her theory of figurative motion.

2 Apoplexy usually refers to a stroke or other incapacitation due to internal bleeding (or a "Stoppage," as Cavendish assumes), but was also used generally to describe death or incapacity following a sudden loss of consciousness.

strive to help or assist the affected or afflicted parts, and those Parts of the Head that are not Irregular, as may be observed by their Motions; but, by the means of some other Parts, there will also be striving and strugling, as may be observed by foaming through the Mouth. The other sort is like ordinary Swounding-Fits, where all the Parts of the Body seem, for a time, to be dead. But this is to be observed, That those that are thus diseased, have certain times of Intermissions, as if the Corporeal Motions did keep a Decorum in being Irregular. But some have had *Epilepsies* from their Birth; which proves, That their Productive Motions was Irregular.

CHAP. XV.

Of Convulsions, and Cramps.

Convulsions and *Cramps* are somewhat alike; and both, in my Opinion, proceed from Cold Contractions: but, *Cramps* are caused by the Contractions of the *Capillary* Veins, or small *Fibers*, rather than of the Nerves and Sinews: for, those Contractions, if violent, are *Convulsions*: so that *Cramps* are *Contractions* of the small *Fibers*; and *Convulsions* are Contractions of the Nerves and Sinews. But the reason (I believe) that these Diseases proceed from Cold Contractions, is, That Hot Remedies produce, for the most part, perfect Cures; but, they must be such sorts of Hot Remedies, that are of dilating or extenuating nature; and not such whose Properties are Hot and Dry, or Contracting: also, the Applications must be according to the strength of the Disease.

CHAP. XVI.

Of CHOLICKS.

Cholicks[1] are like *Cramps* or *Convulsions*; or, *Convulsions* and *Cramps*, like *Cholicks*: for, as *Convulsions* are Contractions of the Nerves and Sinews; and *Cramps*, Contractions of the small *Fibers*: so *Cholicks* are a Contracting of the Gutts: and, for proof, So soon as the Contracting Motions alter, and are turn'd to Dilating or Expelling Actions, the Patient is at ease. But, there are several Causes that produce the *Cholick*: for, some *Cholicks* are produced by Hot and Sharp Motions, as *Bilious Cholicks*; others from Cold and Sharp Motions, as *Splenetick Cholicks*; others from Crude and Raw Humours; some from Hot Winds; some from Cold Winds. The same some sorts

1 Digestive or intestinal pain.

of *Convulsions* and *Cramps* may be: but, though these several *Cholicks* may proceed from several Causes; yet, they all agree in this, To be Contractions: for, as I said, when those Corporeal Motions alter their Actions to Dilation or Expulsion, the Patient is at ease. But, those *Cholicks* that proceed from Hot and Sharp Motions, are the most painful and dangerous, by reason they are, for the most part, more strong and stubborn. As for *Cholicks* in the Stomack, they are caused by the same sorts of Motions that cause some sorts of Contractions: but, those sorts of *Cholick*-Contractions, are after the manner of wreathing, or wringing Contractions. The same in Convulsive-Contractions.

CHAP. XVII.

Of Shaking Palsies.

Shaking Palsies proceed from a Slackness of the Nerves, or Sinew strings, as may be observed by those that hold or lay any heavy weight upon the Arms, Hands or Leggs: for, when the Burdens are removed, those Limbs will be apt to tremble and shake so much, for a short time, (until they have recovered their former strength) that the Leggs cannot go, or stand steadily; nor the Arms, or Hands, do any thing without shaking. The reason of these sorts of Slackness, is, That heavy Burdens occasion the Nerves and Sinews to extend beyond their Order; and being stretched, they become more slack, and loose, by how much they were stretched, or extended; until such time as they contract again into their proper Posture: And the reason that Old Age is subject to *Shaking-Palsies*, is, That the Frame of the whole Body is looser and slacker, than when it was young: As in a decayed House, every Material is looser than when it was first built; but yet, sometimes and old shaking House will continue a great while, with some Repairs: so old shaking Men, with Care, and good Dyet, will continue a great time. But this is to be noted, That trembling is a kind of *Shaking-Palsie*, although of another sort; and so is Weakness after Sickness: but, these sorts are occasioned, as when a House shakes in a great Wind, or Storm; and not through any Fundamental Decay.

CHAP. XVIII.

Of the Muther, Spleen, and Scurvy.

As for those Diseases that are named the *Fits of the Muther*, the *Spleen*, the *Scurvy*,[1] and the like; although they are the most general Diseases, especially amongst the Females; yet, each particular sort is so various, and hath such different Effects, that, I observe, they puzzle the most Learned Men to find out their jugling, intricate, and uncertain Actions. But this is to be observed, That the Richest sorts of Persons are most apt to these sorts of Diseases; which proves, That Idleness and Luxury is the occasion.

CHAP. XIX.

Of Food, or Digestions.

As I have said, *Digestions* are so numerous, and so obscure, that the most Learned Men know not how Food is converted and distributed to all the Parts of the Body: Which Obscurity occasions many Arguments, and much Dispute amongst the Learned; but, in my opinion, it is not the Parts of the Human Body, that do digest the Food, although they may be an occasion (through their own Regularities, or Irregularities) to cause good or bad digestions: but, the Parts of the Food, do digest themselves;[2] that is, alter their actions to the Property and Nature of a Human Body: so that Digestive Parts are only Additional Parts; and, if those Nourishing Motions be Regular, they distribute their several Parts, and joyn their several Parts, to those several Parts of the Body that require Addition. Also, the Digestive Motions are according to the Nature or Property of each several Part of the Human Body, As for example, those Digestive Parts alter into Blood, Flesh, Fat, Marrow, Brains, Humors, and so into any

---

1 All general terms for a mysterious group of mental and physical ailments linked to hysteria, melancholy, and/or spleen, which were often attributed both to idleness and to women ("hysteria" is derived from the Greek word for uterus, while "the muther," or "the suffocation of the mother," is another term for hysteria). In the early seventeenth century, these illnesses were linked to uterine dysfunctions (which would produce "vapors" that rose up and disturbed the brain); by the end of the century, many physicians started to believe that they were related to the nervous system (thus heralding eighteenth-century theories of "nervous" disorders).

2 Self-digestion is an interesting example of Cavendish's thoroughgoing belief in the self-aware, volitional actions of all matter.

other Figurative Parts of the Sensitive Body. The same may be said of the Rational Parts of the Mind: but, if those Digestive Parts be Irregular, they will cause a Disorder in a well-ordered Body: and, if the Parts of the Body be Irregular, they will occasion a Disorder amongst the Digestive Parts: but, according to the Regularities and Irregularities of the Digestive Parts, is the Body more or less nourished. But this is to be noted, That according to the Superfluity or Scarcity of those Digestive Parts, the Body is opprest, or starved.

Chap. XX.
Of SURFEITS.

Surfeits[1] are occasioned after different manners: for, though many Surfeits proceed from those Parts that are received into the Body; yet, some are occasioned through often repetitions of one and the same actions: As for example, The Eyes may surfeit with too often viewing one Object; the Ears, with often hearing one Sound; the Nose, with smelling one Sent; the Tongue, with one Tast. The same is to be said of the Rational Actions; which Surfeits, occasion an aversion to such or such Particulars: but, for those Surfeits that proceed from the Parts that are received into the Body, they are either through the *quantity* that oppresses the Nature of the Body; or, through the *quality* of those Parts, being not agreeable to the Nature of the Body; or, through their Irregularities, that occasion the like Irregularities in the Body: and sometimes, the fault is through the Irregularities of the Body, that hinder those received Parts, or obstruct their Regular Digestions; and sometimes, the fault is both of the Parts of the Body, and those of the Food: but, the Surfeits of the those Parts that receive not Food, are caused through the often repetition of one and the same Action.

CHAP. XXI.
Of Natural Evacuations, or Purgings.

There are many sorts, and several ways or means of Purging actions; whereof some we name *Natural*, which purge the Excremental Parts; and such Natural Purgings, are only of such Parts as are no ways useful to the Body; or of those that are not willing to convert themselves into the Nature and Property of the Substantial Parts. There must of necessity be Purging actions, as well as Digestive actions; because, no Creature can subsist singly of it

1 Weariness, illness, or malaise from overindulgence.

self, but all Creatures subsist each by other; so that, there must be Dividing actions, as well as Uniting actions; only, several sorts of Creatures, have several sorts of Nourishments and Evacuations. But this is to be noted, in the Human Nourishments and Evacuations, that, through their Irregularities, some Men may nourish too much, and others purge too much; and some may nourish too little, and some may purge too little. The Irregularities concerning Nourishments, are amongst the adjoining Parts; the Errors concerning Purging, are amongst the Dividing Parts.

CHAP. XXII.

Of PURGING DRUGGS.

There are many sorts of *Druggs*, whereof some are beneficial, by assisting those particular Parts of the Body that are oppressed and offended, either by Superfluous Humours, or Malignant Humours: but, there are some sorts of Druggs that are as malicious to the Human Life, as the Assistant Druggs are friendly. Several sorts of Druggs, have several sorts of Actions, which causes several Effects; as, some Druggs work by Siege; others, by Urine; some, by Vomit; others, by Spitting; others, by Sweating; some cause sleep; some are hot, others are cold; some dry, others moist. But this is to be noted, That 'tis not the Motions of the Druggs, but the Motion of the Humours, which the Druggs occasion to flow; and not only to flow, but to flow after such or such a manner and way. The Actions of Druggs, are like the Actions of Hounds, or Hawks, that flye at a particular Bird, or run after a particular beast of their own kind, although of a different sort: The only difference is, That Druggs are not only of a different sort, but a different Kind from Animal Kind; at least, from Human Sort.

CHAP. XXIII.

Of the Various Humours of Druggs.

The reason, one and the same Quantity or Dose of one and the same sort of Purging-Druggs or Medicine, will often work differently in several Human Bodies; as also, differently in one and the same Body, at several times of taking the same sorts of Medicines; is, That several Parts of one and the same sort, may be differently humoured: as, some to be duller and slower than others; and some to be more active than others. Also, some Parts may be ill-natured, and cause Factions amongst the Parts of the Body; whereas others will endeavour to rectifie Disorders, or Factions. And sometimes both the Druggs, and the Body, falls out;

and then there is a dangerous strife; the Body striving to expel the Physick,[1] and the Physick endeavouring to stay in the Body, to do the Body some mischief. Also, some Parts of one and the same sort, may be so Irregular, as to hunt not only the superfluous Humours, or the Malignant Humors, but all sorts of flowing Parts; which may cause so great and general Disorder, as may endanger Human Life.

CHAP. XXIV.
Of CORDIALS.

There are many sorts of *Cordials*: for, I take every Beneficial Remedy to be a Cordial: but, many of the Vulgar believe, That there is no Cordial but *Brandy*, or such like Strong-waters; at least, they believe all such Remedies that are virtually Hot, to be Cordials: but, when they take too much of such Cordials, either in Sickness, or Health, they will, in some time, find them as bad as Poyson. But, all such Applications as are named *Cordials*, are not hot: for, some are cool, at least, of a temperate degree. And as there are Regular and Irregular Corporeal Motions; so there are Sympathetical, and Antipathetical Motions; and yet both sorts may be Regular.[2] Also, there is a Neutral sort, that has neither Sympathy nor Antipathy, but is Indifferent. But in Disputes between Two different Parties, a Third may come in to the assistance of one Side, more out of hate to the Opposite, than love to the Assisted. The same may Cordials, or such like Applications, do, when the Corporeal Motions of Human Life are in disorder, and at variance: for, oftentimes there is as great a Mutiny and Disorder amongst the Corporeal Motions, both in the Mind and Body of a Man, as in a Publick State in time of Rebellion: but, all Assistant Cordials, endeavour, to assist the Regular Parts of the Body, and to perswade the Irregular Parts.[3] As for Poysons, they are like Forrein Warr, that endeavours to destroy a Peaceable Government.

---

1 I.e., medicine.

2 Cavendish often associates "antipathetical" motions with irregularity (as in the next chapter); here, however, she acknowledges that both "sympathetical" and "antipathetical" motions can be "regular."

3 Thus Cavendish again suggests that disease is the result of the volitional motion of organic matter, which must be "perswaded" from its rogue actions by neighboring parts (as well as drugs, cordials, etc.).

CHAP. XXV.

Of the different Actions of the several Sensitive Parts of a Human Creature.

Some Parts of a Human Creature will be Regular, and some Irregular: as, some of the Sensitive Parts will be Regular, and some Irregular; that is, some Parts will be Painful, or Sick, others well: some Parts will make false Perceptions; others, true Perceptions: some Parts be Temperate; others, Intemperate: some Parts be Madd, other Parts Sober: some Parts be Wise; others, Foolish: and the same is to be said of the Rational Motions. But, in a Regular Society, every Part and Particle of the Body, is Regularly agreeable, and Sympathetical.

CHAP. XXVI.

Of the Antipathy of some Human Creatures, to some Forrein Objects.

As I have often said, There is often both Sympathy and Antipathy between the Parts of some particular Human and Forrein Object; in so much, that some will occasion such a general Disturbance, as will cause a general Alteration, *viz.* cause a Man to swound, or at least, to be very faint, or sick: as for example, Some will Swound at some sorts of Sounds, some sorts of Scents, some sorts of Tast, some sorts of Touches, and some sorts of Sights. Again, on the other side, some Human Creatures will so sympathize with some sorts of Forrein Objects, as some will Long for that, another will Swound to have.

CHAP. XXVII.

Of the Effects of Forrein Object, on the Human Mind.

As there is often Antipathy of the Parts of a Human Creature, to Forrein Objects; so there are often Sympathetical Effects produced from Forrein Objects, with the Parts of a Human Creature. As for example, A timely, kind, and discreet Discourse from a Friend, will compose or quiet his troubled Mind: Likewise, an untimely, unkind, hasty, malicious, false, or sudden Discourse, will often disorder a well-temper'd, or Regular Mind, the Mind imitating the smooth or harsh strains of the Object: and the same Effects hath Musick, on the Minds of many Human Creatures.

CHAP. XXVIII.

Of CONTEMPLATION.

Human *Contemplation,* is a Conversation amongst some of the Rational Parts of the Human Mind; which Parts, not regarding present Objects, move either in devout Notions, or vain Fancies,

Remembrances, Inventions, Contrivances, Designs, or the like. But the question is, Whether the Sensitive Parts of a Human Society, do, at any time, Contemplate? I answer, That some of the Sensitive Parts are so sociable, that they are, for the most part, agreeable to the Rational: for, in deep Contemplations, some of the Sensitive Parts do not take notice of Forrein Objects, but of the Rational Actions. Also, if the Contemplations be in devout Notions, the Sensitive Parts express Devotion by their Actions, as I have formerly mentioned. Also, when the Rational Parts move in Actions of Desire, straight the Sensitive move in Sympathetical Appetites: Wherefore, if the Society be Regular, the Sensitive and Rational Parts are agreeable and sociable.

CHAP. XXIX.

Of Injecting of the Blood of one Animal, into the Veins of another Animal.

To put Blood of one Animal, into another Animal; as for example, Some Ounces of Blood taken, by some Art, out of a Dogg's Veins, and, by some Art, put into a Man's Veins, may very easily be done by *Injection*;[1] and certainly, may as readily convert it self to the Nature of Human Blood, as Roots, Herbs, Fruit, and the like Food; and probably, will more aptly be transformed into Human Flesh, than Hogg's Blood, mixt with many Ingredients, and then put into Gutts, and boyled, (an ordinary Food amongst Country People;) but Blood being a loose Humourish Part, may encrease or diminish, as the other Humors, viz. *Flegm*, *Choler*, and *Melancholy*, are apt to do. But this is to be observed, That by reason Blood is the most flowing Humor, and of much more, or greater quantity than all the rest of the Humours, it is apt (if Regular) to cause, not only more frequent, but a more general Disturbance.

THE ELEVENTH PART.

CHAP. I.

Of the different Knowledges, in different Kinds and Sorts of Creatures.

If there be not Infinite Kinds, yet, it is probable, there are Infinite several Sorts; at least, Infinite particular Creatures,

1 The Fellows of the Royal Society performed blood transfusions on dogs and other animals; this eventually segued into animal-to-human and human-to-human transfusions, which were believed not only to cure illnesses but also to cause personality changes.

in every particular Kind and Sort; and the Corporeal Motions moving after a different manner, is the cause there are different Knowledges, in different Creatures; yet, none can be said to be *least knowing*, or *most knowing*: for, there is (in my opinion) no such thing as *least* and *most*, in Nature: for, several kinds and sorts of Knowledges, make not Knowledg to be more, or less; but only, they are different Knowledges proper to their kind, (as, Animal-kind, Vegetable-kind, Mineral-kind, Elemental-kind) and are also different Knowledges in several sorts: As for example, Man may have a different Knowledg from Beasts, Birds, Fish, Flies, Worms, or the like; and yet be no wiser than those sorts of Animal-kinds. The same happens between the several Knowledges of Vegetables, Minerals, and Elements: but, because one Creature doth not know what another Creature knows, thence arises the Opinion of *Insensibility*, and *Irrationability*, that some Creatures have of others.[1] But there is to be noted, That Nature is so Regular, or wise, in her Actions, that the *Species* and Knowledg of every particular Kind, is kept in an Even, or Equal Balance: For example, The Death or Birth of Animals, doth neither add or diminish from, or to the Knowledg of the Kind, or rather the Sort. Also, an Animal can have no Knowledg, but such as is proper to the *species* of his Figure: but, if there be a Creature of a mixt *Species*, or Figure, then their Knowledg is according to their mixt Form: for, the Corporeal Motions of every Creature, move according to the Form, Frame, or *Species* of their Society: but, there is not only different Knowledges, in different Kinds and Sorts of Creatures; but, there are different Knowledges in the different Parts of one and the same; as, the different Senses of Seeing, Hearing, Smelling, Tasting, and Touching, have not only different Knowledges in different Sensitive Organs, but in one Sense, they have several Perceptive Knowleges: and though the different Sensitive Organs of a Human Creature, are ignorant of each other; yet, each Sense is as knowing as another. The same (no question) is amongst all the Creatures in Nature.

---

1 I.e., the opinion that some creatures lack sense, reason, and/or consciousness. Cavendish refers to contemporary debates about whether non-human entities can think and know (according to her, of course, they can).

CHAP. II.

Of the Variety of Self-actions in particular Creatures.

There are numerous Varieties of Figurative Motions in some Creatures; and in others, very few, in comparison: but, the occasion of that, is the manner of the Frame and Form of a Creature: for, some Creatures that are but small, have much more variety of Figurative Motions, than others that are very bigg and large Creatures: so that, it is not only the Quantity of Matter, or Number of Parts, but the several Changes of Motion, by the Variety of their Active Parts, that is the cause of it: for, Nature is not only an Infinite Body, but, being Self-moving, causes Infinite Variety, by the altered Actions of her Parts; every altered Action, causing both an altered Self-knowledg, and an altered Perceptive Knowledg.

CHAP. III.

Of the Variety of Corporeal Motion, of one and the same sort or kind of Motion.

There is Infinite Variety of Motion of the same sorts and kinds of Motions; as for example, Of Dilations, or Extensions, Expulsions, Attractions, Contractions, Retentions, Digestions, Respirations: There is also Varieties of Densities, Rarities, Gravities, Levities, Measures, Sizes, Agilness, Slowness, Strength, Weakness, Times, Seasons, Growths, Decays, Lives, Deaths, Conceptions, Perceptions, Passions, Appetites, Sympathies, Antipathies, and Millions the like kinds, or sorts.

CHAP. IV.

Of the Variety of particular Creatures.

Nature is so delighted with *Variety*, that seldom two Creatures (although the same sort, nay, from the same Producers) are just alike; and yet Human Perception cannot perceive above four kinds of Creatures, viz. *Animals*, *Vegetables*, *Minerals*, and *Elements*: but, the several sorts seem to be very numerous; and the Varieties of the several Particulars, Infinite: but, Nature is necessitated to divide her Creatures into Kinds and Sorts, to keep Order and Method: for, there may be numerous Varieties of sorts; as for example, Many several Worlds, and infinite Varieties of Particulars in those Worlds: for, Worlds may differ from each other, as much as several sorts of Animals, Vegetables, Minerals, or Elements; and yet be all of that sort we name *Worlds*: but, as for the Infinite Varieties of Nature, we may say, That every Part of Nature is Infinite, in some sort; because every Part of Nature is a perpetual Motion, and makes Infinite Varieties, by change or alteration of Action: but, there is so much Variety of the several Shapes, Figures, Forms, and Sizes, as Bigger, and Less; as also, several sorts of Heats, Colds, Droughts, Moistures, Fires, Airs, Waters, Earths, Animals, Vegetables, and Minerals, as are not to be expressed.

CHAP. V.

Of Dividing, and Rejoyning, or Altering Exterior Figurative Motions.

The Interior and Exterior Figurative Motions of some sorts of Creatures, are so united by their Sympathetical Actions, as they cannot be separated without a Total Dissolution; and some cannot be altered without a Dissolution; and other Figurative Motions may separate, and unite again; and others, if separate, cannot unite again, as they were before: As for example, The Exterior Parts of a Human Creature, if once divided, cannot be rejoyned; when as some sorts of Worms may be divided, and if those divided Parts meet, can rejoyn, as before. Also, some Figurative Motions of different sorts, and so different, that they are opposite, may unite in agreement, in one Composition, or Creature; yet, when the very same sorts of Figurative Motions, are not so united, they are, as it were, deadly Enemies.

CHAP. VI.

Of Different Figurative Motions in particular Creatures.

There are many Creatures that are composed of very opposite Figurative Motions; as for example, Some Parts of Fire and Water; also, all Cordials, Vitriols,[1] and the like Waters; also, Iron and Stone, and Infinite the like: But, that which is composed of the most different Figurative Motions, is *Quicksilver*,[2] which is exteriorly Cold, Soft, Fluid, Agil, and Heavy: also, Divisible, and Rejoynable; and yet so Retentive of its Innate Nature, that although it can be rarified, yet not easily dissolved; at least, not that Human Creatures can perceive; for, it hath puzzled the best *Chymists*.[3]

---

1 I.e., sulfuric acid.

2 Mercury.

3 Chemists, and specifically those like van Helmont who were interested in what is now called iatrochemistry, which had its roots in alchemy and aimed to cure diseases via chemical substances (see Introduction, pp. 33–35).

CHAP. VII.

Of the Alterations of Exterior and Innate Figurative Motions of several sorts of Creatures.

The Form of several Creatures, is after several manners and ways, which causes several Natures or Properties: As for example, The Exterior and Innate Corporeal Motions of some Creatures, depend so much on each other, That the least Alteration of the one, causes a Dissolution of the whole Creature; whereas the Exterior Corporeal Motions of other sorts of Creature, can change and rechange their actions, without the least disturbance to the Innate Figurative Motions: In other sorts the Innate Motions shall be quite altered, but their Exterior Motions be in some manner consistent: As for proof, Fire is of the Nature, that both the Exterior and Innate Motions, are of one and same sort; so that the Alteration of the one, causeth a Dissolution of the other; that is, Fire loses the Property of Fire, and is altered from being Fire. On the other side, the Exterior Figurative Motions of Water, can change and rechange, without any disturbance to the Innate Nature: but, though the Alteration of the Innate Figurative Motions of all Creatures, must of necessity alter the Life and Knowledg of that Creature; yet there may be such consistent Motions amongst the Exterior Parts of some sorts of Creature, that they will keep their Exterior Form: As for example, A Tree that is cut down, or into pieces, when those pieces are withered, and, as we say, dead; yet, they remain of the Figure of Wood. Also, a dead Beast doth not alter the Figure of Flesh or Bones, presently. Also, a dead Man doth not presently dissolve from the Figure of Man; and some, by the Art of embalming, will occasion the remaining Figurative Motions of the dead Man to continue, so that those sorts of Motions, that are the Frame and Form, are not quite altered: but yet, those Exterior Forms are so altered, that they are not such as those by which we name a *Living Man*. The same of Flyes, or the like, intomb'd in *Amber*: but by this we may perceive, That the Innate Figurative Motions may be quite altered, and yet the Exterior Figurative consistent Motions, do, in some manner, keep in the Figure, Form, or Frame of their Society. The truth is, (in my opinion) That all the Parts that remain undissolved, have quite altered their Animal actions; but only the Consistent actions, of the Form of their Society, remains, so as to have a resemblance of their Frame or Form.

CHAP. VIII.

Of LOCAL MOTION.

All Corporeal Motion is *Local*; but only they are different Local Motions; and some sorts or kinds, have advantage of others, and some have power over others, as, in a manner, to inforce them to alter their Figurative motions; as for example, When one Creature doth destroy another, those that are the *Destroyers*, occasion those that we name the *Destroyed*, to dissolve their Unity, and to alter their actions: for, they cannot annihilate their actions; nor can they give or take away the Power of Self-motions; but, as I said, some Corporeal motions can occasion other Corporeal motions to move so, or so. But this is to be noted, That several sorts of Creatures have a mixture of several sorts of Figurative motions; as for example, There are Flying Fish, and Swimming Beasts; also, there are some Creatures that are partly Beasts, and partly Fish, as *Otters*, and many others; also, a *Mule* is partly a Horse, and an Ass; a *Batt* is partly a Mouse, and a Bird; and *Owle* is partly a Cat and a Bird; and numerous other Creatures there are, that are partly of one sort, and partly of another.[1]

CHAP. IX.

Of several manners, or way of Advantages, or Disadvantages.

Not only the Manner, Form, Frame, or Shape of particular Creatures; but also, the Regularity or Irregularity of the Corporeal motions of particular Creatures, doth cause that which Man names *Strength* or *Weakness*, *Obedience* or *Disobedience*, *Advantages* or *Disadvantages* of Power and Authority, or the like: As for example, A greater Number will overpower a lesse: for, though there be no Differences (as being no Degrees) of Self-strength amongst the Self-moving Parts, or Corporeal motions; yet, there may be stronger and weaker Compositions, or Associations; and a greater Number of Corporeal motions, makes a stronger Party: but, if the greater Part be Irregular, and the lesser Party be Regular, a hundred to one, but the weaker Party is victorious.[2] Also, the manner of the Corporeal motions; as, a Diving-motion may get the better

---

1 Various animals remained difficult for natural philosophers to classify. For instance, since antiquity the bat had been considered a bird, despite giving birth to live offspring, and was not classified as a mammal until 1693.

2 In this egalitarian view of natural matter, no parts are intrinsically stronger, except by way of forming "associations" of moving, well-functioning (or "regular") parts.

of a Swimming-motion; and, in some cases, the Swimming, the better of the Diving. Jumping may have the advantage over Running; and, in other cases, Running, over Jumping. Also, Creeping may have the advantage over Flying; and, in other cases, Flying, over Creeping. A Cross Motion may have the advantage over a Straight; and, in other cases, a Straight, over a Cross. So it may be said, of Turning and Lifting, of Contracting and Dilating Motions. And many the like Examples may be had; but, as I have often said, There is much Advantage and Disadvantage in the manner and way of the Composed Form and Figure of Creatures.

CHAP. X.

Of the Actions of some sorts of Creatures, over others.

Some sorts of Creatures are more Exteriorly active, than other sorts; and some more Interiorly active; some more rare, some more dense, and the like: also, some dense Creatures are more active than the rare; and some rare, are more active than other sorts that are dense. Also, some Creatures that are rare, have advantage of some that are dense; and some that are dense, over some sorts that are rare; some leight Bodies, over some heavy Bodies; and some heavy Bodies, over some sorts of leight Bodies. Also, several sorts of Exterior Motions, of several sorts of Creatures, have advantage and disadvantage of each other; as for example, Springs of Water, and Air, will make Passages, and so divide hard strong Rocks. And, on the other side, a Straw will divide Parts of Water; and a small Flye, will divide Parts of the Air: but, mistake me not, I mean, that they occasion the Airy or Watry Parts, to divide.

CHAP. XI.

Of GLASSIE BODIES.

Tis impossible, as I have said, to describe the Infinite Corporeal Figurative Motions: but, amongst those Creatures that are subject to Human Perception, there are some that resemble each other, and yet are of different Natures; as for example, *Black Ebony*, and *Black Marble*, they are both Glassie, smooth, and black; yet, one is Stone, the other Wood. Also, there be many light and shining Bodies, that are of different Natures; as for example, Metal is a bright shining Body; and divers sorts of Stones, are bright shining Bodies: also, clear Water is a bright shining Body; yet, the Metal and Stones are Minerals, and Water is an Element. Indeed, Most Bodies are of a Glassie Hue, or, as I may say, Complexion; as may be observed in most Vegetables; as also, Skins, Feathers, Scales, and the like.

But some may say, *That Glassiness is made by the Brightness of the Light that shines upon them.*[1]

I answer: If so, then the ordinary Earth would have the like Glassiness: but, we perceive the Earth to appear dull in the clearest Sun-shining Day: wherefore, it is not the Light, but the nature of their own Bodies. Besides, every Body hath not one and the same sort of Glassiness, but some are very different: 'Tis true, some sorts of Bodies do not appear Glassie, or shining, until they be polished: but, as for such sorts of shining Bodies that appear in the dark, there is not many of them perceiv'd by us, besides the Moon and Starrs; but yet some there are, as Fire; but that is an Element. There are also Glow-worms Tayles, Cats Eyes, Rotten Wood, and such like shining-Bodies.

CHAP. XII.

Of Metamorphoses, or Transformations of Animals and Vegetables.

There are some Creatures that cannot be Metamorphosed: as for example, Animals and Vegetables, at least, most of those sorts, by reason they are composed of many several and different Figurative Motions, and I understand *Metamorphose*, to be a change and alteration of the Exterior Form, but not any change or alteration of the Interior or Intellectual Nature: and how can there be a general change of the Exterior Form or Shape of a Human Creature, or such like Animal, when the different Figurative Motions of his different Compositions, are, for the most part, ignorant of each other's particular Actions? Besides, as Animals and Vegetables require degrees of time for their Productions, as also, for their Perfections; so, some Time is requir'd for their Alterations: but, a sudden alteration amongst different Figurative Motions, would cause such a Confusion, that it would cause a Dissolution of the *whole* Creature, especially in actions that are not natural, as being improper to their kind, or sort: The same of Vegetables, which have many different Figurative Motions. This considered, I cannot chuse but wonder, that wise men should believe (as some do) the Change or Transformation of Witches, into many sorts of Creatures.

---

1 The nature and properties of light were a subject of great debate in the late seventeenth century, in large part due to the advent of microscopy.

CHAP. XIII.

Of the Life and Death of several Creatures.

That which Man names *Life*, and *Death*, (which are some sorts of Compositions and Divisions of Parts of Creatures) is very different, in different kinds and sorts of Creatures, as also, in one and the same sort: As for example, Some Vegetables are old and decrepit in a Day; others are not in Perfection, or in their Prime, in less than a hundred years. The same may be said of Animal kinds. A *Silk-worm* is no sooner born, but dyes; when as other Animals may live a hundred years. As for Minerals, Tinn and Lead seem but of a short Life, to Gold; as a Worm to an Elephant, or a Tulip to an Oak for lasting; and 'tis probable, the several Productions of the Planets and Fixed Starrs, may be as far more lasting, than the parts of Gold more lasting than a Flye: for, if a Composed Creature were a Million of years producing, or Millions of years dissolving, it were nothing to Eternity: but, those produced Motions that make Vegetables, Minerals, Elements, and the like, the subtilest Philosopher, or Chymist, in Nature, can never perceive, or find out; because, Human Perception is not so subtile, as to perceive that which man names *Natural Productions*: for, though all the Corporeal Motions in Nature are perceptive; yet, every Perceptive Part doth not perceive all the actions in Nature: for, though every different Corporeal Motion, is a different Perception; yet, there are more Objects than any one Creature can perceive: also, every particular kind or sort of Creatures, have different Perceptions, occasioned by the Frame and Form of their Compositions, or unities of their Parts: So as the Perceptions of Animals, are not like the Perceptions of Vegetables; nor Vegetables, like the Perceptions of Minerals; nor Minerals, like the Perceptions of Elements: For, though all these several kinds and sorts, be perceptive; yet, not after one and the same way, or manner of Perception: but, as there is infinite variety of Corporeal Motions, so there are infinite varieties of Perceptions: for, Infinite Self-moving Matter, hath infinite varieties of Actions. But, to return to the Discourse of the Productions and Dissolutions of Creatures; The reason, that some Creatures last longer than others, is, That some Forms or Frames of their Composition, are of a more lasting Figure. But this is to be observed, That the Figures that are most solid, are more lasting than those that are more slack and loose: but mistake me not; I say, *For the most part*, they are more lasting. Also, this is to be noted, That some Compositions require more labour; some, more curiosity; and some are more full of variety, than others.

CHAP. XIV.
Of CIRCLES.

A *Circle* is a Round Figure, without End; which Figure can more easily and aptly alter the Exterior Form, than any other Figure. For example, A Circular Line may be drawn many several ways, into different and several sorts of Figures, without breaking the Circle: also, it may be contracted or extended into a less or wider compass; and drawn or formed into many several sorts of Figures, or Works; as, into a Square, or Triangle, or Oval, or Cylinder, or like several sorts of Flowers, and never dissolve the Circular Line. But this is to be noted, that there may be several sorts of Circular Lines; as, some Broad, some Narrow, some Round, some Flat, some Ragged or Twisted, some Smooth, some Pointed, some Edged, and numbers of the like; and yet the compass be exactly round.

But some may say, that, *When a Circle is drawn into several Works, it is not a Circle: as for example, When a Circle is squared, it is not a Circle, but a Square.*

I answer: It is a Circle squar'd, but not a Circle broken, or divided: for, the Interior Nature is not dissolved, although the Exterior Figure is altered: it is a Natural Circle, although it should be put into a Mathematical Square. But, to conclude this Chapter, I say, That all such sorts of Figures that are (like Circular Lines) of one piece, may change and rechange their Exterior Figures, or Shapes, without any alterations of their Interior Properties.

CHAP. XV.
Human Creatures cannot so probably treat of other sorts of Creatures, as of their own.

To treat of the Productions of Vegetables, Minerals, and Elements, is not so easie a Task, as to treat of Animals; and, amongst Animals, the most easie Task is, to treat of Human Productions; by reason one Human Creature may more probably guess at the Nature of all Human Creatures (being of the same Nature) than he can of other kinds of Creatures, that are of another Nature. But, mistake me not, I mean not of another Nature, being not of the same kind of Creature, but concerning Vegetables, Minerals, and Elements. The Elements may more easily be treated of, than the other Two kinds: for, though there be numerous sorts of them, at least, numerous several Particulars; yet, not so many several Sorts, as of Vegetables: and though Minerals are not, as to my knowledg, so numerous as Vegetables; yet, they are of more, or at least, of as many Sorts as Elements are. But, by reason I am unlearned, I shall only give my Opinion of the Productions of some sorts; in which, I fear, I shall rather discover my Ignorance, than the Truth of their Productions. But, I hope my *Readers* will not find fault with my Endeavour, though they may find fault with my little Experience, and want of Learning.

THE TWELFTH PART.

CHAP. I.

Of the Equality of ELEMENTS.

As for the Four Elements, *Fire*, *Air*, *Water*, and *Earth*; they subsist, as all other Creatures, which subsist by each other: but, in my opinion, there should be an Equality of the Four Elements, to balance the World:[1] for, if one sort should superabound, it would occasion such an Irregularity, that would cause a Dissolution of this World; as, when some particular Humour in Man's Body superabounds, or there is a scarcity of some Humours, it causes such Irregularities, that do, many times, occasion his Destruction. The same may be said of the Four Elements of the World: as for example, If there were not a sufficient quantity of Elemental Air, the Elemental Fire would go out; and if not a sufficient quantity of Elemental Fire, the Air would corrupt: also, if there were not a sufficient quantity of Elemental Water, the Elemental Fire would burn the Earth; and if there were not a sufficient quantity of Earth, there would not be a solid and firm Foundation for the Creatures of the Earth: for, if there were not Density, as well as Rarity; and Levity, as well as Gravity; Nature would run into Extreams.

CHAP. II.

Of several TEMPERS.

Heat doth not make Drought: for, there is a *Temper* of Hot and Moist. Nor Cold doth not make Drought: for, there is a *Temper* of Cold and Moist. Neither doth Heat make Moisture: for, there is a

---

1 In the Aristotelian tradition, all sublunary natural matter was composed of either one of or a combination of these four elements, each with its own properties that were thought to correspond to the four humors of the body. Cavendish adopts this view but also subordinates it to her organic materialism (e.g., see Part 8, Chapter III, p. 118, where she suggests that there are likely more than four humors). By contrast, van Helmont provocatively claimed that there were only two primary elements (air and water); see *Oriatrike* 45–62. See also Appendix C2.

Temper of Hot and Dry. Nor doth Cold make Moisture: for, there is a *Temper* of Cold and Dry. But, such or such sorts of Corporeal Figurative Motions, make Hot, Cold, Moist, Dry; Hot and Dry, Hot and Moist; Cold and Dry, Cold and Moist; and, as those Figurative Motions alter their Actions, those *Tempers* are altered: the like happens in all Creatures. But this is to be observed, That there is some opposite or contrary *Tempers*, which have a likeness of Motions: as for example, A Moist Heat, and a Moist Cold, have a likeness or resemblance of Moistness; and the same is in dry Heats and Cold: but surely, most sorts of Moistures, are some sorts of dilative Motions; and most Droughts, are some sorts of Contractive Motions: but, there are several sorts of Dilations, Contractions, Retentions, Expulsions, and the like: for, there are Cold Contractions, Hot Contractions; Cold Dilations, Hot Dilations; Hot Retentions, Cold Retentions; and so of Digestions, Expulsions, and the like: But, as I said, Moist Heats, and Moist Cold, seem of a Dilative Nature; as Dry, of a Contractive Nature. But, all Cold and Heat, or Dry and Moist, may be made by one and the same Corporeal Motions: for, though the Actions may vary, the Parts may be the same: yea, the like Actions may be in different Parts. But, no Part is bound to any particular Action, having a free Liberty of Self-motion. But, concerning Hot and Cold, and the like Actions, I observe, That Extream Heat, and Extream Cold, is of a like Power, or Degree: neither can I perceive the Hot Motions to be quicker than Cold: for Water, in little quantity, shall as suddenly freeze, as any leight Fewel or Straw, burn: and Animals will as soon freeze to death, as be burned to death: and Cold is as powerful at the Poles, as Heat in the *Torrid Zone*. And 'tis to be observed, That Freezing is as quick and sudden, as Thawing: but sometimes, nay every often, Cold and Hot Motions will dispute for Power; and some sorts of Hot, with other sorts. The like Disputes are amongst several sorts of Cold Motions; Dry with Moist, Dry with Dry, Moist with Moist. And the like Disputes are also often amongst all Creatures. As for Density, it doth not make Gravity: for, there may be Dense Bodies, that are not Grave; as for example, Feathers, and Snow.[1] Neither doth Gravity make Density: for, a quantity of Air hath some weight, and yet is not dense. But mistake me not; for, I mean by *Grave*, *Heavy*; and not for the Effects of Ascending, and

1 Discussions of density and gravity were ongoing at this time; Isaac Newton (1643–1727) did not publish his theory of gravity until 1687.

Descending: for Feathers, though Dense, are more apt to ascend, than descend; and Snow, to descend. Also, all sorts of Fluidity, do not cause Moist, Liquid, or Wet; nor all Extenuations, cause Light: but, they are such and such sorts of Fluidities and Extenuations, that cause such and such Effects. And so for Heats, Colds, Droughts, Moistures, Rarities. The same for Gravities, Levities, and the like. So that, Creatures are Rare, Fluid, Moist, Wet, Dry, Dense, Hard, Soft, Leight, Heavy, and the like, according to their Figurative Motions.

CHAP. III.

Of the Change and Rechange; and of Dividing and Joyning of the Parts of the Elements.

Of all Creatures subject to Human Perception, the Elements are most apt to Transform, *viz.* to *Change* and *Rechange*; also, to Divide and *Joyn* their Parts, without altering their Innate Nature and Property. The reason is, because the Innate Figurative Motions of Elements, are not so different as those of Animals and Vegetables, whose Compositions are of many different Figurative Motions; in so much, that dis-joining any Part of Animals, or Vegetables, they cannot be joined again, as they were before; at least, it is not commonly done: but, the Nature and Property of the Elements, is, That every Part and Particle are of one innate Figurative Motion; so that the least grain of Dust, or the least drop of Water, or the least spark of Fire, is of the same Innate Nature, Property, and Figurative Motions, as the whole Element; when as, of Animals, and Vegetables, almost, every Part and Particle is of a different Figurative Motion.

CHAP. IV.

Of the Innate Figurative Motions of Earth.

There are many sorts of *Earth*, yet all sorts are of the same kind; that is, they are all Earth: but (in my opinion) the prime Figurative Motions of Earth, are Circles;[1] but not dilated Circles, but contracted Circles: neither are those Circles smooth, but rugged; which is the cause that Earth is dull, or dim, and is easily divided into dusty Parts: for all, or at least, most Bodies that are smooth,

---

1 Now that Cavendish has established that all things exist via the unique figurative motions of a unique conglomeration of natural parts, she begins to speculate about the different types of motion that animate different things. However, across the following chapters, she seems to recognize that this exercise is purely speculative.

are more apt to joyn, than divide; and have a Glassie Hew or Complexion; which is occasioned by the smoothness, and the smoothness occasioned by the evenness of Parts, being without Intervals: but, according as these sorts or Circular Motions are more or less contracted, and more or less rugged, they cause several sorts of Earth.

CHAP. V.

Of the Figurative Motions of Air.

There are many sorts of *Airs*, as there is of other Creatures, of one and the same kind: but, for Elemental Air, is composed of very Rare, Figurative Motions; and the Innate Motions, I conceive to be somewhat of the Nature of Water, *viz*. Circular Figurative Motions, only of a more Dilating Property; which causes Air, not to be Wet, but extraordinary Rare; which again cause it to be somewhat of the nature of Light: for, the Rarity occasions Air to be very searching and penetrating; also, dividable and compoundable: but, the Rarity of Air, is the cause that it is not subject to some sorts of Human Perception; but yet, not so Rare, as not to be subject to Human Respirations; which is one sort of Human Perception: for, all Parts of all Creatures, are perceptive one way, or another: but, as I said, there are many sorts of Air; as, some Cold, some Hot; some Dry, some Moist; some Sharp; some Corrupt, some Pure, some Gross; and numbers more: but, many of these sorts are rather Metamorphosed Vapours, and Water, than pure Elemental Air: for, the pure Elemental Air, is, in my opinion, more searching and penetrating, than Light; by reason Light may be more easily eclipsed, or stopt; when as Air will search every Pore, and every Creature, to get entrance.

CHAP. VI.

Of the Innate Figurative Motion of Fire.

The Innate Figurative Motions of Elemental Fire, seem the most difficult to Human Perception, and Conception: for, by the Agilness, it seems to be more pure than the other sorts of Elements; yet, by the Light, or Visibleness, it seems more gross than Air; but, by the dilating Property, it seems to be more rare than air, at least, as rare as Air. By the Glassie or Shining Property, it seems to be of Smooth and Even Parts: also, by the piercing and wounding Property, Fire, seems to be composed of sharp-pointed Figurative Motions: Wherefore, the Innate Figurative Motions of Fire, are, Pure, Rare, Smooth, Sharp Points, which can move in Circles, Squares, Triangles, Parallels, or any other sorts of Exterior Figures, without an alteration of its Interior Nature; as may be observed by many sorts of Fuels: as also, it can contract and dilate its Parts, without any alteration of its Innate Property.

CHAP. VII.

Of the Productions of Elemental Fire.

It is to be observed, That Points of Fire are more numerous, and more suddenly propagating, than any other Element, or any other Creature that is subject to Human Perception. But, Sparks of Fire, resemble the Seeds of Vegetables, in this, That as Vegetables will not encrease in all sorts of Soyles, alike; neither will the Points of Fire, in all sorts of Fuel, alike. And, as Vegetables produce different Effects in several Soyls; so doth Fire on several Fuels: As for example, The Seeds of Vegetables do not work the same Effect in a Bird's Crop,[1] as in the Earth: for, there they encrease the Bird by digestion; but, in the ground, they encrease their own Issue (as I may say): So Fire, in some Fuels, doth destroy it self, and occasions the Fuel to be more consumed; when as, in other sorts of Fuel, Fire encreases extreamly. But Fire, as all other Creatures, cannot subsist single of it self, but must have Food and Respiration; which proves, Fire is not an Immaterial Motion. Also, Fire hath Enemies, as well as Friends; and some are deadly, namely, Water, or Watry Liquors. Also, Fire is forced to comply with the Figurative Motions of those Creatures it is joyned to: for, all Fuels will not burn, or alter, alike.

CHAP. VIII.

Of FLAME.

Flame is the Rarest Part of Fire: and though the Fuel of Flame be of a vaporous and smoaky Substance; yet surely, there are pure Flames, which are perfect Fires: and, for proof, we may observe, That Flame will dilate and run, as it were, to catch Smoak: but, when the Smoak is above the Flame, if it be higher than the Flame can extend, it contracts back to the Fiery Body. But, Flame doth somewhat resemble that we name *Natural Light*: but yet, in my opinion, Light is not Flame; nor hath it any Fiery Property, although it be such a sort of Extenuating or Dilating Actions, as Flame hath.

---

1 A muscular pouch connected to a bird's esophagus.

CHAP. IX.

Of the two sorts of Fire most different.

There are many sorts of Fires: but two sorts are most opposite; that is, the Hot, Glowing, Burning, Bright, Shining Fire; and that sort of Fire we name a *Dead, Dull Fire*; as, Vitriol Fires, Cordial Fires, Corrosive Fires, Feverish Fires, and numerous other sorts;[1] and every several sort, hath some several Property: as for example, There is greater difference between the Fiery Property of Oyl, and the Fiery Property of Vitriol: for, Oyl is neither Exteriorly Hot, nor Burning; whereas Vitriol is Exteriorly Burning, though not Exteriorly Hot: but, the difference of these sorts of Fires, is, That the Actions of Elemental Fire, are to ascend, rather than to descend: and the Dull, Dead Fire, is rather apt to descend, than ascend; that is, to pierce, or dilate, either upwards, or downwards: but, they are both of Dilating and Dividing Natures. But this is to be noted, That all sorts of Heats, or Hotness, are not Fire. Also it is to be noted, That all Fires are not Shining.

CHAP. X.

Of Dead or Dull Fires.

Of *Dull, Dead Fires*, some sorts seem to be of a mixt sort: as for example, Vitriol, and the like, seem to be Exteriorly, of the Figurative Motions of Fire; and Interiorly, of the Figurative Motions of Water, or of Watry Liquors: And Oyl is of Fiery Figurative Motions, Interiorly; and of Liquid Figurative Motions, Exteriorly; which is the cause that Fiery Properties of Oyl cannot be altered, without a Total Dissolution of their Natures. But, such sorts whose Fiery Figurative Motions are Exterior, as being not their Innate Nature, may be divided from those other Natural Parts they were joyned to, without altering their Innate Nature.

CHAP. XI.

Of the Occasional Actions of Fire.

All Creatures have not only Innate figurative Motions that cause them to be such or such a sort of Creature; but, they have such and such actions, that cause such and such Effects: also, every Creature is occasioned to particular Actions, by forrein Objects; many times to improper actions, and sometimes to ruinous

1 Cavendish considers the effects of vitriol, or sulfuric acid; cordials and liqueurs; and fevers in the category of "fire" because of their burning qualities.

actions, even to the dissolution of their Nature: And, of all Creatures, Fire is the most ready to occasion the most Mischief; at least, Disorders: for, where it can get entrance, it seldom fails of causing such a Disturbance, as occasions a Ruine. The reason is, that most Creatures are porous: for, all Creatures, subsisting by each other, must of necessity have *Egress* and *Regress*, being composed of Interior and Exterior Corporeal Motions. And Fire, being the sharpest figurative Motion, is apt to enter into the smallest Pores.

But some may ask, Whether Fire is porous it self?

I answer: That having Respiration, it is a sufficient proof that it is Porous: for, Fire dyes if it hath not Air.

But some may say, *How can a Point be porous?*

I answer, That a Point is composed of Parts, and therefore may very well be porous: for, there is no such thing as a Single Part in Nature, and therefore, not a Single Point.

Also, some may say, *If there be Pores in Nature, there may be Vacuum.*

I answer, That, in my opinion, there is not; because there is no empty Pores in Nature: Pores signifying only an *Egress* and *Regress* of Parts.

CHAP. XII.

Fire hath not the Property to Change and Rechange.

Of all the Elemental Creatures, *Fire* is the least subject to change: for, though it be apt to occasion other Creatures to alter; yet it keeps close to its own Properties, and proper Actions: for, it cannot change, and rechange, as Water can. Also, Natural Air is not apt to change and rechange, as Water: for, though it can (as all the Elements) divide and join its Parts, without altering the Property of its Nature: yet, it cannot readily alter, and alter again, its Natural Properties, as Water can. The truth is, Water and Fire, are opposite in all their Properties: but, as Fire is, of all the Elements, the furthest from altering: so Water is, of all the Elements, the most subject to alter: for, all Circular Figures are apt to variety.

CHAP. XIII.

Of the Innate Figurative Motions of Water.

The Nature of *Water* is, Rare, Fluid, Moist, Liquid, Wet, Glutinous, and Glassie. Likewise, Water is apt to divide and unite its Parts, most of which Properties are caused by several sorts of Dilations, or Extenuations: but, the Interior, or Innate Figure of Water, is a Circular Line. But yet, it is to be observed, That there are many several sorts of Waters, as there are many several sorts of Airs, Fires, and Earths, and so of all Creatures: for, some Waters are more rare than others, some more leight, and some more heavy; some more clear, and some more dull; some salt, some sharp; some bitter, some more fresh, or sweet; some have cold Effects, some hot Effects: all which is caused by the several Figurative Motions of several sorts of Waters: but, the nature of Water is such, as it can easily alter, or change, and rechange, and yet keep its Interior, or Innate Nature or Figure. But this is also to be observed, That the Dilating or Extenuating Circle of Water, is of a middle Degree, as between Two Extreams.

CHAP. XIV.

The Nature or Property of Water.

Wetness, which is the Interior or Innate Property, or Nature of Water, is, in my opinion, caused by some sort of Dilations or Extenuations. As, all Droughts, or Dryness, are caused by some sorts of Contractions; so, all Moistures, Liquors, and Wets, by Dilations: yet, those Extenuations, or Dilations, that cause Wet, must be of such a sort of Dilations, as are proper to Wet; *viz.* Such a sort of Extenuations, as are Circular Extenuations; which do dilate, or extenuate, in a smooth, equal dilation, from the Center, to the Circumference; which Extenuations, or Dilations, are of a middle Degree; for otherwise, the Figure of Water might be extended beyond the Degree of Wet; or, not extended to the Degree of Wet. And it is to be observed, That there is such a Degree as only causes moistness, and another to cause liquidness, the third to cause wetness: for, though Moistness and Liquidness are in the way of Wetness; yet, they are not that which we name *Wet*: also, all that is Soft, or Smooth, is not Wet; nor is all that is Liquid, or Flowing, Wet: for, some sorts of Air are liquid and flowing, but not wet: nay, Flame is liquid and flowing, but yet quite opposite from wet. Dust is flowing, but neither liquid or wet, in its Nature. And Hair and Feathers are soft and smooth, but neither liquid, nor wet. But, as I said, Water is of such a Nature, as to have the Properties of Soft, Smooth, Moist, Liquid, and Wet; and is also of such flowing Properties, caused by such a sort of Extenuating Circles as are of a Middle or Mean Degree: but yet, there are many several sorts of Liquors, and Wets, as we may perceive in Fruit, Herbs, and the like: but, all sorts of Wets, and Liquors, are of a watry kind, though of a different sort. But, as I have said, all things that are Fluid, are not Wet; as, Melted Metal, Flame, Light, and the like, are fluid, but not wet: and Smoak and Oyl are of another sort of Liquidness, than Water, or Juyce; but yet they are not wet: and that which causes the difference of different sorts of Waters, and Watry Liquors, are the differences of the watry Circular Lines; as, some are edged, some are pointed, some are twisted, some are braided, some are flat, some are round, some ruff, some smooth; and so after divers several Forms or Figures: and yet are perfect Circles, and of some such a Degree of Extenuations or Dilations.

CHAP. XV.

Of the Alteration of the Exterior Figurative Motion of Water.

As I formerly said, The Figurative Motions of the Innate Nature of Water, is a sort of Extenuating; as being an equal, smooth Circle: which is the cause Water is rare, fluid, moist, liquid, and wet. But, the Exterior Figurative Motions of the watry Circle, may be edged, pointed, sharp, blunt, flat, round, smooth, ruff, or the like; which may be either divided, or altered, without any alteration of the Innate Nature, or Property: As for example, Salt-water may be made fresh, or the Salt Parts divided from the watry Circle: The like of other sorts of Waters; and yet the Nature of Water remains.

CHAP. XVI.

Of OYL, and VITRIOL.

The Exterior Figurative Motions of *Oyl*, are so much like those of *Water*, as, to be fluid, smooth, soft, moist, and liquid, although not perfectly wet: but, the Interior Figurative Motions of Oyl, are of that sort of Fire, that we name a *Dull, Dead Fire*: and the difference between *Salt Waters*, *Vitriol* or the like, and *Oyl*, is, That the Exterior Figurative Motions of *Vitriol* and *Salt Waters*, are of a sort of Fire; whereas it is the Interior Figurative Motions of Oyl, or the like, that are of those sorts of Fire; and that is the reason that the fiery Motions of Oyl cannot be altered, as the fiery Motions of *Vitriol* may. But this is to be noted, That although the Interior Figurative Motions of Oyl, are of such a sort of fiery Motions; yet, not just like those of *Vitriol*; and are not burning, corroding, or wounding, as *Vitriols*, *Corrosives*, and the like, are: for, those are somewhat more of the Nature of bright shining Fires, than Oyls.

CHAP. XVII.

Of Mineral and Sulphureous Waters.

In *Sulphureous* and *Mineral Waters*, the *Sulphureous* and *Mineral* Corporeal Motions, are Exterior, and not Interior, like Salt waters: but there are several sorts of such waters; also, some are occasionally, others naturally so affected: for, some waters running through Sulphureous, or Mineral Mines, gather, like a rowling Stone, some of the loose Parts of Gravel, or Sand; which, as they stick or cleave to the rowling Stone; so they do to the running Waters; as we may perceive by those waters that spring out of Chalk, Clay, or Lime Grounds, which will have some Tinctures of the Lime, Chalk, or Clay; and the same happens to Minerals. But, some are naturally Sulphureous; as for example, Some sorts of hot Baths are as naturally Sulphureous, as the Sea-water is Salt: but, all those Effects of Minerals, Sulphurs, and the like, are dividable from, and also may be joyn'd to, the Body of water, without any disturbance to the nature of water; as may be proved by Salt-water, which will cause fresh Meat to be salt; and salt Meat will cause Fresh-water to be salt. As for hot Baths, those have hot figurative Motions, but not burning: and the moist, liquid, and wet Nature of water, makes it apt to joyn, and divide, to, and from other sorts of Motions; as also, to and from its own sort.

CHAP. XVIII.

The Cause of the Ebbing and Flowing of the Sea.[1]

The Nature of water is to flow; so that all sorts of waters will flow, if they be not obstructed: but it is not the Nature of Water, to ebb. Neither can water flow beyond the Power of its Quantity: for, a little water will not flow so far as a great one. But, I do not mean by flowing, the falling of water from some Descent; but, to flow upon a Level: for, as I have said, all waters do naturally flow, if they be not obstructed; but, few sorts of water, besides Sea-water, ebbs. As for the Exterior Figurative Motions of water, in the action of flowing, they are an Oval, or a half Circle, or a half Moon; where the middle parts of the half Moon, or Circle, are fuller than the two Ends. Also, the figure of a half Moon, or half Circle, is concave on the inside, and convex on the outside of the Circle: but, these Figurative Motions, in a great quantity of water, are bigg and full, which we name *Waves of Water*; which waves flowing

1 The operations of the tides remained mysterious until Newton's theory of gravity, which appeared in his *Principia* (1687), became known and accepted in the early eighteenth century.

fast upon each other, presses each other forward, until such time as the half Circle divides: for, when the Bow of the half Circle is over-bent, or stretched, it divides into the middle, which is most extended: and when a half Circle (which is a whole wave of water) is divided, the divided Parts fall equally back on each side of the flowing waves: so, every wave dividing, after that manner, in the full extension, it causes the motion of ebbing, that is, to flow back, as it flow'd forward: for, the divided Parts falling back, and joining as they meet, makes the head of the half Circle, where the Ends of the half Circle were; and the Convex, where the Concave was; by which action, the ebbing Parts are become the flowing Parts. And the reason that it ebbs and flows by degrees, is, That the flowing half Circles require so much time to be at the utmost extension. Also, every wave, or half Circle, divides not all at one time, but one after another: for, two Bodies cannot be in one place at one point of time; and until the second, third, and so the rest, flow as far as the first, they are not at their full extension. And thus the Sea, or such a great Body of Water, must flow, and ebb, as being its nature to flow; and the flowing Figure, being over-extended, by endeavouring to flow beyond its power, causes a dividing of the Extended Parts, which is the Cause of the Ebbing.

But, whether this Opinion of mine, be as probable as any of the former Opinions concerning the Ebbing and Flowing of the Sea, I cannot judg: but I would not be mistaken; for the flowing of the water, is according to its Quantity; for, the further it flows, the fainter, or weaker it is.

CHAP. XIX.
Of OVERFLOWS.

As for *Overflows*,[1] there be many; and many more would be, if the waters were not hindred and obstructed by Man's Inventions. But, some Overflows are very Uncertain and Irregular; others, Certain and Regular, as, the flowing of *Nilus* in *Egypt*: but as for the distance of time of its flowing, it may proceed from the far Journey of those flowing-waters: and, the time of its ebbing, may be attributed to the great Quantity of Water; so that the great quantity of water, will cause a longer or a shorter time in the flowing or ebbing; and certainly the waters are as long a flowing back, as flowing forward.

As for Spring Tides, they are only in such a time when there is a Natural Issue of a greater quantity of water: so that

1 Floods.

Spring-Tides are but once a Month, and Single-Tides in so many hours: but, many several occasions, may make the Tides to be more or less full.

As for Double-Tides, they are occasioned through the Irregular dividing of the Half-Circle; as, when they divide not orderly, but faster than they orderly should do; which, falling back in a Crowd, and being, by that means, obstructed, so that they cannot get forward, they are necessitated to flow, where they ebb'd.

The reason the Tides flow through Streams of Running-waters, is, That the Tide is stronger than the Stream: but, if the Stream and Tides pass through each other, then the Tide and Stream are somewhat like Duellers together, which make Passes and Passages for their conveniency.

CHAP. XX.

Of the Figure of Ice and Snow.[1]

A Circle may not only extend and contract it self without dividing; but may draw it self into many several Figures, as Squares, or Triangles: as also, into many other Figures mix'd of Squares, Triangles, Cubes, or the like; being partly one, and partly, another; and into several ways, and after several manners; which is the reason, Water may appear in many several Postures of Snow, Ice, Hail, Frost, and the like: and, in my Opinion, when the Water-Circle is Triangular, it is Snow; when the Circle is Square, it is Ice: as for Hail, they are but small pieces of Ice; that is, small Parts, or few Drops of Water, changed into Ice; and those several Parts moving after several manners, make the Exterior Figures, after several shapes; as, great Bodies of Ice will be of many several shapes, occasioned by many or fewer Parts, and by the several Postures of those Parts: but, such Figures, though they are of Ice, yet, are not the Innate Figures of Ice. The same is to be said of Snow. But, the reason of these my Opinions concerning the Figures of Ice and Snow, is, That Snow is leighter than the Water it self; and Ice is heavier, at least, as heavy. And the reason Snow is so leight, is, That a Triangular Figure hath no poyse, being an odd Figure; whereas a Square is poysed by Even and Equal

---

1 Another topic frequently discussed by the members of The Royal Society. For example, in *Micrographia* (1665), Robert Hooke (1635–1703) suspected that snowflakes were fragments of ice crystals. Cavendish may also have had in mind Robert Boyle's *New Experiments and Observations Touching Cold* (1665), which theorizes the formation of ice.

Lines, and just Number of Points, as, Two to Two: but, a Triangle is Two to One. Also, a Circle is a poysed Figure, as being equal every way, from the Center to the Circumference; and from the Circumference to the Center, all the Lines drawing to one Point. But, mistake me not; for I treat (concerning the Figures of Snow and Ice) only of those Figures that cause Water to be Snow or Ice; and not of the Exterior Figures of Snow and Ice, which are occasioned by the Order or Disorder of Adjoining Parts: for, several Parts of Water, may order themselves into numerous several Figures, which concern not the nature of Water, as it is Water, Snow, or Ice: As for example, Many Men in a Battel, or upon Ceremony, joyn into many several Figures or Forms; which Figures or Forms, are of no concern to their Innate Nature. Also, the several Figures or Forms of several Houses, or several sorts of Building in one House, are of no concern to the Innate Nature of the Materials. The like for the Exterior Figures of Ice and Show; and therefore *Microscopes* may deceive the Artist, who may take the Exterior for the Interior Figure; but there may be great difference between them.[1]

CHAP. XXI.

Of the Change and Rechange of Water.

Water being of a Circular Figurative Motion, is, as it were, but one Part, having no divisions; and therefore can more easily change and rechange it self into several Postures, *viz.* into the Posture of a Triangle, or Square; or can be dilated or extended into a larger compass, or contracted into a lesser compass; which is the cause it can turn into Vapour and Vaporous Air; or into Slime, or into some grosser Figure: For example, Water can extend it self beyond the proper degrees of Water, into the degree of Vapour; and the Circle, extending further than the degree of a Vaporous Circle, is extended into a Vaporous Air; and if the Vaporous Airy Circle be extreamly extended, it becomes so small, as it becomes to be a sharp Edg, and so, in a degree, next to Fire; at least, to have a hot Effect: but, if it extends further than an Edg, the Circle breaks into Flashes of Fire, like Lightning, which is a flowing Flame: for, being produced from Water, it hath the property of Flowing, or Streaming, as Water hath,

1 Cavendish frequently expresses her distrust of optical instruments, which she believed to distort rather than to augment vision. This skepticism is one important aspect of her larger critique of experimental practice and its over-reliance on sense perception. See also *Observations* 50–53; *Blazing World* 78–80.

as we may perceive by the Effects of some few Parts of Water flung on a bright Fire; for those few drops of Water being not enough to quench the Fire, straight dilate so extreamly, that they break into a Flame; or else cause the Fire to be more brisk and bright: and as the Water-Circle can be turned into Vapour, Air, and Flame, by Extension; so, it can be turned into Snow, Hail, or Ice, by Contraction.

CHAP. XXII.

Of Water Quenching Fire; and Fire Evaporating Water.

There is such an Antipathy betwixt *Water* and *Fire*, (I mean bright shining Fire) that they never meet Body to Body, but Fire is in danger to be quenched out, if there be a sufficient Quantity of Water. But it is to be observed, That it is not the actual Coldness of Water, that quenches out Fire; for, Scalding-water will quench out Fire: wherefore, it is the Wetness that quenches out Fire; which Wetness choaks the Fire, as a Man that is drown'd: for, Water being not fit for Man's Respiration, because it is too thick, choaks and smuthers him; and the same doth Water to Fire: for, though Air is of a proper temper for Respiration, both to some sorts of Animals, such as Man; as also, to Fire: yet, Water is not: which is most proper for other sorts of Animals, namely, Fish; as also, for some sorts of Animals that are of a mixt kind or sort, partly Fish, and partly Flesh: to which sort of Creatures, both Air and Water are both equally proper for their Respiration; or, their Respiration equal to either: for certainly, all sorts of Creatures have Respiration, by reason all Creatures subsist by each other; I say, *By each other*, not *Of each other*. But, there are many several sorts and kinds of Respirations; as concerning Water and Fire, though a sufficient quantity of Water, to Fire, doth always choak, smuther, or quench out the Fire's Life, if joyn'd Body to Body; yet, when there is another Body between those two Bodies, water is in danger to be infected with the Fire's heat; the Fire first infecting the Body next to it; and that Body infecting the Water: by which Infection, Water is consumed, either by a languishing Hectick Fever; or, by a raging Boyling Fever; and the Life of Water evaporates away.

CHAP. XXIII.

Of Inflamable Liquors.

There are many Bodies of mixt Natures; as for example, Wine, and all Strong Liquors, are partly of a watry Nature, and partly of a fiery Nature; but, 'tis of that sort we name a *Dead*, or *Dull Fire*: but, being of such a mixt Nature, they are both apt to quench Bright Fire, as also, apt to burn or flame; so that such sorts are both Inflamable, and Quenchable. But, some have more of the fiery Nature; and others, more of the watry Nature; and, by those Effects, we may perceive, that not only different, but opposite Figurative Motions, do well agree in one Society.

CHAP. XXIV.
Of THUNDER.

I Observe, that all Tempestuous Sounds have some resemblances to the flowing of waters, either in great and ruffling waves; or, when the waters flow in such sort, as to break in pieces against hard and rugged Rocks; or run down great *Precipices*, or against some Obstruction. And the like Sound hath the Blowings of Wind, or the Clappings of *Thunder*; which causes me to be of opinion, That *Thunder* is occasioned by a Discord amongst some Water-Circles in the Higher Region;[1] which, pressing and beating upon each other in a confused manner, cause a confused Sound, by reason all Circles are Concave within the Bow, and Convex without; which is a Hollow Figure, although no *Vacuum*: which Hollow Figure, causes quick Repetitions and Replies; which Replies and Repetitions, we name *Rebounds* but, Replies are not Rebounds; for, Rebounds are Pressures and Re-actions; whereas Repetitions are without Pressure, but Re-action is not: and, Replies are of several Parts; as, one Part to reply to another. But for *Thunder*, it is occasioned both by Pressures and Re-actions; as also, Replies of Extended Water-Circles, which make a kind or sort of Confusion, and so a confused Sound, which we name *Horrid*; and, according to their Discord, the Sound is more or less terrifying, or violent. But this is to be noted, That as *Thunder* is caused by undivided or broken Circles; so *Lightning* is caused by broken or divided Circles, that are extended beyond the Power of the Nature of the Water-Circle; and when the Circle is extreamly extended, it divides it self into a straight Line, and becomes a flowing Flame.

CHAP. XXV.
Of Vapour, Smoak, Wind, and Clouds.

Vapour and *Smoak* are both fluid Bodies: but, Smoak is more of the Nature of Oyl, than Water; and Vapour more of the Nature of Water, than Oyl; they are dividable: and may be join'd, as other

1 Hobbes argued that thunder occurs when frozen clouds collide (see *De Corpore*, Part IV: Ch. 28), while van Helmont attributes thunder to his concept of elementary motion, or "blas" (see *Oriatrike* 90–91). On "blas," see also Appendix C2, pp. 254–55.

Elements: also, they are of a Metamorphosing Nature, as to change and rechange; but, when they are Metamorphosed into the form of Air, that Air is a gross Air, and is, as we say, a corruptible Air. As for Vapour, it is apt to turn into Wind: for, when it is rarified beyond the Nature of Vapour, and not so much as into the Nature of Air, it turns into some sorts of Wind. I say, some sorts: and certainly, the strongest Winds are made of the grossest Vapours. As for Smoak, it is apt to turn into some sorts of Lightning, I say, apt: for, both Vapour and Smoak can turn into many sorts of Metamorphosed Elements. As for Wind, it proceeds either from Rarified Vapour, or Contracted Air. And there are many sorts of Vapours, Smoaks, and Winds; all which sorts of Vapours and Smoaks, are apt to ascend: but, Wind is of a more level action. As for Clouds, they cannot be composed of a Natural Air; because Natural Air is too rare a Body to make Clouds. Wherefore, Clouds are composed of Vapour and Smoak: for, when Vapour and Smoak ascends up high without transformation, they gather into Clouds, some higher, some lower, according to their purity: for, the purer sort (as I may say for expression-sake) ascends the highest, as being the most agil. But, concerning the Figurative Motions of Vapour and Smoak, they are Circles; but of Winds, they are broken Parts of Circular Vapours: for, when the Vaporous Circle is extended beyond its Nature of Vapour, the Circumference of the Circle breaks into perturbed Parts; and if the Parts be small, the wind is, in our perception, sharp, pricking, and piercing: but, if the Parts are not so small, the wind is strong and pressing: but wind, being rarified Vapour, is so like Air, as it is not perceived by human sight, though it be perceived by human touch. But, as there are hot vapours, cold vapours, sharp vapours, moist vapours, dry vapours, subtil vapours, and the like; so there is such sorts of winds. But, pray do not mistake me, when I say, that some sorts of winds are broken and perturbed Circles, as if I meant, such as those of Lightning: for, those of Lightning, are extended beyond the degree of Air; and those of Vapours, are not extended to the degree of Air: also, those of Lightning, are not perturbed; and those of Wind, are perturbed. Again, those of Lightning, flow in Streams of smooth, small, even Lines; those of Wind, in disordered Parts and Fragments.

CHAP. XXVI.
Of WIND.

Wind and *Fire* have some resemblance in some of their particular actions: as for example, Wind and Fire endeavour the disturbance of other Creatures, occasioning a separating and disjoining of

Parts. Also, Wind is both an Enemy and Friend to Fire: for Wind, in some sorts of its actions, will assist Fire; and in other actions, dissipates Fire, nay, blows it out: but certainly, the powerful Forces of Wind, proceed not so much from Solidity, as Agility: for, soft, weak, if[1] quick Motions, are far more powerful, than strong, slow Motions; because, quick Replies are of great Force, as allowing no time of respit. But this is to be observed, That Wind hath some watry Effects: for, the further water flows, the weaker and fainter it is: so the Wind, the further it blows, the weaker and fainter it is. But this is to be observed, That according to the agilness or slowness of the Corporeal Motions; or, according to the number; or, according to the manner of the compositions, or joynings, or divisions; or, according to the regularity or irregularity of the Corporeal Figurative Motions, so are the Effects.

CHAP. XXVII.
Of LIGHT.

Water, Air, Fire, and Light; are all Rare and Fluid Creatures; but they are of different sorts of Rarities and Fluities: and, though Light seems to be extreamly Rare and Fluid; yet, Light is not so Rare and Fluid, as pure Air is, because it is subject to that sort of Human Perception we name *Sight*; but yet, it is not subject to any of the other Perceptions: and, pure Air is only subject to the Perception of Respiration, which seems to be a more subtil Perception than Sight; and that occasions me to believe, That Air is more Rare and Pure, than Light: but howsoever, I conceive the Figurative Motions of Light, to be extraordinary even, smooth, agil Lines of Corporeal Motions:[2] but, as I said before, there are many sorts of Lights that are not Elemental Lights; as, Glow-worms' Tails, Cats' Eyes, Rotten

1 In the corrected text, Cavendish replaced "or" with "if."

2 Like everything else in nature, then, light is material and consists of "Corporeal Motions." In subsequent chapters, Cavendish claims the same for darkness and color. In this, she argues against the "dioptrical writers" of her era (*Observations* 10)—e.g., Boyle, Descartes, Hobbes, Hooke, and Henry Power (1623–68)—who were all invested in studying the theoretical and practical aspects of light, vision, and microscopy. Her opinions are most similar to those of Hobbes, whose theory of light and vision centered on the motion of material bodies. However, Cavendish sees motion as internal to matter, whereas Hobbes views motion as the result of external force.

Wood, Fish Bones, and that Human Light which is made in Dreams, and Infinite other Lights, not subject to our Perception: which proves, That Light may be without Heat.[1] But, whether the Light of the Sun, which we name *Natural Light*, is naturally hot, may be a dispute: for, many times, the Night is hotter than the Day.

CHAP. XXVIII.
Of DARKNESS.

The Figurative Motions of *Light* and *Darkness*, are quite opposite; and the Figurative Motions of Colours, are as a Mean between both, being partly of the Nature of both: but, as the Figurative Motions of Light, in my opinion, are rare, straight, equal, even, smooth Figurative Motions: those of Darkness are uneven, ruff, or rugged, and more dense. Indeed, there is as much difference between Light and Darkness, as between Earth and Water; or rather, between Water and Fire; because each is an Enemy to other; and, being opposite, they endeavour to out-power each other. But this is to be noted, That Darkness is as visible to Human Perception, as Light; although the Nature of Darkness is, To obscure all other Objects besides it self: but, if Darkness could not be perceived, the Optick Perception could not know when it is dark; nay, particular dark Figurative Motions, are as visible in a general Light, as any other Object; which could not be, if Darkness was only a privation of Light, as the Opinions of many Learned Men are:[2] but, as I said before, Darkness is of a quite different Figurative Motion, from Light; so different, that it is just opposite: for, as the property of Light is to divulge Objects; so, the property of Darkness is to obscure them: but, mistake me not; I mean, that Light and Darkness have such properties to our Perception: but, whether it is so to all Perceptions, is more than I know, or is, as I believe, known to any other Human Creature.[3]

---

1 In *De Corpore* (Part IV: Ch. 27, Sect. 6), Hobbes suggested that "Glow-worms" and "Rotten Wood" glow only due to exposure to heat from sources like sunshine or human touch.

2 Cavendish refers to, among others, Hobbes (see *De Corpore*, Part IV: Ch. 27, Section 16) and Hooke (see *Micrographia*, Observation XVI).

3 Thus, what we know of natural phenomena might vary drastically from creature to creature and might or might not be correct.

CHAP. XXIX.
Of COLOURS.

As for *Colour*, it is the same with Body: for surely, there is no such thing in Nature, as a Colourless Body, were it as small as an Atom; nor no such thing as a Figureless Body; or such a thing as a Placeless Body: so that Matter, Colour, Figure, and Place, is but one thing, as one and the same Body:[1] but Matter, being self-moving, causes varieties of Figurative Actions, by various changes. As for Colours, they are only several Corporeal Figurative Motions; and as there are several sorts of Creatures, so there are several sorts of Colours: but, as there are those, Man names Artificial Creatures; so there are Artificial Colours. But, though to describe the several *Species* of all the several sorts of Colours, be impossible; yet we may observe, that there is more variety of Colours amongst Vegetables and Animals, than amongst Minerals and Elements: for, though the Rain-bow is of many fine Colours; yet, the Rain-bow hath not so much Variety, as many particular Vegetables, or Animals have; but every several Colour, is a several Figurative Motion; and the Brighter the Colours are, the Smoother and Evener are the Figurative Motions. And as for Shadows of Colours, they are caused when one sort of Figurative Motions is as the Foundation: for example, If the Fundamental Figurative Motion, be a deep Blew, or Red, or the like, then all the variations of other Colours have a tincture. But, in short, all Shadows have a ground of some sort of dark Figurative Motions. But, the Opinions of many Learned Men, are, That all Colours are made by the several Positions of Light, and are not inherent in any Creature; of which Opinion I am not: For, if that were so, every Creature would be of many several Colours; neither would any Creature produce after their own *Species*: for, a Parrot would not produce so fine a Bird as her self; neither would any Creature appear of one and the same Colour, but their Colour would change according to the Positions of Light; and in a dark day, in my opinion, all fine coloured Birds, would appear like Crows; and fine coloured Flowers, appear like the Herb named *Night-shade*; which is not so. I do not say, That several Positions of Light may not cause

1 Cavendish argues against the existence of any kind of "Figureless Body," or immaterial substance, which she recognized in the work of Neoplatonists like Henry More (1614–87), as well as in van Helmont's notion of substances that existed between body and spirit (i.e., gasses).

Colours; but I say, The Position of Light is not the Maker of all Colours; for, *Dyers* cannot cause several Colours by the Positions of Light.

CHAP. XXX.

Of the Exterior Motions of the Planets.

By the *Exterior Motions of the Planets,* we may believe their Exterior Shape is Spherical: for, it is to be observed, That all Exterior Actions are according to their Exterior Shapes; but, by reason Vegetables and Minerals have not such sorts of Exterior Motions or Actions, as Animals; some Men are of opinion, they have not Sensitive Life; which opinion proceeds from a shallow consideration:[1] neither do they believe the Elements are sensible, although they visibly perceive their Progressive Motions; and yet believe all sorts of Animals to have sense, only because they have Progressive Motions.

CHAP. XXXI.

Of the Sun, and Planets, and Seasons.

The Sun, Moon, Planets, and all those glittering Starrs we see, are several sorts of that Man names *Elemental Creatures*: but Man, having not an infinite Perception, cannot have an infinite perceptive knowledg: for, though the Rational Perception is more subtil than the Sensitive; yet, the particular Parts cannot perceive much further than the Exterior Parts of Objects: but, Human Sense and Reason cannot perceive what the Sun, Moon, and Starrs are; as, whether solid, or rare; or, whether the Sun be a Body of Fire; or the Moon, a Body of Water, or Earth; or, whether the Fixed Starrs be all several Suns; or, whether they be other kinds or sorts of Worlds. But certainly, all Creatures do subsist by each other, because Nature seems to be an Infinite united Body, without *Vacuum*. As for the several Seasons of the Year, they are divided into Four Parts: but the several Changes and Tempers of the Four Seasons, are so various, altering every moment, as it would be an endless work, nay, impossible, for one Creature to perform: for, though the *Almanack-makers*[2] pretend to fore-know all the variations of the Elements; yet, they can tell no more than just what

---

1 Cavendish's thoroughgoing vitalism, in which all natural things, even minerals, are rational and perceptive, as well as her focus on human blindness to this fact, anticipates modern eco-critical critiques of the Anthropocene.

2 I.e., astrologists.

is the constant and set-motions; but not the variations of every Hour, or Minute; neither can they tell any thing, more than their Exterior Motions.

CHAP. XXXII.

Of Air corrupting Dead Bodies.

Some are of opinion, *That Air is a Corrupter, and so a Dissolver of all dead Creatures, and yet is the Preserver of all living Creatures.* If so, Air hath an Infinite Power: but, all the reason I can perceive for this Opinion, is, That Man perceives, that when any Raw (or that we name *Dead*) *Flesh*, is kept from the air, it will not stink, or corrupt, so soon as when it is in the air: but yet it is well known, that extream cold air will keep Flesh from corrupting.

Another Reason is, That a Flye entomb'd in *Amber*, being kept from air, the Flye remains in her Exterior Shape as perfectly as if she were alive.

I answer, The cause of that may be, that the Figurative Motions of *Amber*, may sympathize with the Exterior consistent Motions of the Fly, which may cause the Exterior Shape of the Flye to continue, although the Innate Nature be altered. But Air is, as all other Creatures are, both Beneficial, and Hurtful to each other; for Nature is poysed with Opposites: for we may perceive, that several Creatures are both Beneficial and Hurtful to each other: as for example, A Bear kills a Man; and, on the other side, a Bear's Skin will cure a Man of some Disease. Also, a *Wild-Boar* will kill a Man; and the *Boar*'s Flesh will nourish a Man. Fire will burn a man, and preserve a Man; and Millions of such Examples may be proposed. The same may be said of Air, which may occasion Good or Evil to other Creatures; as, the *Amber* may occasion the death of a Fly; and, on the other side, may occasion the Preservation, or Continuation of the Fly's Exterior Figure, or Form: but, Nature being without *Vacuum*, all her Parts must be joined; and her Actions being poysed, there must be both Sympathetical, and Antipathetical actions, amongst all Creatures.

THE THIRTEENTH PART.

CHAP. I.

Of the Innate Figurative Motions of Metals.

All sorts of *Metals*, in my opinion, are of some sorts of Circular Motions; but not like that sort, that is Water: for, the Water-Circle doth extend outward, from the Center; whereas, in my opinion, the Circular Motion of Metal, draws inward, from the Circumference. Also, in my opinion, the Circular Motions are dense, flat, edged, even, and smooth; for, all Bright and Glassie Bodies are smooth: and, though Edges are wounding Figures; yet, Edges are rather of the Nature of a Line, than of a Point. Again, all Motions that tend to a Center, are more fixt than those that extend to a Circumference: but, it is according to the degree of their Extensions, that those Creatures are more or less fixt; which is the cause that some sorts of Metals are more fixt than others; and that causes Gold to be the most fixt of all other sorts of Metals; and seems to be too strong for the Effects of Fire. But this is to be noted, That some Metals are more near related to some sort, than other: as for example, There is no Lead, without some Silver; so that Silver seems to be but a well-digested Lead. And certainly, Copper hath some near relation to Gold, although not so near related, as Lead is to Silver.[1]

CHAP. II.

Of the Melting of Metals.

Metals may be occasioned, by Fire, to slack their Retentive Motions, by which they become fluid; and as soon as they are quit of their Enemy, *Fire,* the Figurative Motions of Metal return to their proper Order: and this is the reason that occasions Metal to melt, which is, to flow: but yet, the Flowing Motion is but like the Exterior, and not the Innate actions of Mineralls:[2] for, the Melting actions do not alter the Innate actions; that is, they do not alter from the Nature of being Metal: but, if the Exterior Nature be occasioned, by the Excess of those Exterior actions, to alter their Retentive actions, then Metal turns to that we name *Dross;*[3] and as much as Metal loses of its weight, so much of the Metal dissolves; that is, so much of those Innate motions are quite altered: but, Gold hath such an Innate Retentiveness, that though Fire may cause an extream alteration of the Exterior actions; yet, it cannot alter the Interior motions. The like is of Quick-silver. And yet Gold is not a God, to be Unalterable, though man knows not the way, and Fire has not the power to alter the Innate Nature of Gold.

---

1 There was tremendous interest at this time in the composition and transmutation of various metals—or alchemy—as seen in the work of one of Cavendish's primary targets, van Helmont.

2 In the corrected text, Cavendish replaced "Animals" with "Mineralls."

3 Mineral waste, dregs, or scum.

CHAP. III.

Of Burning, Melting, Boyling, and Evaporating.

Burning, Melting, Boyling, and *Evaporating*, are, for the most part, occasioned by Fire, or somewhat that is, in effect, Hot: I say, *occasioned*, by reason they are not the actions of Fire, but the actions of those Bodies that melts, boyls, evaporates, or burns; which being near, or joyned to Fire, are occasioned so to do: as for example, Put several sorts of Creatures, or Things, into a Fire, and they shall not burn alike: for, Leather and Metal do not burn alike; for Metal flows, and Leather shrinks up, and Water evaporates, and Wood converts it self, as it were, into Fire; which other things do not; which proves, That all Parts act their own actions. For, though some Corporeal motions may occasion other Corporeal motions to act after such or such a manner; yet, one Part cannot have another Part's motion, because Matter can neither give nor take motion.

CHAP. IV.

Of STONE.

All Minerals seem to be some kinds of Dense and Retentive motions: but yet, those kinds of Dense and Retentive motions, seem to be of several sorts; which is the cause of several sorts of Minerals, and of several sorts of Stones and Metals. Also, every several sort, hath several sorts of Properties: but, in my opinion, some sorts are caused by Hot Contractions and Retentions; others, by Cold Contractions and Retentions; as also, by Hot or Cold Densations: and the reason why I believe so, is, That I observe that many Artificial Stones are produced by Heat: but Ice, which is but in the first Degree of a Cold Density, seems somewhat like transparent Stones; so that several sorts of Stones, are produced by several sorts of Cold and Hot Contractions and Densations.

CHAP. V.

Of the LOADSTONE.

As for the *Loadstone*,[1] it is not more wonderful in attracting Iron, than[2] Beauty, which admirably attracts the Optick Perception of Human Creatures: and who knows, but the North and South Air may be the most proper Air for the Respiration of the *Loadstone*;

---

1 Lodestone, or a naturally magnetized mineral that attracts iron, was used in early modern navigation.

2 In the corrected text, Cavendish deleted "in its" between "than" and "Beauty."

and, that Iron may be the most proper Food for it. But, by reason there hath been so many Learned Men puzled in their Opinions concerning the several Effects of the *Loadstone*, I dare not venture to treat of the Nature, and Natural Effects of that Mineral; neither have I had much experience of it: but I observe That Iron, and some sorts of Stone, are nearly allied; for, there is not any Iron, but what is growing, or is intermixt and united in some sorts of Stone, as that which we call *Iron-stone*. Wherefore, it is no wonder if the *Loadstone*, and Iron, should be apt to embrace one another.

CHAP. VI.

Of Bodies, apt to ascend or descend.

There are so many several Causes that occasion some sorts of Creatures to be apt to *ascend*, and others to *descend*, as they are neither known, or can be conceived by one finite Creature: for, it is not Rarity or Density, that causes Levity and Gravity; but, the Frame or Form of a Creature's Exterior Shape, or Parts. As for example: A Flake of Snow is as Rare as a Downy Feather; yet, the Feather is apt to ascend, and the Flake of Snow to descend. Also Dust, that is hard and dense, is apt to ascend; and Water, that is soft and rare, is more apt to descend. Again, a Bird, that is both a bigger, and a more dense Creature by much, than a small Worm; yet, a Bird can flye up into the air, when as a leight Worm cannot ascend, or flye, having not such a sort of Shape. Also, a great heavy Ship, as big as an ordinary House, fraughted with Iron, will swim upon the face of the Water; when as a small Bullet, no bigger than a *Hasle-Nut*, will sink to the bottom of the Sea. A great Bodied Bird will flye up into the air; when as a small Worm lies on the earth, with a slow kind of crawling, and cannot ascend. All which is caused by the manner of their Shapes, and not the matter of Gravity and Levity.

CHAP. VII.

Why Heavy Bodies descend more forcibly than Leight Bodies ascend.

Although the manner of the Shape of several Creatures, is the chief cause of their *Ascent*, and *Descent*; yet, Gravity and Levity, doth occasion more or less Agility: for, a Heavy Body shall descend with more force, than a Leight Body ascend: and the reason is, not only that there may be more Parts in a Heavy Body, than a Leight; but, that in a Descent, every Corporeal Motion seems to press upon each other; which doubles and trebles the Strength, Weight, and Force, as we may perceive in the

Ascending and Descending of the Flight of Birds, especially of Hawks; of which, the weight of the Body is some hindrance to the Ascent, but an advantage to the Descent: but yet, the Shape of the Bird hath some advantage by the Weight, in such sort, that the Weight doth not so much hinder the Ascent, as it doth assist the Descent.

CHAP. VIII.

Of several sorts of Densities and Rarities, Gravities and Levities.

There are different sorts of Densities and Rarities, Softness and Hardness, Levities and Gravities: as for example, The density of Earth is not like the density of Stone; nor the density of Stone, like the density of Metal: nor are all the Parts of the Earth dense alike; nor all Stones, nor all Metals; as we may perceive in Clay, Sand, Chalk, and Lime-Grounds. Also, we may perceive difference between Lead, Tynne, Copper, Iron, Silver, and Gold; and between Marble, Alablaster, Walling-Stone, Diamonds, Crystals, and the like: and so much difference there is between one and the same kind, that some particulars of one sort, shall more resemble another kind, than their own: as for example, Gold and Diamonds resemble each other's Nature, more than Lead doth Gold; or Diamonds, Crystal; I say, in their Densities. Also, there is a great difference of the Rarity, Gravity, and Levity of several sorts of Waters, and of several sorts of Air.

CHAP. IX.

Of VEGETABLES.

Vegetables are of numerous sorts, and every sort of very different Natures: as for example, Some are Reviving Cordials; others, Deadly Poyson; some are Purgers, others are Nourishers: some have Hot Effects, some Cold; some Dry, some Moist; some bear Fruit, some bears no Fruit; some appear all the year Young; others appear but part of the year Young, and part Old; some are many years a producing; others are produced in few hours; some will last many hundred years; others will decay in the compass of few hours: some seem to dye one part of the year, and revive again in another part of the year: some rot and consume in the Earth, after such a time; and will continue in perfection, if parted from the Earth. Others will wither and decay, as soon as parted from the Earth. Some are of a dense Nature, some of a rare Nature; some grow deep into the Earth; others grow high out of the Earth; some will only produce in dry Soyls, some in moist: some will produce only in Water, as we may perceive by some Ponds; others on Houses of Brick or Stone. Also, some grow out of Stone; as, many Stones will have a green Moss: some are produced by sowing their Seed into the Earth; others, by setting their Roots, or Slips, into the Earth: others again, by joyning or engrafting one Plant into another: so that there is much variety of Vegetables, and those of such different Natures, that they are not only different Sorts, but are variety of Effects of one and the same sort; and it requires not only the study of one Human Creature, or many Human Creatures; but, of all the Human Creatures in all Nations and Ages, to know them; which is the reason, that those that have writ of the Natures of Herbs, Flowers, Roots, and Fruits, may be such mistaken. But I, living more constantly in my Study, than in my Garden, shall not venture to treat much of the particular Natures, and Natural Effects of Vegetables.

CHAP. X.

Of the Production of Vegetables.

Tis no wonder, that some sorts of *Vegetables* are produced out of Stone or Brick, (as some that will grow on top of Houses) by reason that Brick is made of Earth, and Stone is generated in the Bowels of the Earth; which shows they are of an Earthly Nature or Substance. Neither is it a wonder that Vegetables will grow upon some sorts of Water, by reason some sorts of Waters may be mixt with some Parts of Earth. But, I have been credibly informed, That a Man whose Legg had been cut, and a Seed of an Oat being gotten into the Wound by chance, the Oat did sprout out into a green Blade of Grass: which proves, that Vegetables may be produced in several Soyls. But 'tis probable, that though many sorts of Vegetables may sprout, as Barly in Water; yet, they cannot produce any of the off-spring of the same Sort or Kind.

But, my Thoughts are, at this present, in some dispute; as, Whether the Earth is a Part of the Production of Vegetables, as being the Breeder? or, whether the Earth is only Parts of Respiration, and not Parts of Production; and so, rather Breathing-Parts, than Breeding-Parts, as Water to Fishes?

But, if so, then every particular Seed must encrease, not only by a bare Transformation of their Parts into the first Form of Production; but, by division of their united Parts, must produce many other Societies of the same sort; as Religious

Orders, where one Convent divides into many Convents of the same Order; which occasions a numerous Encrease. So the several Parts of one Seed, may divide into many Seeds of the same sort, as being of the same *Species*; but then, every Part of that Seed, must be increased by additional Parts; which must be, by Nourishing Parts: which Nourishing Parts are, in all probability, Earthy Parts; or, at least, partly of Earthy Parts; and partly, of some of the other Elemental Parts: but, as I have often said, all Creatures in Nature are Assisted, and do Subsist, by each other.

CHAP. XI.

Of Replanting Vegetables.

Replanting of Vegetables, many times, occasions great Alterations; in so much as a Vegetable, by often Replanting, will be so altered, as to appear of another sort of Vegetable: the reason is, that several sorts, or parts of Soyls, may occasion other sorts of Actions, and Orders, in one and the same Society. But this is to be noted in the Lives of many Animals, That several sorts of Food, make great alterations in their Temper and Shape; though not to alter their *Species*, yet so as to cause them to appear worse or better: but, this is most visible amongst Human Creatures, whom some sorts of Food will make weak, sick, faint, lean, pale, old, and withered: other sorts of Food will make them strong, and healthy, fat, fair, smooth, and ruddy. So some sorts of Soyls will cause some Vegetables to be larger, brighter, smoother, sweeter, and of more various and glorious Colours.

CHAP. XII.

Of Artificial Things.

Artificial Things, are Natural Corporeal Figurative Motions: for, all Artificial Things are produced by several produced Creatures.[1] But, the differences of those Productions we name *Natural* and *Artificial*, are, That the Natural are produced from the Producer's own Parts; whereas the Artificial are produced by composing, or joyning, or mixing several Forrein Parts; and not any of the particular Parts of their composed Society: for, Artificial things are not produced as Animals,

1 Thus, artificial things are created when organic matter is assembled or manipulated to produce entities that are not indigenous to the natural world.

Vegetables, Minerals, or the like: but only, they are certain several Mixtures of some of the divided, or dead Parts, as I may say, of Minerals, Vegetables, Elements, and the like. But this is to be noted, That all, or at least most, are but Copied, and not Originals.

But some may ask, *Whether Artificial Productions have Sense, Reason, and Perception?*

I answer: That if all the Rational and Sensitive Parts of Nature, are Perceptive, and that no part is without Perception; then all Artificial Productions are Perceptive.

CHAP. XIII.

Of several Kinds and Sorts of Species.

According to my Opinion, though the *Species* of this World, and all the several Kinds and Sorts of *Species* in this World, do always continue; yet, the particular Parts of one and the same Kind or sort of *Species*, do not continue: for, the particular Parts are perpetually altering their Figurative Actions. But, by reason some Parts compose or unite, as well as some Parts dissolve or disunite; all kinds and sorts of *Species*, will, and must last so long as Nature lasts. But mistake me not, I mean such kinds and sorts of *Species* as we name *Natural*, that is, the Fundamental *Species*; but not such *Species*, as we name *Artificial*.

CHAP. XIV.

Of Different WORLDS.

Tis probable if Nature be Infinite, there are several kinds and sorts of those Species, Societies, or Creatures, we name *Worlds*; which may be so different from the Frame, Form, Species, and Properties of this World, and the Creatures of this World, as not to be any ways like this World, or the Creatures in this World. But mistake me not, I do not mean, not like this World, as it is Material and Self-moving; but, not of the same Species, or Properties: as for example, That they have not such kind of Creatures, or their Properties, as Light, Darkness, Heat, Cold, Dry, Wet, Soft, Hard, Leight, Heavy, and the like.

But some may say, *That is impossible: for, there can be no World, but must be either Light or Dark, Hot or Cold, Dry or Wet, Soft or Hard, Heavy or Leight; and the like.*

I answer, That though those Effects may be generally beneficial to most of the Creatures in this World; yet, not to all the Parts of the World: as for example, Though Light is beneficial to the Eyes of Animals; yet, to no other Part of an Animal Creature. And, though Darkness is obstructive to the Eyes of Animals; yet, to no other Parts of an Animal Creature. Also, Air is no proper Object for any of the Human Parts, but Respiration. So Cold and Heat, are no proper Objects for any Part of a Human Creature, but only the Pores, which are the Organs of Touch. The like may be said for Hard and Soft, Dry and Wet: and since they are not Fundamental actions of Nature, but Particular, I cannot believe, but that there may be such Worlds, or Creatures, as may have no use of Light, Darkness, and the like: for, if some Parts of this World need them not, nor are any ways beneficial to them, (as I formerly proved) surely a whole World may be, and subsist without them: for these Properties, though they may be proper for the Form or Species of this World; yet, they may be no ways proper for the Species of another kind or sort of World: as for example, The Properties of a Human Creature are quite different from other kinds of Creatures; the like may be of different Worlds: but, in all Material Worlds, there are Self-moving Parts, which is the cause there is self joyning, uniting, and composing; self dividing, or dissolving; self-regularities, and self-irregularities; also, there is Perception amongst the Parts or Creatures of Nature; and what Worlds or Creatures soever are in Nature, they have Sense and Reason, Life and Knowldg: but, for Light and Darkness, Hot and Cold, Soft and Hard, Leight and Heavy, Dry and Wet, and the like; they are all but particular actions of particular Corporeal Species, or Creatures, which are finite, and not infinite: and certainly, there may be, in Nature, other Worlds as full of varieties, and as glorious and beautiful as this World; and are, and may be more glorious or beautiful, as also, more full of variety than this World, and yet be quite different in all kinds and sorts, from this World: for, this is to be noted, That the different kinds and sorts of Species, or Creatures, do not make Particulars more or less perfect, but according to their kind. And one thing I desire, That my *Readers* would not mistake my meaning, when I say, *The Parts dissolve*: for, I do not mean, that Matter dissolves; but, that their particular Societies dissolve.

APPENDIX TO THE GROUNDS OF Natural Philosophy.

THE FIRST PART.

CHAP. I.

Whether there can be a Substance, that is not a Body.

What a *Substance*, that is not *Body*, can be, (as I writ in the First Chapter of this Book) I cannot imagine; nor, that there is any thing between *Something* and *Nothing*.[1]

But, some may say, That Spiritual Substances are so.

I answer: That Spirits must be either Material, or Immaterial: for, it is impossible for a thing to be between Body and no Body.

Others may say, *There may be a Substance, that is not a Natural Substance; but, some sort of Substance that is far more pure than the purest Natural Substance.*

I answer: Were it never so pure, it would be in the List or Circle of Body: and certainly, the purest Substance, must have the Properties of Body, as, to be divisible, and capable to be united and compounded; and being divisible and compoundable, it would have the same Properties that grosser Parts have: but, if there be any difference, certainly the purest Substance would be more apt to divide and unite, or compound, than the grosser sort. But, as to those sorts of Substance, which some Learned Men have imagined; in my opinion, they are but the same sort of Substance that the Vulgar call, *Thoughts*, and I name, the *Rational Parts*; which, questionless, are as truly Body, as the grossest Parts in Nature: but, most Human Creatures are so troubled with the Thoughts of Dissolving, and Dis-uniting, that they turn Fancies and Imaginations, into Spirits, or Spiritual Substances;[2] as if all the other Parts of their Bodies, should become Rational Parts; that is, that all their Parts should turn into such Parts as Thoughts, which I name, the *Rational Parts*. But that Opinion is impossible: for, Nature cannot alter the nature of any Part; nor can any Part alter its own Nature; neither can the Rational Parts be divided from the Sensitive and Inanimate Parts, by reason

---

1 Cavendish refers to the spirits that animate nature for More and the Neoplatonists, but also van Helmont's notion of gasses, which are both "something" and "nothing." For More's "spirit of nature," see Appendix C1.

2 Again, Cavendish targets More, among others. For her debate with Joseph Glanvill about this topic, see Appendix A1; for More's take, see Appendix C1.

those Three sorts constitute but one Body, as being Parts of one Body. But, put the case that the Rational Parts might divide and subsist without the Sensitive and Inanimate Parts; yet, as I said, they must of necessity have the Properties and Nature of a Body, which is, to be divisible, and capable to be united, and so to be Parts: for, it is impossible for a Body, were it the most pure, to be indivisible.

CHAP. II.

Of an IMMATERIAL.

I cannot conceive how an Immaterial can be in Nature: for, first, An Immaterial cannot, in my opinion, be naturally created; nor can I conceive how an Immaterial can produce particular Immaterial Souls, Spirits, or the like. Wherefore, an Immaterial, in my opinion, must be some uncreated Being; which can be no other than GOD alone.[1] Wherefore, Created Spirits, and Spiritual Souls, are some other thing than an Immaterial: for surely, if there were any other Immaterial Beings, besides the Omnipotent God, those would be so near the Divine Essence of God, as to be petty gods; and numerous petty gods, would, almost, make the Power of an Infinite God. But, God is Omnipotent, and only God.

CHAP. III.

Whether an Immaterial be Perceivable.

Whatsoever is Corporeal, is Perceivable; that is, may be perceived in some manner or other, by reason it hath a Corporeal Being: but, what Being an Immaterial hath, no Corporeal can perceive. Wherefore, no Part in Nature can perceive an Immaterial, because it is impossible to have a perception of that, which is not to be perceived, as not being an Object fit and proper for Corporeal Perception. In truth, an Immaterial is no Object, because no Body.

But some may say, that, *A Corporeal may have a Conception, although not a Perception, of an Immaterial.*

I answer, That, surely, there is an innate Notion of God, in all the Parts of Nature; but not a perfect knowledg: for if there was, there would not be so many several Opinions, and Religions, amongst one Kind, or rather, sort of Creatures, as Mankind, as there are; insomuch, that there are but few of one and the same

1 Cavendish is careful to accommodate divine entities, which exist outside of nature and are therefore not subject to natural laws.

Opinion, or Religion: but yet, that Innate Notion of God, being in all the Parts of Nature, God is infinitely and eternally worshipped and adored, although after several manners and ways; yet, all manners and ways, are joyned in one Worship, because the Parts of Nature are joyned into one Body.

CHAP. IV.

Of the Differences between God, and Nature.

GOD is an Eternal Creator; Nature, his Eternal Creature. GOD, an Eternal Master: Nature, GOD's Eternal Servant. GOD is an Infinite and Eternal Immaterial Being: Nature, an Infinite Corporeal Being. GOD is Immovable, and Immutable: Nature, Moving, and Mutable. GOD is Eternal, Indivisible, and of an Incompoundable Being: Nature, Eternally Divisible and Compoundable. GOD, Eternally Perfect: Nature, Eternally Imperfect. GOD, Eternally Inalterable: Nature Eternally Alterable. GOD, without Error: Nature, full of Irregularities. GOD knows exactly, or perfectly, Nature: Nature doth not perfectly know GOD. GOD is Infinitely and Eternally worshipped: Nature is the Eternal and Infinite Worshipper.

CHAP. V.

All the Parts of Nature worship God.

All Creatures (as I have said) have an Innate Notion of GOD; and as they have a Notion of God, so they have a Notion to worship GOD: but, by reason Nature is composed of Parts; so is the Infinite Worship to God: and, as several Parts are dividing and uniting after several kinds, sorts, manners and ways; so is their Worship to GOD: but, the several manners and ways of Worship, make not the Worship to GOD less: for certainly, all Creatures Worship and Adore GOD; as we may perceive by the Holy Scripture, where it says, *Let the Heavens, Earth, and all that therein is, praise God.* But 'tis probable, that some of the Parts being Creatures of Nature, may have a fuller Notion of GOD than others; which may cause some Creatures to be more Pious and Devout, than others: but, the Irregularity of Nature, is the cause of Sin.

CHAP. VI.

Whether GOD's Decrees are limited.

In my opinion, though God is Inalterable, yet no ways bounded or limited: for, though GOD's Decrees are fixt, yet, they are not bound: but, as GOD hath an Infinite Knowledg, He hath also an Infinite Fore-knowledg; and so, fore-knows Nature's Actions, and what He will please to decree Nature to do: so that, GOD knows what Nature can act, and what she will act; as also, what He will decree: and this is the cause, that some of the Creatures or Parts of Nature, especially Man, do believe *Predestination*. But surely, GOD hath an Omnipotent Divine Power, which is no ways limited: for GOD, being above the nature of Nature, cannot have the Actions of Nature, because GOD cannot make Himself no GOD; neither can He make Himself more than what he is, He being the All-powerful, Omnipotent, Infinite, and Everlasting Being.

CHAP. VII.

Of GOD's Decrees concerning the particular Parts of Nature.

Though Nature's Parts have Free-will, of Self-motion; yet, they have not Free-will to oppose *GOD's Decrees*: for, if some Parts cannot oppose other Parts, being over-power'd, it is probable, that the Parts of Nature cannot oppose the All-powerful Decrees of *GOD*.[1] But, if it please the All-powerful *GOD* to permit the Parts of Nature to act as they please, according to their own natural Will; and, upon condition, if they act so, they shall have such Rewards as Nature may be capable to receive; or such Punishments as Nature is capable of; then the Omnipotent *GOD* doth not predestinate those Rewards, or Punishments, any otherwise than the Parts of Nature do cause by their own Actions.[2] Thus all Corporeal Actions, belong to Corporeal Parts; but, the Rewards and Punishments, to *GOD* alone: but, what those Punishments and Blessings are, no particular Creature is capable to know: for, though a particular Creature knows there is a *GOD*; yet, not what *GOD* is: so, although particular Creatures know there are Rewards and Punishments; yet, not what those Rewards and

---

1 The relationship between free will and providential design was a perennial concern of early modern theological debates. Today, there is some debate about Cavendish's views on free will. See the Introduction (p. 23, note 1); see also Appendix B, esp. p. 238.

2 Thus Cavendish outlines a kind of conditional free will: natural creatures could not likely violate God's will if he were inclined to stop them, yet God allows them to "act as they please, according to their own natural Will" (i.e., their behavior is not "predestinated"). Similarly, their future states remain dependent on their choices ("*GOD* doth not predestinate those Rewards, or Punishments"). See also Introduction (pp. 23–24, 27–29).

Punishments are.[1] But mistake me not; for I mean the general Rewards and Punishments to all Creatures: but 'tis probable, that *GOD* might decree Nature, and her Parts, to make other sorts of Worlds, besides this World; of which Worlds, this may be as ignorant, as a particular Human Creature is of *GOD*. And therefore, it is not probable (since we cannot possibly know all the Parts of Nature, of which we are parts) that we should know the Decrees of *GOD*, or the manners and ways of Worship, amongst all kinds and sorts of Creatures.

CHAP. VIII.

Of the Ten Commandments.

In my opinion, the Notions Man hath of *GOD's Commands* concerning their Behaviour and Actions to Himself, and their Fellow-Creatures, is the very same that *Moses* writ, and presented to all those of whom he was Head and Governour. But, mistake me not, I mean only the *Ten Commandments*; which Commandments are a sufficient Rule for all Human Creatures: and certainly, *GOD* had decreed, that *Moses* should be a wise Man, and should publish these wise Commands. But, the Interpretation of the Law must be such, as not to make it no such Law: but, by reason Nature is as much Irregular, as Regular, Human Notions are also Irregular, as much as Regular; which causes great variety of Religions: and their Actions being also Irregular, is the cause that the practice of Human Creatures is Irregular; and that occasions Irregular Devotions, and is the cause of SIN.

CHAP. IX.

Of Several RELIGIONS.

Concerning the *several Religions*, and several Opinions in Religions, which are like several Kinds and Sorts; the Question is,

Whether all Mankind could be perswaded to be of one Religion, or Opinion?

The opinion of the Minor part of my Thoughts, was, That all men might be perswaded.

And, the opinion of the Major part of my Thoughts, was, That Nature, being divisible and compoundable, and having Free-will, as well as Self-motion; and being Irregular, as well as Regular; as

1 That is, we know that rewards and punishments exist, but not what they are.

also, Variable, taking delight in variety; it was impossible for all Mankind to be of one *Religion*, or Opinion.

The opinion of the Minor part of my Thoughts, was, That the Grace of GOD could perswade all Men to one Opinion.

The Major part of my Thoughts was of the opinion, That GOD might decree or command Nature: but, to alter Nature's nature, could not be done, unless GOD, by his Decree, would annihilate this Nature, and create another Nature, and such a Nature as was not like this Nature: for, it is the nature of this Material Nature, to be Alterable; as also, to be Irregular, as well as Regular; and, being Regular, and Irregular, was a fit and proper Subject for GOD's Justice, and Mercies; Punishments, and Rewards.

CHAP. X.

Of Rules and Prescriptions.

As Saint *Paul* said, *We could not know Sin, but by the Law*; so, we could not know what Punishment we could or should suffer, but by the Law; not only Moral, but Divine Law.

But, some may ask, *What is Law?*

I answer: Law is, Limited Prescriptions and Rules.

But, some may ask, *Whether all Creatures in Nature, have Prescriptions and Rules?*

I answer: That, for any thing Man can know to the contrary, all Creatures may have some Natural Rules: but, every Creature may chuse whether they will follow those Rules; I mean, such Rules as they are capable to follow or practise: for, several kinds and sorts of Creatures, cannot possibly follow one and the same Prescription and Rule. Wherefore, Divine Prescriptions and Rules, must be, according to the sorts and kinds of Creatures; and yet, all Creatures may have a Notion, and so an Adoration of God, by reason all the Parts in Nature, have Notions of God. But, concerning particular Worships, those must be Prescriptions and Rules; or else, they are according to every particular Creature's conception or choice.

CHAP. XI.

Sins and Punishments, are Material.

As all *Sins* are *Material*, so are *Punishments*: for, Material Creatures, cannot have Immaterial Sins; nor can Material Creatures be capable of Immaterial Punishments; which may be proved out of the Sacred Scripture: for, all the Punishments that are declared to be in Hell, are Material Tortures: nay, Hell it self is described to be Material; and not only Hell, but Heaven, is described to be Material. But, whether Angels, and Devils, are Material, that is not declared: for, though they are named Spirits, yet we know not whether those Spirits be Immaterial. But, considering that Hell and Heaven is described to be Material, it is probable, Spirits are also Material: nay, our blessed Saviour Christ, who is in Heaven, with God the Father, hath a Material Body; and in that Body will come attended by all the Hosts of Heaven, to judg the quick and the dead;[1] which quick and dead, are the Material Parts of Nature: which could not be actually judged and punished, but by a Material Body, as Christ hath. But, pray mistake me not; I say, They could not be actually judged and punished; that is, not according to Nature, as Material Actions: for, I do not mean here, Divine and Immaterial Decrees. But Christ, being partly Divine, and partly Natural; may be both a divine and Natural Judg.

CHAP. XII.

Of Human Conscience.

The Human Notions of GOD, Man calls *Conscience*: but, by reason that Nature is full of Varieties, as having Self-moving Parts; Human Creatures have different Notions, and so different Consciences, which cause different Opinions and Devotions: but, Nature being as much compoundable as dividable, it causes unity of some, as also, divisions of other Opinions, which is the cause of several Religions: which Religions, are several Communities and Divisions. But, as for Conscience, and holy Notions, they being Natural, cannot be altered by force, without a Free-will: so that the several Societies, or Communicants, commit an Error, if not a Sin, to endeavour to compel their Brethren to any particular Opinion: and, to prove it is an Error, or Sin, the more earnest the *Compellers* are, the more do the *Compelled* resist; which hath been the cause of many Martyrs. But surely, all Christians should follow the Example of Christ, who was like a meek Lamb, not a raging Lyon: neither did Christ command his Apostles to Persecute; but, to suffer Persecution patiently. Wherefore, *Liberty of Conscience* may be allowed, conditionally, it be no ways a prejudice to the Peaceable Government of the State or Kingdom.

1 "The quick and the dead" is a biblical idiom derived from William Tyndale's 1526 translation of the New Testament; "quick" means "living."

THE SECOND PART.

CHAP. I.

Whether it is possible there could be Worlds consisting only of the Rational Parts, and others only of the Sensitive Parts.[1]

The Parts of my Mind did argue amongst themselves, *Whether there might not be several kinds and sorts of Worlds in Infinite Nature?*

And they all agreed, That probably there might be several kinds and sorts of Worlds.

But afterwards, the Opinion of the Major parts of my Mind, was, That it is not possible: for, though the Rational parts of Nature move free, without Burdens of the Inanimate Parts; yet, being Parts of the same Body, (*viz.* of the Body of Nature) they could not be divided from the Sensitive and Inanimate Parts; nor the Sensitive and Inanimate Parts, from the Rational.

The Opinion of the Minor Parts of my Mind, was, That a Composed World, of either degree, was not a division from the Infinite Body of Nature, though they might divide so much, as to compose a World meerly of their own Degree.

The Major's Opinion was, That it was impossible; because the three Degrees, Rational, Sensitive, and Inanimate, were naturally joyned as one Body, or Part.

The Minor's Opinion was, That a World might be naturally composed only of Rational Parts, as a Human Mind is only composed of Rational Parts; or, as the Rational Parts of a Human Creature, could compose themselves into several Forms, *viz.* into several sorts and kinds of Worlds, without the assistance of the Sensitive or the Inanimate Parts: for, they fancy Worlds which are composed in Human Minds, without the assistance of the Sensitive.

The Major Part agreed, That the Rational Corporeal Actions, were free; and all their Architectors were of their own Degree: but yet, they were so joyned in every Part and Particle, to the Sensitive and Inanimate, as they could not separate from these two Degrees: for, though they could divide and unite from, and to

---

1 This is an important question in the context of Cavendish's materialist account of natural matter, which consists of three elemental "degrees" that cannot be separated from each other (no matter how many times matter is divided). It is also notable that Cavendish considers this question in her appendix, where she tends to speculate about issues that are untenable in more formal contexts.

Particulars, as either of their own Degrees, or the other Degrees; yet, the Three Degrees being but as one united Body, they could not so divide, as not to be joyned to the other Degrees: for, it was impossible for a Body to divide it self from it self.

After this Argument, there followed another; *That, if it were possible there could be a World composed only of the Rational Parts, without the other two Degrees; Whether that World would be a Happy World?*

The Major Part's Opinion was, That, were it possible there could be such unnatural Divisions, those divided Parts would be very unhappy: for, the Rational Parts would be much unsatisfied without the Sensitive; and the Sensitive very dull without the Rational: also, the Sensitive Architectors would be very Irregular, wanting their Designing Parts, which are the Rational Parts.

Upon which Argument, all the Parts of my Mind agreed in this Opinion, That the Sensitive was so Sociable to the Rational, and the Rational so Assisting to the Sensitive, and the Inanimate Parts so necessary to the Sensitive Architectors, that they would not divide from each other, if they could.[1]

CHAP. II.

Of Irregular and Regular Worlds.

Some Parts of my Mind were of opinion, *That there might be a World composed only of Irregularities; and another, only of Regularities: and some, that were partly composed of the one, and the other.*

The Minor Part's Opinion was, That all Worlds were composed partly of the one, and partly of the other; because all Nature's Actions were poysed with Opposites, or Contraries: wherefore, there could not be a World only of Irregularities, and another of Regularities.

The Major Part's Opinion, was, That Nature's Actions were as much poysed by the contrary Actions of Two Worlds, as by the contrary Actions of the Parts of One World, or one Creature: As for example, The Peace and Trouble, Health and Sickness, Pain and Ease, and the like, of one Human Creature; and so of the contrary Natures of several kinds and sorts of Creatures of one and the same World.

After which Discourse, they generally agreed, There might be Regular and Irregular Worlds; the one sort to be such happy Worlds, as that they might be named *Blessed Worlds*; the other so miserable Worlds, as might be named *Cursed Worlds*.

---

1 For more on how the three degrees of matter balance each other's actions, see *Observations* 33.

CHAP. III.

Whether there be Egress and Regress between the Parts of several Worlds.

There arose a Third Argument, viz. *Whether it was possible for some of the Creatures of several Worlds, to remove, so as to remove out of one World, into another?*

The Major Part's Opinion was, That it was possible for some Creatures: for, if some particular Creatures could move all over the World, of which they were a part, they might divide from the Parts of the World they were of, and joyn with the Parts of another World.

The Minor Part's Opinion was, That they might travel all over the World they were part of, but not to joyn with the Parts of another World, to which they belong not.

The Major's Opinion was, That every Part and Particle, belonged to the Infinite Body of Nature, and therefore not any Part could account it self not of the Infinite Body; and being so, then every Part of Nature may joyn, and divide from and to particular Parts, as they please, if there were not Obstructions and Hindrances, and some Parts did not obstruct other Parts: Wherefore, if there were not Obstructions, there might be Egress and Regress amongst the particular Parts of several Worlds.

The Minor's Opinion was, That if it could be according to the Major's Opinion, it would cause an Infinite Confusion in Infinite Nature: for, every Creature of every World, was composed according to the Nature and Compositions of the World they were of: wherefore, the Products of one kind or sort of Worlds, would not be sutable, agreeable, and Regular, to the productions of another kind.

The Major Part's Opinion was, That it was impossible, since Nature is one united Body, without *Vacuum*, but that the Parts of all Worlds must have Egress and Regress.

CHAP. IV.

Whether the Parts of one and the same Society, could, after their Dissolution, meet and unite.[1]

The Fifth Argument, was partly of the same Subject, *viz. Whether the particular Parts of a Creature, (such as a Human*

---

1 The term "dissolution" is important, as it registers for Cavendish how the natural matter that composes particular societies or creatures "dissolves" or disassembles before migrating into new compositions. This, then, opens the possibility that it could reunite (as she considers here).

Creature is) could travel out of one World into another, after the dissolution of his Human Life?

The Major Part's Opinion was, That they could.

The Minor's Opinion was, They could not; because the particular Parts so divided and joyned to and from other particular Parts and Societies, as it was impossible, if they would, so to agree, as to divide from those Parts and Societies they are joyned to, and from those they must joyn with, to meet in another World, and joyn as they would, in the same Society they were of, when the whole Society is dissolved. Neither can Parts divide and joyn, as they would: for, though Self-moving Parts have a Free will to move; yet, being subject to Obstructions, they must move as they can: for, no particular Part hath an absolute Power. Wherefore, the Dispersed Parts of a Dissolved Society, cannot meet and joyn as they would. Besides, every Part is as much affected to one Sort, Kind, or Particular, they are Parts of, as to another. Besides, the Knowledg of every Part alters, according as their Actions alter: so that the Parts of one and the same Society, after division, have no more knowleg of that Society.

CHAP. V.

Whether, if a Creature being Dissolved, and could Unite again, would be the same.

The Sixth Argument was, *That, put the case it were possible all the several Parts belonging to one and the same Society; as for example, To one Human Creature, after his Human Life was dissolved, and his Parts dispersed, and afterwards, all those Parts meeting and uniting; Whether that Human Creature would be the same?*

The Minor Part's Opinion was, That it could not be the same Society: for, every Creature was according to the nature of their Kind or Sort; and so according to the Form and Magnitude of one of their Kind or Sort.

The Major Part's Opinion was, That though the Nature of every particular Creature had such Forms, Shapes, and Properties, as was natural to that sort of Creatures they were of; yet, the Magnitude of particular Creatures of one and the same sort, might be very different.

The Minor Part's Opinion was, That if all the Parts of one Society, as for example, a Man, from the first time of his Production, to the time of his Dissolution, should, after division, come to meet and unite; that Man, or any other Creature, would be a

Monstrous Creature, as having more Parts than was agreeable to the nature of his Kind.

The Major Part's Opinion was, That though the Society, *viz.* The MAN, would be a Society of greater Magnitude; yet, not any ways different from the Nature of his Kind.

CHAP. VI.

Of the Resurrection of Human Kind.

The Seventh Argument, was, *Whether all the particular Parts of every Human Creature, at the time of the Resurrection, be, to meet and joyn, as being of one and the same Society?*

The Minor Part's Opinion was, They shall not: for, if all those Parts that had been of the same Body and Mind of one Man, from his first Production, to the last of his Dissolution; or, from his Birth, to the time of his Death, (supposing him to have liv'd long) should meet and joyn, as one Society, that is, as one Man; that Man, at the time of his Resurrection, would be a Gyant; and if so, then old Men would be Gyants; and young Children, Dwarfs.[1]

The Major Part's Opinion was, That, if it was not so, then every particular Human Society would be imperfect at the time of their Resurrection: for, if they should only rise with some of their Parts, as (for example) when they were in the strength of their Age, then all those Parts that had been either before, or after that time, would be unjustly dealt with, especially if Man be the best Product in Nature. Besides, if a dead Child did rise a Man, as at his most perfect Age, it could not be said, He rises according to a Natural Man, having more Parts than by Nature he ever had; and an old Man, fewer Parts than naturally he hath had: so, what by Adding and Diminishing the Parts of particular Men, it would not cause only Injustice; but, not any particular Human Creature, would be the same he was.

---

1 That is, human bodies consist of natural parts that are constantly moving, changing, and translating into other forms; reassembling them all, from across our lives, might result in a monstrously large amalgamation of parts.

CHAP. VII.

Of the Dissolution of a World.

The Eighth Argument was, *That when all Human Creatures that were dissolved, should rise, Whether the World they were of, should not be dissolved?*

All the Parts of my Mind agreed, That when all the Human Creatures that had been dissolved, should rise, the whole World, besides themselves, must also dissolve, by reason they were Parts of the World: for, when all those numerous dissolved and dispersed Parts, did meet and joyn, the World wanting those Parts, could not subsist: for, the Frame, Form, and Uniformity of the World, consisted of Parts; and those Parts that have been of the Human Kind, are, at several times, of other kinds and sorts of Creatures, as other sorts and kinds are of Human Kind; and all the Sorts and Kinds, are Parts of the World: so that the World cannot subsist, if any kind or sort of Creatures, that had been from the first time of the Creation, should be united; I mean, into one and the same sort or kind of Creatures; as it would be, if all those that are Quick, and those that have been *Dissolved*, (that is, have been dead) should be alive at one time.

CHAP. VIII.

Of a New Heaven, and a New Earth.

The Ninth Argument was, *That if a World could be dissolved, and that the Human Creatures should rise, and reunite; what World should they reside in?*

All the Parts of my Thoughts generally agreed, That the Omnipotent GOD would command the Parts of His Servant NATURE, to compose other Worlds for them, into which Worlds they should be separated; the Good should go into a Blessed World; the Bad, into a Cursed World: and the Sacred Scripture declares, That there shall be a *New Heaven*, and a *New Earth*;[1] which, in their opinion, was a Heaven and a Hell, for the Blessed and Cursed Human Kind of this World.

1 Revelation 21:1.

CHAP. IX.

Whether there shall be a Material Heaven and Hell.

The Tenth Argument was, *Whether the Heaven and Hell that are to be produced for the Blessed and Cursed, shall be Material?*

The Minor Part's Opinion was, That they shall not be Material.

The Major Parts were of opinion, They shall be Material, by reason all those Creatures that did rise, were Material; and being Material, could not be sensible either of Immaterial Blessings, or Punishments: neither could an Immaterial World, be a fit or proper Residence for Material Bodies, were those Bodies of the purest Substance. But, whether this Material Heaven and Hell, shall be like other Materials Worlds, the Parts of my Mind could not agree, and so not give their Judgment. But, in this they all agreed, That the Material Heaven and Hell, shall not have any other Animal Creatures, than those that were of Human kind, and those not produced, but raised from Death.

But when they came to argue, Whether there might be Elements, Minerals, and Vegetables, they could not agree; but some did argue, and offer to make proof, That there might be Mynes of Gold, and Rocks of Diamonds, Rubies, and the like; all which, were Minerals. Also, some were of opinion, there were Elements: for, Darkness and Light, are Elemental Effects: and, if Hell was a World of Darkness; and Heaven, a World of Light; it was probable there were Elements.

CHAP. X.

Concerning the Joys or Torments of the Blessed and Cursed, after they are in Heaven, or Hell.

As for the *Joys of Heaven*, and the *Torments of Hell*, all the Parts of my Mind agreed, they could not conceive any more probably, than those they had formerly conceived: which former Conceptions they had occasioned the Sensitive Parts to declare; and having been formerly divulged in the Book of my *Orations*,[1] their Opinion was, *That it would be a superfluous Work to cause them to be repeated in this Book*. But, the Ground or Foundation of those Conceptions, is, That God may decree, *That both the Sensitive and Rational Parts of those that are restored to Life, should move in variety of Perceptions, or Conceptions, without variety of Objects*: and, *that those Creatures* (viz. *Human Creatures*) *that are raised from Death to Life, should subsist without any Forrein Matter, but should*

---

1 *Orations of Divers Sorts* (London, 1662).

be always the same in Body and Mind, without any Traffick, Egress, or Regress of Forrein Parts. And the proof, that the Sensitive and Rational Parts of Human Creatures, may make Perceptions, or rather Conceptions, without Forrein Objects, is, *That many men in this world have had Conceptions, both amongst the Rational and Sensitive, which Man names* Visions, *or* Imaginations; *whereof some have been Pleasing and Delightful; others, Displeasing, and Dreadful.*[1]

THE THIRD PART.

The PREAMBLE.

The Parts of my Mind, after some time of respite from *Philosophical Arguments*, delighting in such harmless Pastimes; did begin to argue about a *Regular* and *Irregular* World; having formerly agreed, there might be such Worlds in Nature; and that the Regular Worlds, were Happy Worlds; the Irregular, Miserable Worlds. But, there was some division amongst the Parts of my Mind, concerning the choice of their Arguments; as, Whether to argue, first, of the particular Parts of the Regular, or of the Irregular World. But, at last, they agreed to argue, first, of the Regular World. But, pray mistake not these Arguments; for they are not Arguments of such Worlds as are for the reception of the Blessed and Cursed Humans, after their Resurrections: but, such as these Worlds we are of, only freely Regular, or Irregular. Also, though I treat but only of one Regular World, and one Irregular World; yet, my opinion is, there may be a great many Irregular Worlds, and a great many Regular Worlds, of several kinds and sorts: but, these I shall treat of, are such as are somewhat like this World we are of.

CHAP. I.

Of the Happy and Miserable Worlds.

The First Argument was, *Whether there might not be such Worlds in Nature, as were in no kind or sort like this World we are of?*

They all agreed, That it was probable there was.

The Second Argument was, *Whether it was probable that the Happy and Miserable Worlds were, in any kind, like this we are of.*

They all agreed, It was probable that this World was somewhat like both one, and the other; and so, both those were somewhat

1 That is, because there is no longer anything to perceive, humans in the afterlife will only conceive and imagine.

like this: for, as the *Happy World* was no ways Irregular; and the *Miserable World* no ways Regular: so this World we are of, was partly Irregular, and partly Regular; and so it was a *Purgatory World.*[1]

CHAP. II.

Whether there be such kinds and sorts of Creatures in the Happy and Blessed World, as in this World.

The Third Argument was, *Whether it was probable, the Happy and Miserable Worlds, had Animal, Vegetable, Mineral, and Elemental Kinds?*

They agreed, It was probable there were such Kinds: but yet, those Kinds, and particular sorts of those Kinds, might be different from those of this World.

The Fourth Argument was, *Whether there was Human sorts of Creatures in those Worlds.*

They all agreed, There was.

CHAP. III.

Of the Births and Deaths of the Heavenly World.

The Fifth Argument was, *Whether there could be Births and Deaths in the Happy World?*

Some Part of my Mind were of opinion, That if there was so Regular a World, as that there were no Irregularities in it, there could not be *Deaths*: for, Death was a Dissolution; and if there was no Death, there could be no Birth, or Production: for, if any particular sort of Creatures should Encrease, and never dissolve, they would become Infinite; which every particular kind or sort of Creatures, may be, for time, and be Eternal; as also, be Infinite for Number; because, as some dissolve, others are produced. And so, if particular sorts or kinds of Creatures, be Eternal; the particular Production and Dissolution, is Infinite: but, if any Sort, or Kind, should encrease, without decrease, not any particular World could contain them: As for example, If all the Human Creatures that have been produced from our Father *Adam*, (which hath not been above Six thousand years) should be alive, this World could not contain them; much less, if this World, and the Human sorts of Creatures, had been of a longer date. And besides, if there should be a greater Encrease, by the Number of Human Creatures: in truth, the numerous Encrease,

---

1 Here, not a religious concept per se but merely a place "between" worlds.

would have caused Mankind, in the space of Six thousand years, to be almost Infinite.

But, the Minor Parts of my Mind was of opinion, That then the *Happy World* could not be so perfectly Regular, if there was Death.

The Major Part's opinion was, That some sorts of Deaths were as regular, as the most Regular Births: for, though Diseases were caused by Irregular Actions, yet, Death was not: for, as it is not Irregular, to be old; so it is not Irregular, to dye. But, this Argument broke off for that time.

CHAP. IV.

Whether those Creatures could be named Blessed, *that are subject to dye.*

The Sixth Argument was, *Whether those Creatures could be called Blessed, or Happy, that are subject to dye?*

The Major Parts of my Mind was of opinion, That, if Death was as free from Irregularities, as Birth; then it was as happy to Dye, as to be Born.

The Minor Parts were of opinion, That though Dissolution might be as Regular as Composition; yet, it was an Unhappiness for every particular Society, to be dissolved.

The Major Part's Opinion, was, That though the particular Societies were dissolved; yet, by reason the general Society of the Kind, did continue, it was not so much Unhappiness; considering, particular Parts, or Creatures, did make the General Society; and not, the General, the Particular Societies: so that, the Parts of the Particulars, remained in the General, as in the Kind or Sort.

The Minor Parts were of opinion, That the Particulars of the same Kind or Sort, (as *Mankind*) did contribute but little to the General: for, other sorts of Creatures did contribute more than they; only Mankind was the Occasion, or Contributor of the First Foundation, but no more: but, the other Parts or Creatures of the World, did contribute more to their Kind, than the Creatures of the same Kind did: and, as other Kinds, and Sorts, did contribute to Mankind; so Mankind, to other Kinds or Sorts: for, all Kinds and Sorts, did contribute to the Subsistance and Assistance of each other.

The Major Part's Opinion was, That if all the Parts of a World did assist each other, then Death could be no Unhappiness, especially in the Regular World; by reason all Creatures in that World, of what Kind or Sort soever, was Perfect and Regular: so that, though the particular Human Creatures did dissolve from being Humans; yet, their Parts could not be Unhappy, when they did unite into other Kinds, and Sorts, or particular Societies: for, those other sorts and kinds of Creatures, might be as happy as Human Creatures.

CHAP. V.

Of the Productions of the Creatures of the Regular World.

The Seventh Argument was, of Productions of the Creatures of the Regular World, *viz. Whether their Productions were frequent, or not?*

The Minor Part's Opinion, was, That they were frequent.

The Major Part's Opinion, was, That they were not *frequent*, or *numerous*, by reason the World was Regular, and so all the Productions or Generations, were Regular; but could not exceed such a Number as was, regularly, sufficient for a World, of such a Dimension as the Regular World; and according to the Dimensions, must the Society or Creatures be, let them be large or little.

CHAP. VI.

Whether the Creatures in the Blessed World, do Feed, and Evacuate.

The Eighth Argument, was, *Whether the Blessed Humans, in the Happy World, did Eat, and Evacuate?*

They agreed, That, if they did feed, they must evacuate.

Then there was a Dispute, *Whether those Happy Creatures did eat?*

They all agreed, That, if they were Natural Human Creatures, they had Natural Appetites: but, by reason there were no Irregularities in this World, the Human Creatures had not any Irregular Appetites, nor Irregular Digestions; Irregular Passions, or Irregular Pastimes.

Then there arose a Dispute, Whether those Blessed Creatures did sleep?

Some were of opinion, They did not sleep: for, Sleep was occasioned through a weariness of the Sensitive Organs, making perceptions of Forrein Objects; and all Weariness, or Tiredness, was Irregular.

The Major part of my Mind, was of a contrary Opinion; because the delight of Nature, is in Variety: and therefore, Regular Sleeps were delightful.

The Minor was of opinion, That Sleep was like Death, and therefore it could not be Happy.

But, at last, they did conclude, That Sleep, being a soft and quiet Repose, (as being retired from all Actions concerning Forrein Parts, and had only Actions at Home, and of private Affairs; and that all Parts of Body and Mind, were then most sociable amongst themselves) that the Blessed Humans did sleep.

CHAP. VII.

Of the Animals, and of the Food of the Humans of the Happy World.

The Ninth Argument, was, *Whether there were all sorts of Animals in the Regular World?*

All the Parts of my Mind agreed, That if there were such Creatures as Human Creatures, it was probable there was other Animal Creatures: but, by reason there was no Irregularities, there could not be Cruel or Ravenous Animal Creatures: for, a Lyon, Leopard, or Wolf, in that World, would be as harmless as a Sheep in this; and all Kites, Hawks, and the like ravenous Birds, would be as harmless as those Birds that only feed on the Berries, and Fruit of the Earth.

CHAP. VIII.

Whether it is not Irregular, for one Creature to feed on another.

The Tenth Argument was, *Whether it was not Irregular, for one Creature to feed on another?*

Some were of opinion, That it was natural for one Creature to subsist by another, and so assist each other; but not cruelly to destroy each other.

Upon this Argument, the Parts of my Mind divided into a Minor and a Major part.

The Minor Part's opinion, was, That, since all the Creatures in Nature, had Life; then, all Creatures that did feed, did destroy each other's Life.

The Major Part's Opinion, was, That they might be assisted by the Lives of other Creatures, and not destroy their Lives: for, Life could not be destroyed, though Lives might be occasionally alter'd: but, some Creatures may assist other Creatures, without destruction or dissolution of their Society: as for example, The Fruits and Leaves of Vegetables, are but the Humorous Parts of Vegetables, because they are divisible, and can encrease and decrease, without any dissolution of their Society; that is, without the dissolution of the Plant. Also, Milk of Animals, is a superfluous Humor of Animals: and, to prove it to be a superfluous Humor, I alledg, That much of it oppresses an Animal. The same I say of the Fruits and Leaves of many sorts of Vegetable Creatures. Besides, it is natural for such sorts of Creatures to have their Fruits and Leaves to divide from the Stock.

The Minor Part's Opinion, was, That the Milk of Animals, and the Fruits of Vegetables, and the Herbs of the Earth, had as much Life as their Producers.

The Major Part's Opinion, was, That though they had as much Life as their Producers; yet, it was natural for such off-springs to change and alter their Lives, by being united to other sorts of Creatures: as for example, An Animal eats Fruit and Herbs; and those Fruits and Herbs convert themselves into the nature of those Animals that feed of them. The same is of Milk, Eggs, and the like; out of which, a condition of Life is endeavoured for: and, for proof, such sorts of Creatures account an Animal Life the best; and therefore, all such superfluous Parts of Creatures, endeavour to unite into an Animal Society; as we may perceive, that Fruits and Herbs, are apt to turn into Worms, and Flies; and some Parts of Milk, as Cheese, will turn into Maggots; so that when Animals feed of such Meats, they occasion those Parts they feed on, to a more easie Transformation; and not only such Creatures, but Humans also, desire a better Change: for, what Human would not be a glorious Sun, or Starr?

After which Discourse, all the Parts of my Mind agreed unanimously, That Animals, and so Human Creatures, might feed on such sorts of Food, as aforesaid; but not on such Food as is an united Society: for, the Root and Foundation of any kind and sort of Creature, ought not to be destroyed.

CHAP. IX.

Of the Continuance of Life in the Regular World.

The Opinion of the Parts of my Mind, was, That, it was probable, that all Societies in the Regular World, (that is, all such Parts of Nature as are united into particular Creatures) are of long life, by reason there are not Irregularities to destroy them, before their natural time.

But then a Dispute was raised amongst the Parts of my Mind, concerning the natural time, that is, the proper time of the Lives of those Creatures: for, all Creatures were not of the same time of Production; nor, after their Production, of the same time of Continuance. But the Parts of my Mind concluded, That though they could not judg by observation of any Creature, no, not of their own Sort; yet, they did believe they could judg better of Human Creatures, as being, at that time, of a Human Society, than of any other: but, by reason they were of this World (that is, Irregular in part) they did believe they might very much err in their Judgment, concerning the continuance of Human Lives, in the *Happy World*. But, after much debate, they concluded, That a Human Creature, in the Regular World, might last as long as the Productions did not oppress or burden that World, (for that would be irregular) but how long a time that might be, they could not possibly conceive or imagine.

CHAP. X.

Of the Excellency and Happiness of the Creatures of the Regular World.

The Parts of my Mind could not possibly, being Parts of a Purgatory World, conceive the happy condition of all Creatures in the Regular World; but only, conceiving there was no Irregularities, they did also conceive, that all Creatures there, must be in perfection; and that the Elemental Creatures were purer, without drossie[1] mixtures; so that their Earth must needs be so fruitful, that it produces all sorts of excellent Vegetables, without the help of Art; and their Minerals as pure, as all sorts of Stone that are transparent, and as hard as Diamonds; the Gold and Silver, more pure than that which is refined in our World. The truth is, that, in their Opinions, the meanest sorts of Metal in the Regular World, were more pure than the richest sort in this World: so that then, their richest Metal must be as far beyond ours, as our Gold is beyond our Iron, or Lead. As for the Elemental Waters in the Regular World, they must be extraordinary smooth, clear, flowing, fresh, and sweet; and the Elemental Air only, a most pure, clear, and glorious Light; so that there could be no need of a Sun: and, by reason all the Air was a Light, there could be no Darkness; and so, no need of a Moon, or Starrs. The Elemental Fire, although it was Hot, yet it was not Burning. Also, there could neither be scorching Heats, nor freezing Colds, Storms, nor Tempest: for, all Excess is irregular. Neither could there be Clouds, because no Vapours. But, not to be tedious; it was my Mind's Opinion, That all the Parts of the *Happy World*, being Regular, they could not obstruct each other's Designs or Actions; which might be a cause, that both the Sensitive and Rational Parts may not only make their Societies more curious, and their Perceptions more perfect; but their Perceptions more subtile: for, all the actions of that World being Regular, must needs be exact and perfect; in so much, that every Creature is a perfect Object to each other; and so every Creature must have, in some sort, a perfect Knowldg of each other.

CHAP. XI.

Of Human Creatures in the Regular World.

The Opinion of my Mind, was, That the *Happy World*, having no Irregularities, all Creatures must needs be Excellent, and most Perfect, according to their Kind and Sort; amongst which, are Human Creatures, whose Kinds, or Sorts, being of the Best,

1 Impure, muddy, or worthless.

must be more excellent than the rest, being Exactly formed, and Beautifully produced: there being, also, no Irregularities, Human Creatures cannot be subject to Pains, Sickness, Aversions, or the like; or, to Trepidations, or Troubles; neither can their Appetites, or Passions, be irregular: wherefore, their Understanding is more clear, their Judgments more poysed; and by reason their Food is Pure, it must be Delicious, as being most tastable: also, it must be wholsome, and nourishing; which occasion the Parts of Body and Mind, to be more Lively and Pleasant.

CHAP. XII.

Of the Happiness of Human Creatures in the Material World.

The Happiness that Human Creatures have in the *Regular World*, is, That they are free from any kind or sort of Disturbance, by reason there are no Irregular Actions; and so, no Pride, Ambition, Faction, Malice, Envy, Suspition, Jealousie, Spight, Anger, Covetousness, Hatred, or the like; all which, are Irregular Actions among the Rational Parts: which occasions Treachery, Slander, false Accusations, Quarrels, Divisions, Warr, and Destruction; which proceeds from the Irregularities of the Sensitive Parts, occasioned by the Rational, by reason the Sense executes the Mind's Designs: but, there are no Plots or Intrigues, neither in their State, nor upon their Stage; because, though they may act the parts of Harmless Pleasures; yet, not of Deceitful Designs: for, all Human Creatures, live in the Regular World, so united, that all the particular Human Societies, (which are particular Human Creatures) live as if they were but one Soul, and Body; that is, as if they were but one Part, or particular Creature. As for their pleasures, and pleasant Pastimes; in my opinion, they are such, as not any Creature can express, unless they were of that World, or Heaven: for, all kinds and sorts of Creatures, and all their Properties or Associations, in this World we are of, are mixt; as, partly Irregular; and partly, Regular; and so it is but a *Purgatory-World*. But surely, all Human Creatures of that World, are so pleasant and delightful to each other, as to cause a general Happiness.

THE FOURTH PART.

CHAP. I.

Of the Irregular World.

After the Arguments and Opinions amongst the Parts of my Mind, concerning a Regular World; their Discourse was, of an

Irregular World: Upon which they all agreed, That if there was a World that was not in any kind or sort, Irregular; there must be a World that was not in any kind or sort, Regular. But, to conceive those Irregularities that are in the Irregular World, is impossible; much less, to express them: for, it is more difficult to express Irregularities, than Regularities: and what Human Creature of this World, can express a particular Confusion, much less a World of Confusions? Which I will, however, endeavour to declare, according to the Philosophical Opinions of the Parts of my Mind.

CHAP. II.

Of the Productions and Dissolutions of the Creatures of the Irregular World.

According to the Actions of Nature, all Creatures are produced by the Associations of Parts, into particular Societies, which we name, *Particular Creatures*: but, the Productions of the Parts of the Irregular World, are so Irregular, that all Creatures of that World are Monstrous: neither can there be any orderly or distinct kinds and sorts; by reason that Order and Distinction, are Regularities. Wherefore, every particular Creature of that World, hath a monstrous and different Form; insomuch, that all the several Particulars are affrighted at the Perception of each other: yet, being Parts of Nature, they must associate; but, their Associations are after a confused and perturbed manner, much after the manner of Whirlwinds, or Ætherial Globes, wherein can neither be Order, nor Method: and, after the same manner as they are produced, so are they dissolved: so that, their *Births* and *Death*s are *Storms*, and their *Lives* are *Torments*.

CHAP. III.

Of Animals, and of Humans, in the Irregular World.

It has been declared in the former Chapter, *That there was not any perfect Kind or Sort of Creatures in the Irregular World*: for, though there be such Creatures as we name *Animals*; and amongst Animals, Humans: yet, they are so Monstrous, that, being of confused Shapes, or Forms, none of those Animal Creatures can be said to be of such, or such a sort; because they are of different disordered Forms. Also, they cannot be said to be of a perfect Animal-kind, or any Kind; by reason of the variety of their Forms: for, those that are of the nature of Animals, especially of Humans, are the most miserable and unhappy of all the Creatures of that World; and the Misery is, That Death doth not help them: for, Nature being a perpetual Motion, there is no rest either alive or dead. In this World, it's true, some Societies (*viz.* some Creatures) may, sometimes, after their Dissolutions, be united into more Happy Societies, or Forms; which, in the Irregular World, is impossible; because all Forms, Creatures, or Societies, are miserable: so that, after dissolution, those dispersed Parts cannot joyn to any other Society, but what is as bad as the former; and so those Creatures may dissolve out of one Misery, and unite into another; but cannot be released from Misery.

CHAP. IV.

Of Objects, and Perceptions.

The Opinions amongst the Parts of my Mind, were, That in the Unhappy, or Miserable World, all the actions of that World, being irregular, it must needs be, that all sorts of Perceptions of that World, must also be irregular: not only because the Objects are all irregular; but, the perceptive actions are so too; in such manner, that, what with the irregularity of the Objects, and the irregularity of the Perceptions, it must, of necessity, cause a horrid confusion, both of the Sensitive and Rational Parts of all Creatures of that World, in so much, that not only several Creatures may appear as several Devils to each other; but, one and the same Creature may appear, both to the Sense and Reason, like several Devils, at several times.

CHAP. V.

The Description of the Globe of the Irregular World.

The Opinion of my Mind was, That the Globe of the Irregular World was so irregular, that it was a Horrid World: for though, being a World, it might be somewhat like other Worlds, both Globous, and a Society of it self, by its own Parts; and therefore might have that which we name *Earth*, *Air*, *Water*, and *Fire*: but, for Sun-light, Moon-light, Starr-light, and the like, they are not parts of the World they appear to; and are Worlds of themselves. But, there can be no such Appearances in the Irregular World: for, the Irregularities do obstruct all such Appearances; and the Elemental Parts (if I may name them so) are as irregular, and therefore as horrid as can be: so that it is probable, that the Elemental Fire is not a bright shining Fire, but a dull, dead Fire, which hath the Effects of a strong Corrosive Fire, which never actually Heats, but actually Burns; so that some Creatures may both freeze and burn at once. As for the Earth of that World, it is probable that it is like corrupted Sores, by reason all Corruptions are produced by Irregular Motions; from which Corruptions, may proceed such stinking Foggs, as may be as far beyond the scent of Brimstone, or any the worst of Scents that are in this World, as *Spanish* or *Roman* Perfumes, or Essences, are beyond the scent of Carion, or *Assafœtida*;[1] which causes all Creatures (of Airy Substances) that breathe, to be so infected, as to appear like Poysoned Bodies. As for their Elemental Water, 'tis probable, that it is as black as Ink, as bitter as Gaul, as sharp as *Aquafortis*,[2] and as Salt as Brine, mixt irregularly together, by reason the Waters there, must needs be very troubled Waters. As for the Elemental Air, I shall declare the Opinion of my Rational Parts, in the following Chapter.

CHAP. VI.

Of the Elemental Air, and Light of the Irregular WORLD.

Tis probable, that the Elemental Air of the Irregular World, is neither perfectly Dark, nor perfectly Light; for, either would be, in some part or kind, a Perfection or Regularity: but, being irregular, it must be a perturbed Air; and, being perturbed, it is probable it produces several Colours. But, mistake me not, I do not mean such Colours as are made by perturbed Light; but, such as are made by perturbed Air: and, through the Excess of Irregularities, may be Horrid Colours; and, by reason of the Ætherial whirling Motions, which are Circular Motions, the Air may be of the colour of Blood, a very horrid Colour to some sorts of Creatures: but 'tis probable, this Bloody Colour is not of a pure Bloody Colour, but of a corrupted Bloody Colour: and so the Light of the Irregular World, may, probably, be of a corrupt Bloody Colour: but, by the several Irregular Motions, it may be, at several times, of several corrupted Bloody Colours; and by reason there are no intermissions of *Air*, there can be no intermissions of this *Light*, in the Irregular World.

CHAP. VII.

Of Storms, and Tempests, in the Irregular World.

As for *Storms*, and *Tempests*, and such irregular Weather, 'tis probable there are continual Winds and Thunders, caused by the disturbance of the Air; and those Storms and Tempests, being irregular, must needs be violent, and therefore very horrid. There

---

1 A perennial herb that produces a resin-like sap known for its foul odor.

2 Latin: strong water; i.e., acid.

may also be Lightnings, but they are not such as those that are of a fiery colour; but such as are like the colour of Fire and Blood mixt together. As for *Rain*, being occasioned by the Vapours from the Earth and Waters, it is according as those Vapours gather into Clouds: but, when there is Thunder, it must needs be violent.

CHAP. VIII.

Of the several Seasons, or rather, of the several Tempers in the Irregular World.

As for *several Seasons*; there can be no constant Season, because there is no Regularity; but rather, a great Irregularity, and Violence, in all Tempers and Seasons; for there is no mean Degree: and surely, their Freezing is as sharp and corroding, as their Corrosive Burnings; and it is probable, that the Ice and Snow in that world, are not as in this world, *viz.* the Ice to be clear, and the Snow white; because there the water is a troubled, and black water; so that the Snow is black, and the Ice also black; not clear, or like black polished Marble: but 'tis probable, that the Snow is like black Wool; and the Ice, like unpolished black Stone; not for Solidity, but for Colour and Roughness.

CHAP. IX.

The Conclusion of the Irregular and Unhappy or Cursed World.

I have declared in my former Chapter, concerning the *Irregular World*, That there could not be any exact, or perfect kind or sort, because of the Irregularities; not that there is not Animal, Vegetable, Mineral, and Elemental Actions, and so not such Creatures; but, by reason of the Irregularities, they are strangely mixt and disordered, so that every Particular seems to be of a different Kind, or sort, being not any ways like each other; and yet, may have the nature of such Kinds, and Sorts, by reason they are Natural Creatures, although irregularly Natural: but, those irregular Natural Creatures, cannot chuse, by the former Descriptions, but be Unhappy, having, in no sort or kind, Pleasure, or Ease: and for such Creatures that have such Perceptions as are any way like ours, they are most Miserable: for, by the Sense of Touch, they freeze and burn: by the sense of Tast, they have Nauseousness, and Hunger, being not satisfied: by the sense of Scent, they are suffocated, by reason of irregular Respiration: by the sense of Hearing, and sense of Seeing, they have all the horrid Sounds and Sights, that can be in Nature: the Rational Parts are, as if they were all distracted or mad; and the Sensitive Parts tormented with Pains, Aversions, Sicknesses, and Deformities; all which is caused through the Irregular Actions of the Parts of the Irregular World; so that the Actions of all sorts of Creatures, are Violent, and Irregular.

But, to conclude: As all the Creatures of our World, were made for the Benefit of Human Creatures; so, 'tis probable, all the Creatures of the Irregular World, were produced for the Torment and Confusion of Human Creatures in that World.

THE FIFTH PART,
Being divided into FIFTEEN SECTIONS.

Concerning Restoring-Beds, or Wombs.

I.

At the latter end of my *Philosophical Conceptions*, the Parts of my Mind grew sad, to think of the dissolving of their Society: for, the Parts of my Mind are so friendly, that although they do often Dispute and Argue for Recreation and Delight-sake; yet, they were never so irregular, as to divide into Parties, like Factious Fellows, or Unnatural Brethren: which was the reason that they were sad, to think their kind Society should dissolve, and that their Parts should be dispersed and united to other Societies, which might not be so friendly as they were. And, after many several Thoughts, (which are several Rational Discourses: for, Thoughts are the Language of the Mind) they fell into a Discourse of *Restoring Beds*, or *Wombs*, viz. *Whether there might not be Restoring Beds, as well as Producing Beds, or Breeding Beds*. And, to argue the case, they agreed to divide into Minor and Major Parts.

II.

The Major Parts of my Mind were of the opinion, That there are Beds, or Wombs, of Restoration, as well as Beds of Production: for, if Nature's actions be poysed, there must be one, as well as the other.

The Minor Part's Opinion, was, That, as all Creatures were produced, so all Creatures were subject to dissolve: so that, the poyse of Nature's Productions, was Nature's Dissolutions, and not Restorations.

The Major Part's Opinion, was, That there are Restorations in Nature: for, as some dissolved, others united in every kind and sort of Creature, which as a Restoration to the kinds and sorts of Creatures.

The Minor Part's Opinion, was, That though every sort and kind of Creatures, continued as the *Species* of each sort and kind; yet, they did not continue by such Restorations as they were arguing about: for though, when some Creatures dye, others of the same Sort or *Species*, are born or bred; yet, they are Produced, not restored: for, they conceived, that Restoration was a reviving and re-uniting the Parts of a Dissolved Society or Creature; which Restoration was not natural, at least, not usual.

The Major Part's Opinion, was, That Restoration was natural, and usual: for, there were many things, or Creatures, restored, in some sort, after they were dead.

The Minor Part's Opinion, was, That some Creatures might be restored from some Infirmities, or Decays; but, they could not be restored after they were dissolved, and their Parts dispersed.

The Major Part's Opinion, was, That if the Roots, Seeds, or Springs of a Society, or Creature, were not dissolved and dispersed, those Creatures might be restored to their former condition of Life, if they were put, or received, into the Restoring Beds: As for example, A dry and withered Root of some Vegetable, although the Parts of that Vegetable be, as we say, dead; yet, they are often restored by the means of some Arts: also, dead Sprigs will, by Art, receive new Life.

The Minor Part's Opinion, was, That if there were such actions of Nature, as Restoring actions; yet, they could not be the Poysing Actions, nor the Artificial Actions: for, not any dead Creature can be restored by Art.

III.

Some of the Gravest Parts of my Mind, made this following Discourse to some other Parts of my Mind.

Dear Associates, There hath been many Human Societies, that have perswaded themselves, That there are such Restoring Actions of Nature, which will restore, not only a Dead, but a Dispersed Society; by reason they have observed, That Vegetables seem to dye in one Season, and to revive in another: as also, that the Artificial Actions of Human Creatures, can produce several Artificial Effects, that resemble those we name *Natural*; which hath occasioned many Human Creatures to wast their Time and Estates, with Fire and Furnace, cruelly torturing the Productions of

Nature, to make their Experiments.[1] Also, they trouble themselves with poring and peeing through Telescopes, Microscopes, and the like Toyish Arts, which neither get Profit, nor improve their Understanding: for, all such Arts prove rather ignorant Follies, than wise Considerations; Art being so weak and defective, that it cannot so much assist, as it doth hinder Nature:[2] but, there is as much difference between Art and Nature, as between a Statue and a Man; and yet Artists believe they can perfect what by Nature is defective; so that they can rectifie Nature's Irregularities; and do excuse some of their Artificial actions, saying, they only endeavour to hasten the actions of Nature: as if Nature were slower than Art, because a Carver can cut a Figure or Statue of a Man, having all his Materials ready at hand, before a Child can be finished in the Breeding-Bed. But, Art being the sporting and toyish actions of Nature, we will not consider them at this time.

But, *Dear Associates*, if there be any such things in Nature, as *Restoring-Beds*, which most of our Society are willing to believe; yet, those Beds cannot possibly be *Artificial*, but must be *Natural Beds*. Nor can any one particular sort of Bed, be a general Restorer: for, every several Sort or Kind, requires a Bed, or Womb, that is proper for their Sorts or Kinds: so that, there must be as many sorts, at least, and kinds of Beds, as there are kinds of Creatures: but, what those Wombs or Beds are, we Human Creatures do not know; nor do we know whether there be any such things in this World: but, if there be such things in this World, we cannot conceive where they are.

IV.

After the former Discourse, the Parts of my Mind were a little sad: but, after many and frequent Disputes and Arguments, they all agreed, That there are *Restoring Beds*, or *Wombs*, in Nature: but that to describe their Conceptions of those *Restoring Beds*, was only to describe Opinions, but no known Truths: and their Opinions were, That those Beds are as lasting as Gold, or Quick-silver:[3] for, though they may be occasioned to alter their

1 Cavendish targets alchemists like van Helmont and Paracelsus, who habitually employed "fire and furnace" in their chemical pursuits, while also likely taking a jab at the experimental culture of The Royal Society of London.

2 Another jab at Royal Society members like Hooke and Power, who promoted the use of optical instruments in their work.

3 Mercury.

Exterior Form; yet, not their Interior or Innate Nature. But, mistake not my Mind's Opinion: for, their Opinion is not, That those Beds are Gold, or Quicksilver: for, their Opinion was, That neither Gold, or Quicksilver, were Restorers of Life: but, if they were Restorers, they could restore no other Creatures, but only dead Metals, by reason several Creatures require several Restoring Beds proper to their Sorts or Kinds: so that a Mineral Kind or Sort, could not restore an Animal Kind or Sort; because there was no such thing in Nature, as the *Elixir*, or *Philosophers-Stone*,[1] which the *Chymists* believe to be some Deity, that can restore all Sorts and Kinds.

V.

As it has formerly been declared, The Parts of my Mind were generally of opinion, That it was, at least, probable, there were such things in Nature as *Restoring-Beds*, or *Wombs*. The next Opinion was, That these Beds were of several Kinds or Sorts, *viz*. Animal, Vegetable, Mineral, and Elemental: so that every Kind or Sort, is a general Restorer of the Lives of their Kind or Sort. As for example, An Animal *Restoring-Bed*, may restore any dead Animal, to his former Animal Life, in case the Animal Roots or Seeds, (which we name, the *Vital Parts*) were not divided and dispersed, but inclosed, or inurned,[2] so that no other Animal could come to feed on those Roots and Seeds of the dead Animal Body; and in case the Body was so closely kept, though dead many years, if it was put into a *Restoring-Bed*, that Animal Creature would reunite to the former Animal Life and Form.

But then there arose this Argument, *That if the Bodies of the dead Animals, did corrupt and dissolve of themselves, as most dead Animal Bodies do; Whether, after their Dissolution, they could be Restored?*

The Minor Part's Opinion was, That those dissolved Bodies, being dissolved, or divided, and their Parts out of their places, could not be restored.

The Major Part's Opinion, was, They might be restored; first, Because, though the Parts may be divided; yet, they were not annihilated. The next, That those divided Parts were not

---

1 A fabled alchemical substance thought to turn base metals into gold or silver. Cavendish likely specifically targets van Helmont, who thought that quicksilver treated with a certain elixir would produce gold.

2 I.e., encased (or "put in an urn").

so separated and dispersed, as to be united to other Societies: Wherefore, if all those dead Animal Parts were put into a *Restoring-Womb*, or *Bed*; the Bed would occasion those Parts to place themselves into their proper Order and Form.

VI.

After the former Discourse, some of the Parts of my Mind were sad, to think, that those that had been embowelled, were made incapable of ever being restored; and, that it was a greater cruelty to murder a dead man, and to rob him of his Interior Parts; than to murder a living man, and yet suffer his whole Body to lye peaceably in the Urn, or Grave.

But, the other Parts endeavouring to comfort those sad Parts, made this Argument, *viz. Whether it might not probably be, that the Bones or Carcase or a Human Creature, were the Root of Human Life? and if so, then if all the Parts were dissolved, and none were left undissolved, but the bare Carcase; they might be restored to life.*

The sad Part's Opinion, was, That it was impossible they could be restored, by reason the Roots of Human Life, were those we name the *Vital Parts*; and those being divided from the Carcase, and dispersed, and united unto other Societies, could not meet and joyn into their former state of Life, or Society, so as to be the same Man.

The Comforting Parts were of opinion, It was not probable that the Fleshy and Spungy Parts, being the Branches of Human Life, could also be the Roots. Wherefore, in all probability, the Bones were the Roots; and the Bones being the Roots, if the bare Carcase of a Man should be put into a Restoring Bed, all the Fleshy and Spungy Parts, both those that were the Exterior, and those that were Interior, would spring and encrease to their full Maturity.

The sad Part's Opinion, was, That if the Bones were the Roots; and that, from the Roots, all the Exterior and Interior Parts, belonging to a Human Creature, should spring, and so encrease to full Maturity; yet, those Branches would not be the same they were, *viz.* the same Parts of the same Man; and besides, those Branches would rather be new Productions, than Restorations.

The Comforting Part's Opinion, was, That though the Branches were new, the Carcase, as the Root, being the same, the Man would be the same: for, though the Spungy and Fleshy Parts, divide and unite from Home, and to Forrein Parts; yet, the Man is the same: and to prove that the Bony Parts are the Roots of Human Life, doth it not happen, That if the Flesh be cut from the Bone, and the Bone be left bare; yet, in time, the bone produces new flesh: but, if any bone be separated from the Body, that Bone cannot be restored; nor can a new bone spring forth, nor can the divided bone be joyned or knit to the body, as it was before: for, although a broken bone may be set; yet, a divided bone cannot be rejoyned: All which Arguments, were a sufficient proof, That the Bones were the Roots of Life.

The Sad Part's Argument, was, That it was well known, that if any of the Vital Parts of a Human Creature, as the Liver, Lungs, Heart, Kidneys, and the like, were decayed, pierced, or wounded, the Human Creature dyed, by reason those Parts are incurable.

The Comforting Parts were of opinion, That there were many less Causes which did often occasion Human Death; yet, those Causes were not the Roots of Life: nor were those Parts the Roots of Life, although those Parts which we name *Vital*, were the chief Branches of Human Life.

But, at last, they all agreed in this opinion, That the *Bones*, were the Root; the *Marrow*, the Sapp, and the *Vitals*, the chief branches of Life. Also, they agreed, That when an Human Life was restored, the bones did first fill with some Oylie Juyces; and from the bones, and the sap or juyce of the bones, did all the Parts belonging to a Human Creature, spring forth, and grow up to Maturity: and certainly, *Not to disturb the Bones of the dead*, was a Holy and Religious Charge to Human Creatures.

VII.

After the pacifying the Sad Parts of my Mind, their Argument was, *That, supposing Creatures could be restored; whether they should be restored as when they were first produced; or, as when they were at the perfection of their Age; or, as when they were at old Age?*

But, after many Disputes, they all agreed, That those that should be restored, should be restored to that degree of Age and Strength, which is the most perfect: and, as all Productions arrived towards Perfection by degrees; so those that were restored, should return to Perfection by degrees, if they were past the perfect time of their age: and those that were not arrived to their Perfection, before they dyed, should arrive to it, however, as those that had it: so that, both *Youth* and *Age*, shall meet in Perfection: for, as the one encreases, as it were, forward; so the other return to their Strength and Perfection of their past Age.

VIII.

After the former Opinions, the Parts of my Mind were somewhat puzled in their *Arguments* concerning the degrees of the

Restoring Times; as, *Whether Restoration was done by a General Act, or by Degrees?*

The most Doubting Part's Opinion, was, That it was not natural to Restore, although it was natural to Produce; and, that all Natural Productions, were by degrees: but, for Restorations, (being not Natural Productions) they could not be done by degrees: and therefore the Action of Restoration, was but as one Action, although of many Parts.

The Believing Parts of my Mind were of opinion, That all Nature's Actions, being by degrees, all Restorations were also by degrees.

The Doubting Part's Opinion was, That there were some actions that had no degrees: for, One action might signifie a Thousand.

The other Part's Opinion was, That a Thousand actions, or degrees, were in the figure of One.

The Doubting Parts were of opinion, That it was impossible. But, at last, they agreed, That the Restoring actions were by degrees.

IX.

The Parts of my Mind were divided into Minor and Major Parts, about the Time or Degrees of Restoration of Human Creatures.

The Minor's Opinion was, That the Restoring actions of Nature, were so much quicker than the Producing actions, that a Human Creature might be restored in a Month's time; whereas the production of a Human Creature was in ten Months: for, though a Human Creature may Quicken at Three Months' time; yet, it was not fully Ripe for Birth, before the time of Ten Months.

The Major Part's Opinion was, That Restoration was according as the Creature was Dissolved: for, a Man that was newly dead; or not so long dead, that his Parts were not yet divided; that Man might be restored to Life in an Hour's time, or less: but, if all the Parts, excepting the bare Carcase, were dissolved, there would require as long a time in Restoring, as in Producing.

The Minor's Opinion, was, That the Restoring-time, was no longer than the time of Quickning.

The Major Part's Opinion, was, That though the Exterior Form or Frame of a Child, might be before the Quickning; yet, it was not a perfect Animal, until it was Quick: and although it might be a perfect Animal when it was Quick; yet, not ripe, that is, not at the full Perfection of a Human Creature. As it is with

Fruits: for, a Green Plumb is not like a Ripe Plumb; but, any Green Fruit, is like a Dead Fruit, in comparison of a Ripe Fruit.

At last, the Parts of my Mind did agree, That if a Human Creature was dissolved, excepting the bare Carcase; it would require Ten Months' time ere it could perfectly be restored: for, the Springing Parts would require so long a time ere they could come to full Maturity.

X.

The Question being stated, *Whether the Restoring-Bed, was a Fleshy Bed*; All the Parts of my Mind, after many Disputes, agreed, That it could not be a Fleshy Bed, by reason the nature of Flesh is so corruptible, dissolvable, and easie to be dissolved, that it could not possibly be of such a lasting nature, as is required for *Restoring-Beds*. But yet, they agreed, they were like Flesh, for Softness, or Spunginess; as also, for Colour. Also, they agreed, That the Animal *Restoring-Bed*, was of such a Nature or Property, that it could dilate and contract, as it had occasion; in so much, that it could contract to the compass of the smallest, or extend to the magnitude of the largest Animal. Also, they did agree, That it was somewhat like the Stomack of a Human Creature, or of the like Animal, that could open and shut the Orifice; and that when an Animal Creature was put into the *Restoring-Bed*, it would immediately inclose the Animal: and when it had caused a perfect Restoration, the *Restoring-Bed* would open it self, and deliver it to its own Liberty.

XI.

Another Question amongst the Parts of my Mind concerning *Restoring-Beds*, or *Wombs*, was: *That in case there were such Restoring-Beds in Nature, as in all probability there were; Where could those Restoring-Beds be? viz. Whether there were any in this World? If not in this World, in any other World?*

The Minor Parts were of opinion, There were none in this World; but, that there were some in other Worlds.

The Major Part's Opinion, was, That there were such Beds; but, that Human Creatures would not know them, though they could perceive them: nor, if they could perceive them, could they tell how to make use of them.

At last they all agreed, That those *Restoring-Beds* were in the Center of the World: but, where the Center is, no Human Creature, no, not the most Subtile and Learned *Mathematicians*, *Geometricians*, or *Astrologers*, could, with their most Laborious

Arts, and Subtile Observations, know; and therefore, unless by a special Decree from God, no such Restoration can be made.

XII.

The Parts of my Mind were very studious to conceive where the Center of the World was: Some of the Parts of my Mind was of opinion, That there were four Centers, *viz.* A Center in the Earth, a Center in the Air, a Center in the Sea, and a Center in the Element of Fire.

Upon which Opinion, the Parts of my Mind divided into Minor and Major Parts.

The Minor Parts were of opinion, That there were Centers in all the Four Elemental Parts; and that the *Restoring-Beds,* were only of four Kinds: but yet, there might be many several sort of each particular Kind; and that each particular Kind, with all the several Sorts, was produced in each particular Elemental Center.

The Major Part was of opinion, That there might be infinite Centers, if there were infinite Worlds: also, there might be many Centers in this World; for, every round Globe hath a Center. But, their Opinion concerning the *Restoring-Beds,* was, That they were in the Center of the Globe of our whole World, and not of any of the Parts of the World: for, the *Air* could have but an uncertain Center; neither could the *Water* have a very solid Center; and the *Earth* was too solid to have a Center, consisting of the Four kinds of Elements: neither could the Elemental *Fire* have such a Center, as to breed such different kinds and sorts of *Beds,* as the *Restoring-Beds* are, because many of them are quite of a different nature from the nature of Elemental Fire: wherefore, it must be the Center of the World, which must consist of all the Elemental kinds.

XIII.

After the former *Argument,* the Parts of my Mind were very studious in conceiving, where the Center of the whole Universe of this our World, might be: at last they all agreed, It was the *Sea,* which is the Watry Element: for, the *Sea* is inclosed with the *Airy, Fiery,* and *Earthy* Parts of the Universe, and therefore must be the Center. And, though the Sea was the Center of the World; yet, there was a Center of the Sea: so that, there was a Center in a Center; in which Center, were the *Restoring-Beds.*

XIV.

After the former Conceptions, the Parts of my Mind were very studious, to conceive where the Center's Center might be. But, they could not possibly conceive it, by reason they could not possibly imagine how large, and of what compass the Sea may be of: for they did verily believe, that the utmost extension of the Sea, is not, as yet, known to Human-Kind: for, that Circle about which the Ships of *Cavendishe*, and *Drake*,[1] did swim, might be, in comparison to the whole Body of the Sea, but such a Circle as a Boy may occasion, with throwing a small Stone, or such like thing, into a Pond of Water.

XV.

The last Conception of my Mind, concerning *Restoring-Bed*s, was, That the Parts of my Mind did conceive, That the Center of the whole Universe, was the Sea; and in the Center of the Sea, was a small Island; and in the Center of the Island, was a Creature, like (in the outward Form) to a great and high Rock: Not that this Rock was Stone; but, it was of such a nature, (by the natural Compositions of Parts) that it was compounded of Parts of all the principal Kinds and Sorts of the Creatures of this World, *viz.* Of *Elemental*, *Animal*, *Mineral*, and *Vegetable* kinds: and, being of such a nature, did produce, out of it self, all kinds and sorts of *Restoring-Beds*; whereof, some sorts were so loose, that they only hung by Strings, or Nerves: others stuck close. Some were produced at the top, or upper parts: others were produced out of the middle parts; and some were produced from the lower parts, or at the bottom. In short, the Opinion of the Parts of my Mind, was, That this Rocky Creature was all covered with its own Productions; which Productions were of all Kinds and Sorts: not that they were numerous; but, various Productions: also, that these various Productions, were *Restoring-Beds*: for, the nature of this Rocky Creature, is as lasting as the Sun, or other Planets; which was the reason that those Productions are not subject to decay, as other Productions are: nor can they produce new Creatures; but only restore former Creatures; as, those that had been Produced, and were partly Dissolved.

THE CONCLUSION.

After the Wisest Parts of my Mind had ended their *Arguments*, there being some of the Dullest, and the most Unbelieving, or rather, Strange Parts of my Mind, that had retired into the

1 Sir Thomas Cavendish (1560–92) and Sir Francis Drake (1540–96), English explorers and circumnavigators.

Glandula of my Brain, which is a kind of Kernel;[1] which they made use of, instead of a Pulpit: out of which, they declared their Opinions, thus:

Dear Associates, *We, that were not Parties of your Disputations, or Argumentations, concerning* Restoring-Beds*; being retired into the* Glandula *of the Brain, where we have been informed by the Nerves, and Sensitive Spirits, of your wise Opinions, and subtile Arguments. Considering that your Conclusion was as improbable, if not as impossible, as the Chymical* Philosophers-Stone, *or* Elixir*; We desire you (being Parts of one and the same Society) not to trouble the whole Society, in the search of that, which, if it was in Nature, will never be found. But to prevent, that your painful Studies, and witty Arguments, be not buried in Oblivion; We advise you, To perswade the Sensitive Parts of our Society, to record them, so that they may be divulged to all the Societies of our own Kind or Sort of Creatures; as* Chymists *do, who, after they have wasted their Times and Estates, to gain the* Philosopher-Stone, *or* Elixir*; write Books to teach it to the Sons of Art: which is impossible, at least, very improbable, ever to be learn'd, there being no such Art in Nature: but, were it possible such an Art was to be obtained; yet, when obtained the Artist would never divulge it in Print. But, those great Practitioners, finding, after much Loss and Pains, nothing but Despair, write Books of that Art; which, instead of the* Elixir, *did produce* Despair*; which again, though produced by Art, did produce, naturally, that Vice, named* Malice*; and* Malice, *being a Pregnant Seed, sowed upon the Fertile Ground of their Writings, produces so much Mischief, that many men of good Estates, have been undone, in following their Rules in* Chymistry*: And if your Books should be as successful as* Chymistry *hath been (I dare not say, among* Fools*; but) amongst Credulous Men; your Books will cause as much Mischief as theirs have done; not by the ways of* Fire, *but by the ways of* Water*: for, your Books send men to* Sea, *a much Cooler Element than* Fire*; but, more Dangerous than* Chymical Fire, *unless* Chymical Fire *be* Hell-Fire.

Upon which Discourse, the rest of my Thoughts were very angry, and pull'd them out of their Pulpit, the *Glandula*; and not only so, but put them out of their Society, believing they were a Factious Party, which, in time, might cause the Society's Dissolution.

1 Cavendish refers to the pineal gland, a tiny organ in the center of the brain which Descartes regarded as the principal seat of the human soul.

Appendix A: Cavendish Correspondence

1. Joseph Glanvill to Cavendish, 13 October 1667[1]

[The following letter from clergyman and philosopher Joseph Glanvill (1636–80) was transcribed from the printed collection *Letters and Poems in Honour of the Incomparable Princess, Margaret, Duchess of Newcastle* (1676), which William Cavendish edited and published after the death of Margaret in 1673. Unlike other prominent philosophers like Thomas Hobbes (1588–1679) and Henry More (1614–87), who refused to engage seriously with Cavendish's work (despite being sent copies of her books), Glanvill exchanged a series of letters with Cavendish in the 1660s that politely but persistently dispute her materialism and debate the pre-existence of souls and other spiritual phenomena like witchcraft. Unfortunately, Cavendish's side of this correspondence is no longer extant.]

MADAM,

I Owe it to your *Grace*[']*s* singular condescention, and goodness, that my Letters are not displeasing, and I see a great deal of Generosity, in your *Grace*[']*s* acceptance, of such mean things, as my slender stock of Knowledge can impart. As for your Inquiry about the Plastick Faculties;[2] I Answer, that they are those, whereby the Body is formed at first, and by which the Alimental Juices,[3] are after, through the whole course of Life, orderly distributed for the purposes of growth and nutrition: But whether, as your *Grace* inquires, they are Faculties inherent, in the Soul, or are only Mechanical Motions of the Body

1 Since William Cavendish edited Glanvill's letter, I have retained original spelling and grammar, with the exception of possessives.

2 Glanvill mentions these faculties in a previous letter not included here; he refers to the vital spirit or force that infuses and animates all natural matter.

3 I.e., bodily fluids. In humans, blood or spinal fluid.

I cannot determine certainly. But I rather incline to the *Platonists,*[1] who will have the Soul to be the Body[']s Maker, and they affirm (as is ordinary; though with some diversity in the Names and Presentation) That there are three sorts of Faculties, which they Phancy as Analogous parts, or Regions in the Soul, *(Viz.)* The *Mind,* so they call the highest Faculties of abstract Reason, and Understanding, which is the *First*. The *Second* they call the *Soul, (Viz.)* as it is united to the Body, and exerciseth the operation of Sense. The *Third,* is the Image of the *Soul,* which is those Faculties, that are called Plastical, that move and turn the Body, but are devoid of Understanding, or Sense; Now how the *Soul,* which is Immaterial, can manage and order Corporeal Motions is a difficulty of which Philosophy as yet hath given no account, as I have particularly taken notice, and proved in my *Sceptis Scientifica,*[2] but yet the thing ought not therefore to be denied, because the manner of the most obvious sensible things is to us unknown; And by this we can only prove, that we have yet no certain Theory of Nature: And, in good earnest, Madam, all that we can hope for, as yet, is but the History of things as they are, but to say how they are, to raise general *Axioms,* and to make *Hypotheses,* must, I think, be the happy priviledge of succeeding Ages; when they shall have gained a larger account of the *Phœnomena,* which yet are too scant and defective to raise Theories upon: so that to be ingenious and confess freely, we have yet no such thing as Natural Philosophy;[3] Natural History is all we can pretend to; and that too, as yet, is but in its Rudiments, the advance of it your *Grace* knows is the design and buisiness of the *Royal Society;*[4] from whom we may reasonably at last expect better grounds for general Doctrines, than any the World yet hath been acquainted with; but this, Madam, is an excursion.[5] I therefore return to your *Grace*[']*s* Letter, which inquires some things,

1 In his *Republic,* Plato asserted that the human psyche consists of three parts: reason, spirit, and appetite. These beliefs were adapted by Henry More (1614–87) and other Neoplatonists of the seventeenth century.

2 *Scepsis scientifica* (1665), an updated edition of Glanvill's *Vanity of Dogmatizing* (1661).

3 These lines express Glanvill's commitment to probabilism, which he shares with Cavendish.

4 The Royal Society of London, a fellowship of natural philosophers committed to revealing nature's ways via experiment and induction.

5 I.e., digression.

about my Notion of the *Soul*['] *s* Original:[1] As to this I would not be understood to affirm peremptorily a thing, which the greatest part of Men, neither have, nor can receive, only I consider it as an *Hypothesis*, that may be taken up to satisfy those minds that are much troubled at the seeming inequalities of Providence; and whether true, or false, this I will take the boldness to be confident in, That the Doctrine of the *Soul*['] *s Præexistence*,[2] doth best suit with the appearances of the World. And best Answers for the Divine Justice and Goodness, in all the affairs of Providence; In this Madam, I am a little *Dogmatical*, and this step further, I think I may take, without immodesty; That the Doctrine hath so much to say for it self, from Reason, and the highest Antiquity, as to render it fit to be considered, and indeed, since the two other wayes,[3] are confessedly desperate, methinks there should be no harm in examining this; which is all I pretend to. But particularly to your *Grace*'s *Quæry*, Whether were *Souls* Created or Uncreated? I Answer, no doubt Created: But then I do not see how that follows, which your *Grace* is pleased to infer, *Viz.* That Sin was then Created, For our *Souls* in their State were Spotless and Innocent, as the Angels of God. That Mankind was so first, and fell by a voluntary Transgression, is the common Doctrine; and how we may suppose it was particularly in the way of *Præexistence*, your *Grace* will see easily, when I shall have procured that Book of mine, I have mentioned, and promised your *Grace*, but cannot yet light on.[4] The other part also of your *Grace*['] *s* Division: *Viz.* That if those *Souls* were Eternal, they are God[']s; is I humbly conceive a mistake likewise, since though

1 I.e., the place from which the soul derives.

2 Glanvill dedicated much of his career to establishing the pre-existence of souls, or the belief that the soul is eternal and migrates into and out of material forms, which was a non-orthodox view at the time. In this, he sides with More and contributes to the larger seventeenth-century debate about the precise relationship between the soul and the body that it animates.

3 The period's theological thinkers isolated three options: creationism, whereby God creates each soul anew and implants it into the human body at conception, birth, or sometime between (this was the orthodox view at the time); traduction, whereby souls perpetuate from parent to child via conception (this was part of Lutheran doctrine); and the pre-existence of souls, whereby souls are pre-created and then incarnated in bodies at some later time. See Lewis 271–72.

4 His book *Lux Orientalis* (1662).

the World, had been Created from Eternity (which even the Schools[1] confess possible) it had nevertheless been a Creature, by reason of its dependence upon another, for its being, and to have been produced, and yet from Eternity, is no absurdity, our Faith affirms it, in the Eternal Generation of the Son, and Procession of the Holy-Ghost, and to take an instance with which we may make more bold: If the Sun had been from Eternity no doubt it would have shone Eternally, and yet it[']s Beams had been effects and dependent; And whereas your *Grace* saith again, That what is Immaterial is a God: I must here also take the boldness, to enter my Dissent to your Proposition; Indeed Mr. *Hobbs* denys all Immateriality to Created Beings,[2] but I think upon grounds precarious and unsafe, That our *Souls* are Immaterial in their Natures, hath been sufficiently proved by some late Philosophers; particularly by the most learned Dr. *H. Moore*,[3] and I also have done something about this, in my Book of *Præexistence*, If your *Grace* demands my Reasons; they shall be ready at the least intimation, of those commands which I shall ever account a singular Honour to observe. For the antiquity of *Præexistence*, which your *Grace* rightly observes, to be no certain Argument of the truth of it, I humbly say I have not alledged it, for a demonstration of the thing, but to take off the prejudice we are apt to have against all supposed Novelties, and to shew that it is not so despicable, an *Hypothesis* but that several great minds of former times, even in the Ages of the best Antiquity have owned a kindness for it, and consequently that we cannot, without some immodesty, deny it a favourable hearing, But madam, I forget my self, and the consideration I ought to have of your *Grace*'s Time and Patience, and therefore only add, that I am,

Bath, Octob. 13. 1667.

Illustrious Madam,
Your Grace[']s
Most Obedient Servant,
Jos. Glanvill

2. Correspondence between Cavendish and Constantijn Huygens

[In 1657, Cavendish and Constantijn Huygens (1596–1687) corresponded about the nature of "Rupert's drops," or spherical

---

1 I.e., the academic and theological establishment.

2 Hobbes was a committed materialist and denied all immaterial substances in nature. Cavendish agreed with him on this point.

3 Henry More.

glass beads with small tails that could sustain great force without breaking. However, if the tail was even gently cracked, the glass would shatter. Huygens seems genuinely interested in Cavendish's opinion on this matter and returns to her for further insight after testing and finding inadequate her original hypothesis of a combustible substance hidden within the glass. By her turn, Cavendish enjoys speculating about this phenomenon and enacts in real time her belief that opinions about nature are always subject to revision. A scholar, poet, composer, and statesman, Huygens was a consummate letter writer. He also assisted Cavendish in placing her books at Leiden University (the subject of the last two letters below).

To facilitate reading, I have modernized typography and spelling but have not changed grammar, with the exception of possessives. My transcriptions are based on those originally made by Nadine Akkerman and Marguérite Corporaal and are adapted here with their full permission.[1] For the originals, see Akkerman and Corporaal.]

a. Huygens to Cavendish, 12 March 1657 (Koninklijke Bibliotheek, The Hague [KA 48, f. 37r])

To the Lady Marchionesse of Newcastle. 12 Mart. 1657.

Madam;

I had the honour to hear so good solutions given by Your Ex*cellency* upon divers questions moved in a whole afternoon she was pleased to bestow upon my unworthy conversation,[2] that I am turning to school with all speed, humbly beseeching Your Ex*cellency* may be so bountiful towards my ignorance, as to instruct me about the natural reason of these wonderful glasses, which, as I told you Madam, will fly into powder if one breaks but the least top of their tails: whereas without that way they are hardly

1 I have included six of the 11 extant letters between Huygens and Cavendish, which span at least 14 years.

2 Likely at the Duarte house in Antwerp, where Cavendish and her husband often spent time while in exile in the 1650s. The Duartes were wealthy gem merchants who became the center of the city's intellectual and artistic life.

to be broken by any weight or strength. The King of france[1] is as yet unresolved in the question notwithstanding he hath been curious to move it to an assembly of the best philosophers of Paris, the microcosm of his Kingdome. Your Ex*cellency* hath no cause to apprehend the cracking blow of these little innoxious[2] guns. If you did, Madam, a servant may hold them close in his fist, and your self can break the little end of their tail without the least danger. But, as I was bold to tell your E*xcellency*, I should be loath to believe any female fear should reign amongst so much over-masculine wisdom as we the world doth admire in her. I pray God to blesse your E*xcellency* with a daily increase of it, and your worthy self to grant that amongst those admirers I may strive to deserve by way of my humble service the honour to be accounted Y[3]

> I have made bold to join unto these a couple of poor Epigrams I did meditate in my journey hither,[4] where Your Ex*cellency*['] s noble Tales were my best entertainment. I hope, Madame, you will perceive the intention of them through the mist of a language I do but harp and guess at.

b. Cavendish to Huygens, 20 March 1657 (Koninklijk Huis-archief, The Hague [G1-9/1])

Noble Sir

I received by mrs de Werts[5] a letter & A Couple of Epigrams wherein you have praised me & my book[6] more th[a]n the Wit, or merit, of either deserves; which expresses your overflowing generosity that chooses rather to give too much praise then too little.

As for your request concerning my Opinion, of the glasses, you have done me the favor to send me, I know not civilly how to deny it, nor prudently to grant it, nor learnedly to give it; for it were A presumption to give my Opinion, after these famous and learned philosophers, as those which are in france; whose brains Nature have so tempered and furnished with such

---

1 Louis XIV (r. 1643–1715).

2 I.e., harmless; innocuous.

3 The page breaks off at this point.

4 The epigrams are not extant.

5 Mrs. Duarte.

6 Likely *Nature's Pictures*, which Huygens added to his library in 1656. See Akkerman and Corporaal 278.

conceptions, reasons, Judgements, & Wit, to find out the truths both of obscure Nature and subtle Arts; that I may rather wonder with the ignorant then give my Opinion with the Learned; but to my Outward sense these glasses do Appear to have in the head, body or belly A Liquid, & oily Substance, which may be the Oily spirits or Essences; of Sulphur, also the glasses do Appear to my senses; Like the nature, or Art of guns and the spirit of Sulphur as the powder; where Although they are charged; yet until they be discharged: gives no report or sound; the discharging of these glasses is by the breaking of A piece or part or end, of the tails where the discharging of guns are by mach, firelocks, serves or the like,[1] which sets fire or gives Vent to the powder; but these Sulphurous spirits, having as it seems A more forceable Nature; it doth violently thrust itself out, where it finds Vent, Like as wind, but rather like fire, being of A fiery Nature, & may have the Effects of bright shining fire, which when it has no Vent, Lies as dead, but As soon as it can eat out A passage or finds A Vent, it breaks forth in A violent crack or thundering noise; I do not say the Effects of these spirits are to flame or to burn after that way but only it hath the like Effects, as to break disperse and Spread abroad as bright shining fire doth, for oily Sulphur, vitriol spirits & the like fiery Natures, are those which are called A cold dead fire, that is the exterior parts is cold & dull, although the interior is hot, & Active,

As for the wonder how this Liquid matter should be put into this glass, for it is Visible A Liquid matter, is therein, which to my senses it must be first put in, to the matter or substance that makes the glasses. And when the glass is blown the Liqueur runs, or crowds to the most hollowest, and Largest place it can get into, Like as wind will blow the Water into A crowd or heap together And fill All hollow places it can get into—as ditches, pits, or the Like, so doth the breath of the glass maker, blow that oily essences, or spirits into the belly of the glass where before it can have so much time to retire back, the end of the little porous tail, is soathred up;[2] Where afterwards when the soadred part is broke of the spirits finding Vent struggles; & strives to get forth, wherein the strife it breaks the glass to pieces, wherewith it makes

1 The diction is confusing here, but Cavendish seems to indicate that matchlocks ("mach"), firelocks, and perhaps sear-pins ("serves") perform the same purpose in self-igniting guns as the tails do in Rupert's drops (that is, they serve as the spark or ignition).

2 Soldered.

A Noise, or report, Like A gun or rather as A fired house, or the like, I mean not for the Loudness of the sound, for the report is small, to such Loud reports, though it be great for so small a body but I compare these Spirits like to fire, and the glass as the house wherein the fiery spirits Are in as much as when they break forth, they rend and disperse the materials of their transparent house several ways, as also the fiery oily spirits spreads itself into vapor & dies, for dilation is the way to desolation and as this glasses breaks when discharged so, I believe guns at their discharging would break; if the barrels were of glass, as they are of Iron, and I know nothing to the contrary but this Liquid substance in these glasses, may be the Oil of saltpetre[1] which is flatious,[2] brimstone and charcoal, which is hot mixt together and so may be A Liquid gunpowder, or rather Gunpowder made Liquid, put into the glasses, as for the sound or report it gives, when discharged by giving the glass Vent, may be by the same cause, yet makes Air give A report for Air Although it be Equal tempered or cold yet when it have been pent up and afterwards have Vent, will make a Loud report; so will Water or Any Liqueur for Air and wind have Vocal Noises; but to draw you towards An end it Appears thus to my senses; that the strife of the Spirits or gunpowder Liqueur and the bricklyness[3] of the Glass is the cause of the breaking and powdering of the same, and the spirits being Airy; and the Liqueur windy,[4] and being first pent up, and then gets Vent is the cause of that sound, or Report, and for the enclosure of the Liqueur is done by the Art of the Artificers; which Art if the philosophers knew or had been bound Apprentice to, might soon have satisfied the King of France's Curiosity, and instructed him in the knowledge thereof, for these glasses more concerns the Artificers than the Natural philosophers or speculators; but Women Wears at their Ears for pendants as great Wonders, Although they make not so great A Report, which are glass bobs, with Narrow necks as these glasses have tails, and yet is filled with several colours silks and course black cotton-wool, which to my senses is more difficult to put into these glass pendants then Liqueur into these glass guns, but Sir I have made A tedious discourse, of what my senses have observed of these glasses you sent me, which discourses may tire or Weary your Sense to read

1 Potassium nitrate.

2 I.e., flatuous or generating wind; in this context, explosive.

3 Brittleness.

4 Generating wind or combustible.

it, but I have only this to excuse me that I chose rather to say too much to show or express my Obedience to your Commands; then to say so little as it may be thought I was Negligent or idle, but if I have committed A fault in being over diligent, pray pardon me, whereby you will As to those favors I have received from you, for which next to your Own Merits hath obliged me to be

Sir

Antwerp 20th March 1657

Your humble friend
& servant
M. NEWCASTLE

c. Huygens to Cavendish, 27 March 1657 (Koninklijke Bibliotheek, The Hague [KA 48, f. 36])

To the Marchionesse
of Newcastle
27. March. 1657

Madam;

I have put your Ex*cellency* to a trouble which I did suppose should be the last upon this subject. But experience having carried me to a new by-way, from whence I do not see how to bring myself upon the path of truth without your gracious assistance, I do presume this second time to inform your Ex*cellency* of what I have found out since you were pleased to bestow a most judicious sheet of paper upon my ignorant curiosity. In order of your Ex*cellency*[']s determination, I did conceive, if the matter enclosed in the hollow parts of these bottles should be a sulphurous liquid Gunpowder, that without question fire would work upon it and make it active. But, Madam, I found myself so far short of my opinion, that firing one of these bottles to the reddest height of heat, I have not only seen it Without any effect, but also being cooled again, I have wondered to see all his virtue spent and spoiled, so that I could break of the whole tail by pieces even to the belly without any motion more than you would see in an ordinary piece of glass. Having also broke the belly a sunder and well observed the little hollow bubbles within it, I have not found the least appearance of any liquor or oily substance should have been enclosed therein. If your Ex*cellency* think it worth her pains to consider of these circumstances, It may be by degrees she will bring herself to the true notice of the mystery. I am the bolder in importuning her with these trifles, for as much I remember your

Ex*cellency* would declare unto me that being today of an opinion in matter of Philosophy, she would not to be bound to it [so] that tomorrow she might not make choice of a better.[1] I leave all to her most ingenious perspicacity, and with her leave do sign me Y.

d. Cavendish to Huygens, 30 March 1657 (British Library, MS Add 28558 f.65)

Monsieur Huijgens de Zulichem
Le Haghue

Sir

I have received your second letter by mrs Dewerts wherein I find your dissatisfaction of the Opinion of those Little glasses; truly Arts are as obscure and hard to find and by those yet are unlearned in them, as Nature[']s Works; but to Clear my Opinion, or rather to Answer your desires I shall Argue something more of them; though my Arguments may be as weak as my Opinions, & my opinions, as weak as my Judgement, & my Judgement as weak as want of Knowledge Can make it. As for the Liqueur you say in your Letter that if it were a Sulphurous Liqueur, or a Liquid gunpowder (as I said) I thought it might be, doubtless it would be active by the help of fire;[2] I Answer for that fire hath several Active Effects both in itself and upon other substances; or subjects[;] wherefore if the Liqueur had been dry powder it might be subject to that effect, of fire, as to flash, flame, or bounce; but if the powder were wet the fire could work no such effects, but as the substance is A Liqueur fire is as subject to that Liquid substance, or matter as that substance or matter is to fire[,] for all Liqueurs although strong with spirits and hot in operation will quench fire as suddenly, as fire shall evaporate Liqueur take quantity for quantity and it is probable that the high fire you did Apply to the glass, did evaporate out the Liqueur in the glass which might be the weakening & changing or altering the former effects; Also you say you cannot perceive the bubble to be a Liqueur[.] I Answer that it is probable the Liqueur, if any be therein was Evaporated out either by the fire, you applied or by the vent of passage, which may soon turn it into Vapour by reason

1 Huygens refers to Cavendish's view that opinions are based on limited knowledge and are therefore always subject to revision, which she also espouses in *Grounds*.

2 It would explode when exposed to flame.

of the Little quantity that is in a glass thus it might be wasted before the truth could possibly be found out;[1] for Certainly to my sense, as also to my reason A Liqueur Appeared to be in those glasses; you sent me; but if there be no Liqueur in those glasses; then it is probable it might be put pent up air enclosed therein, which having vent was the cause of the sound, or report which those glasses gave[.] Thus Sir you may perceive by my Arguing, I strive to make my former opinion, or sense good; Although I do not bind myself to opinions, but truth; and the truth is that though I cannot find out the truth of the glasses; yet

In truth I Am

Sir

Your humble servant

M Newcastle

Antwerp 30th march 1657

Sir I would have written my letters to you in my own hand but be reason my hand writing is not legible I thought you might rather have guessed at what I would say then had read what I had written[.] this is the reason they were written by another hand[2]

e. Cavendish to Huygens, 27 October 1658 (Koninklijk Huis-archief, The Hague [G1-9/1])

Monsieur de Zulichem

noble Sir

give me leave to challenge your promise which was to favor my book and so me by it so much as to present it to the university library of layden,[3] for though my book hath neither wit nor worth enough to disserve a place in that library yet by the honour that it will receive from your hands it may find a good acceptance[.] thus Sir I trouble you[,] but no man lives without some troubles

1 That is, there might actually be an imperceptible explosive substance in the glass that evaporates or dissipates when heated.

2 Apparently, this post-script is in Cavendish's own hand-writing, while the rest of the letter is written by an amanuensis.

3 Huygens helped to place Cavendish's books at the library of the University of Leiden.

and those persons that are most eminent are oftenest solicited to do favours and your favour in this will ever oblige me

to be Sir your
most humble servant
MARGREAT
NEWCASTLE

f. Huygens to Cavendish, 28 November 1658[1]

Hague, the 28th. *of* November, 1658.

MADAM,

According to your Excellency[']s command, I have been of purpose at *Leyden*, and there delivered your Present into the hands of the *Rector Magnificus* (as we call him) of the University, who some days after hath made a solemn exhibition of it to the Lords Curators, in a public meeting of the whole Academic Senate, and, in their name, hath sent me the Letter here enclosed; by which I hope the faithful discharge of my Ambassage[2] shall be testified, and give your Excellency occasion of further Employment to bestow upon the unworthy person,

Madam, of
Your Excellency[*'s*] *Humble*
and Obedient Servant,
Huygens de Zulichem.

This letter came but even now from *Leiden*, so that I hope your Excellency will not suspect any negligence in me.

[Huygens includes here a letter of thanks in Latin and a receipt from the Rector at Leiden University.]

1 This letter does not survive in manuscript but is printed in *A Collection of Letters and Poems*.

2 I.e., ambassadorial role.

Appendix B: Selection from Book I, Chapter XXXV of Observations upon Experimental Philosophy

[*Observations upon Experimental Philosophy* (1666; 1668) critiques the experimental program of The Royal Society of London and, more broadly, offers Cavendish's most thorough expression of her mature natural philosophy. Her views in *Observations* correspond with those we find in *Grounds*, although *Observations* devotes more time to her theory of knowledge and perception, her views on material motion, and her critique of experimental and mechanical philosophy, and less time to health and the human body. The chapter below offers details about knowledge, perception, and free will that supplements her treatment of these topics in *Grounds*.]

1. From Book I, Chapter XXXV: Of Knowledg and Perception in general.[1]

Since Natural Knowledg and Perception, is the Ground and Principle, not onely of Philosophy both Speculative and Experimental, but of all other Arts and Sciences, nay, of all the Infinite particular actions of Nature; I thought it not amiss to joyn to the end of this Part [of *Observations*], a full declaration of my opinion concerning that Subject.

First, It is to be observed, That Matter, Self-motion, and Self-knowledg, are inseparable from each other, and make Nature one Material, Self-moving, and Self-knowing Body. To say *inseparable from each other*, in my opinion, seems as if they were different Parts, and not different properties of the same Part.[2]

2. Nature being Material, is dividable into Parts; and being infinite in quantity or bulk, her Parts are infinite in number.

---

1 I follow the second, 1668 edition of *Observations*, except in the case of printing errors, where I defer to the 1666 edition. I retain original spelling and grammar, although I have corrected errors and modernized usage of both possessives and the conjunction "than."

2 I.e., Cavendish claims that they are *not* separate entities.

3. No Part can subsist singly, or by it self, precised[1] from the rest; but they are all parts of one infinite Body; for though such parts may be separated from such parts, and joined to other parts, and by this means may undergo infinite changes, by infinite compositions and divisions; yet no part can be separated from the Body of Nature.

4. And hence it follows, That the Parts of Nature are nothing else but the particular changes of particular figures, made by Self-motion.

5. As there can be no annihilation, so there can neither be a new Creation of the least part or particle of Nature, or else Nature would not be Infinite.

6. Nature is purely corporeal or material, and there is nothing that belongs to, or is a part of Nature, which is not corporeal; so that natural and material, or corporeal, are one and the same; and therefore spiritual beings, non-beings, mixt-beings, and whatsoever distinctions the Learned do make,[2] are no ways belonging to Nature. Neither is there any such thing as an Incorporeal motion; for all actions of Nature are corporeal, being natural; and there can no abstraction be made of Motion or Figure, from Matter or Body, but they are inseparably one thing. Wherefore no spiritual Being, can have local Motion.[3]

7. As Infinite Matter is divided into Infinite Parts; so Infinite Knowledg is divided into infinite particular Knowledges; and infinite Self-motion, into infinite particular Self-actions.

8. There is no other difference between Self-knowledg, and particular Knowledges, than betwixt Self-motion, and particular Self-actions; or betwixt a Whole, and its Parts; a Cause, and its Effects: for, Self-knowledg is the Ground and Principle of all particular knowledges, as Self-motion is the Ground and Principle of all particular actions, changes and varieties of natural figures.

9. As Infinite Nature has an infinite Self-motion and Self-knowledg; so every part and particle has a particular and finite Self-motion and Self-knowledg, by which it knows it self, and its own actions, and perceives also other parts and actions; which latter is properly called Perception; not as if there were two different Principles of knowledg in every particular Creature

1 Isolated or detached.

2 Cavendish refers especially to the spirits espoused by English Neoplatonist Henry More (1614–87) and the gasses proposed by Flemish alchemist Jan Baptist van Helmont (1580–1644).

3 I.e., physical motion within the natural world.

or part of Nature; but they are two different acts of one and the same interior and inherent Self-knowledg, which is a part of Nature's Infinite Self-knowledg.

10. Thus Perception, or a perceptive knowledg, belongs properly to parts, and may also be called an exterior knowledg, by reason it extends to exterior objects.

11. Though Self-knowledg is the ground and principle of all particular knowledges and perceptions; yet, Self-motion, since it is the cause of all the variety of natural figures, and of the various compositions and divisions of parts; it is also the cause of all perceptions.

12. As there is a double degree of corporeal Self-motion, *viz.* Rational, and Sensitive; so there is also a double degree of Perception, Rational and Sensitive.

13. A Whole may know its Parts; and an Infinite a Finite; but no particular part can know its whole, nor one finite part, that which is infinite: I say, no particular part; for, when parts are regularly composed, they may by a general Conjunction or Union of their particular Knowledges and Perceptions, know more, and so judg more probably of the Whole, or of Infinite; and although by the division of parts, those composed knowledges and perceptions, may be broke asunder like a ruined House or Castle, Kingdom or Government; yet some of the same Materials may chance to be put to the same uses, and some may be joined to those that formerly employed themselves other ways. And hence I conclude, That no particular Parts are bound to certain particular actions, no more than Nature her self, which is self-moving Matter; for, as Nature is full of variety of motions or actions, so are her Parts; or else she could not be said self-moving, if she were bound to certain actions, and had not liberty to move as she pleases: for, though God, the Author of Nature, has ordered her, so that she cannot work beyond her own nature, that is, beyond Matter; yet has she freedom to move as she will; neither can it be certainly affirmed, that the successive propagation of the several species of Creatures, is decreed and ordained by God, so that Nature must of necessity work to their continuation, and can do no otherwise; but human sense and reason may observe, that the same Parts keep not always to the same particular Actions, so as to move to the same species or figures; for, those parts that join in the composition of an Animal, alter their actions in its dissolution, and in the framing of other figures; so that the same Parts which were joined in one particular Animal, may, when they dissolve from that composed

figure, join severally to the composition of other figures; as for example, of Minerals, Vegetables, Elements, *&c.* and some may join with some sorts of Creatures, and some with others, and so produce Creatures of different sorts, when as before they were all united in one particular Creature: for, particular Parts are not bound to work or move to a certain particular action, but they work according to the wisdom and liberty of Nature, which is onely bound by the Omnipotent God's Decree, not to work beyond her self, that is, beyond Matter; and since Matter is dividable, Nature is necessitated to move in Parts; for Matter can be without Parts, no more than Parts can be without a Whole; neither can Nature, being material, make her self void of figure; nor can she rest, being self-moving; but she is bound to divide and compose her several Parts into several particular figures, and dissolve and change those figures again infinite ways: All which proves the variety of Nature, which is so great, that even in one and the same species, none of the particulars resemble one another so much, as not to be discerned from each other.

But to return to Knowledg and Perception: I say, They are general and fundamental actions of Nature; it being not probable that the infinite parts of Nature should move so variously, nay, so orderly and methodically as they do, without knowing what they do, or why, and whether they move; and therefore all particular actions whatsoever in Nature, as Respiration, Digestion, Sympathy, Antipathy, Division, Composition, Pressure, Re-action, *&c.* are all particular perceptive and knowing actions: for, if a Part be divided from other Parts, both are sensible of their division: The like may be said of the composition of Parts: and as for Pressure and Re-action, they are as knowing and perceptive as any other particular actions; but yet this does not prove, that they are the principle of perception, and that there's no Perception but what is made by Pressure and Re-action;[1] or that at least they are the ground of Animal perception; for as they are no more but particular actions, so they have but particular perceptions: and although all Motion is sensible, yet no part is sensible but by its own motions in its own parts; that is, no corporeal

1 Cavendish critiques mechanical accounts of perception, which hinge on the random collision of tiny particles, as seen in the work of ancient atomists like Epicurus (341–270 BCE) and seventeenth-century mechanists like Thomas Hobbes (1588–1679).

motion is sensible but of or by it self. Therefore when a man moves a string, or tosses a ball, the string or ball is no more sensible of the motion of the hand, than the hand is of the motion of the string or ball; but the hand is onely an occasion that the string or ball moves thus or thus. I will not say, but that it may have some perception of the hand, according to the nature of its own figure; but it does not move by the hand's motion, but by its own: for there can be no Motion imparted without Matter or Substance.

Neither can I certainly affirm, that all Perception consists in patterning out exterior objects; for, although the perception of our human senses is made that way, yet Nature's actions being so various, I dare not conclude from thence, that all the perceptions of the infinitely various parts and figures of Nature are all made after the same manner.[1] Nevertheless, it is probable to sense and reason, that the infinite parts of Nature have not onely interior Self-knowledg, but also exterior perceptions of other figures or parts, and their actions; by reason there is a perpetual commerce and intercourse between parts and parts; and the chief actions of Nature, are Composition and Division, which produce all the variety of Nature; which proves, there must of necessity be perception between parts and parts: but, how all these particular perceptions are made, no particular Creature is able to know, by reason of their variety; for, as the actions of Nature vary, so do the perceptions. Therefore it is absurd to confine all perception of Nature, either to Pressure and Re-action, or to the Animal kind of perception; since even in one and the same Animal Sense, (as for example, of Seeing) there are numerous perceptions: for, every motion of the Eye, were it no more than a hair[']s breadth, causes a several perception: besides, it is not onely the Five Organs in an Animal, but every part and particle of his Body, that has a peculiar knowledg and perception, because it consists of Self-moving Matter; which if so, then a Looking-glass, that patterns out the face of a Man; and a Man's Eye, that patterns again the copy from the Glass, cannot be said to have the same perception; by reason a Glass, and an Animal, are different sorts of Creatures: for, though a piece of Wood, Stone, or Metal, may have a perceptive knowledg of Man, yet it hath not a Man's perception; because it is a Vegetable, or Mineral, and cannot have an Animal-knowledg

1 In other words, there might be many types of perception beyond what humans know or experience.

or perception, no more than the Eye patterning out a Tree or Stone, can be said to have a Vegetable or Mineral perception; ... and although sensitive and rational knowledg is general and infinite in infinite Nature, yet every part being finite, has but finite and particular perceptions ...

But some may say, If the particular parts of one composed figure, be so ignorant of each other's knowledg, as I have expressed, How can they agree in some action of the whole figure, where they must all be employed, and work agreeably to one effect? As for example, When the Mind designs to go to such a place, or do such a work, How can all the Parts agree in the performing of this act, if they be ignorant of each other[']s actions? I answer: Although every Part's knowledg and perception, is its own, and not another's, so that every Part knows by its own knowledg, and perceives by its own perception; yet it doth not follow from thence, That no Part has any more knowledg than of it self, or of its own actions: for, as I said before, it is well to be observed, That there being an entercourse and commerce, as also an acquaintance and agreement between Parts and Parts, there must also of necessity be some knowledg or perception betwixt them, that is, one Part must be able to perceive another Part, and the action of that same Part: for, wheresoever is life and knowledg, that is, sense and reason, there is also perception; and though no Part of Nature can have an absolute knowledg, yet it is neither absolutely ignorant; but it has a particular knowledg, and particular perceptions, according to the nature of its own innate and interior figure. In short; As there are several kinds, sorts and particular perceptions, and particular ignorances between parts, so there are more general perceptions between some parts, than between others; the like of ignorance: all which is according to the various actions of corporeal self-motion: But yet no part can have a thorow perception of all other parts and their actions, or be sure that that part which it perceives, has the like perception of it again; for, one part may perceive another part, and yet this part may be ignorant of that part, and its perception: For example, my Eye perceives an object, but that object is not necessitated to perceive my Eye again: also my Eye may perceive the pattern of it self made in a Looking-glass, and yet be ignorant whether the Glass do the like.... and, most commonly, one part judges of another's perception by its own; for, when one man perceives the actions of another man, he judges by those actions, what perceptions he has; so that judgement is but a comparing of actions ... Therefore perception of exterior objects, though it proceeds from an interior principle of Self-knowledg, yet it is nothing else but an observation of exterior parts or actions ...

But it is to be observed, That since there is a double perception[1] in the infinite Parts of Nature, Sensitive and Rational; the perception and information of the rational parts is more general, than of the sensitive, they being the most prudent, designing and governing parts of Nature, not so much encumbred with labouring on the inanimate parts of Matter, as the sensitive: Therefore the rational parts in a composed figure, or united action, may sooner have a general knowledg and information of the whole, than the sensitive, whose knowledg is more particular: As for example, A man may have a pain in one of the parts of his body, although the perception thereof is made by the sensitive corporeal motions in that same part, yet the next adjoining sensitive parts may be ignorant thereof, when as all the rational parts of the whole body may take notice of it. Thus the rational parts having a more general acquaintance than the sensitive, and being also the designing and architectonical parts, they employ the sensitive parts to work to the same effect; but these are not always ready to obey, but force sometimes the Rational to obey them, which we call Irregularity; which is nothing but an opposition or strife between parts: As for example, A man designs to employ the exterior strength and action of his exterior parts; but if through irregularity, the legs and arms be weak, the stomack sick, the head full of pain; they will not agree to the executing of the commands of the Rational Parts. Likewise, the mind endeavours often to keep the sensitive motions of the body from dissolution; but they many times follow the Mode, and imitate other objects, or cause a dissolution or division of that composed figure by voluntary actions.

Thus the Sensitive and Rational Motions do oftentimes cross and oppose each other: for, although several parts are united in one body, yet are they not always bound to agree in one action; nor can it be otherwise; for, were there no disagreement between them, there would be no irregularities, and consequently no pain or sickness, nor no dissolution of any natural figure.[2]

And such an agreement and disagreement, is not onely betwixt the rational and sensitive parts, but also betwixt the rational and

---

1 On "double perception," see *Grounds*, p. 69.

2 Cavendish probably means that certain types of dissolution are irregular, given that she views the uniting and dissolution of parts as a perpetual, necessary, and hence regular function of natural matter.

rational, the sensitive and sensitive. For some rational Parts, may in one composed figure, have opposite actions; As for example, the Mind of man may be divided, so as to hate one person, and love another: nay, hate and love one and the same person, for several things, at the same time: as also, rejoice and grieve at the same time.... also, there are advantages and disadvantages amongst Parts, according to the several sorts of corporeal figurative motions; so that some sorts of corporeal motions, although fewer or weaker, may overpower others that are more numerous and strong; but the rational being the most subtil, active, observing and inspective Parts, have, for the most part, more power over the sensitive, than the sensitive have over them; which makes that they, for the most part, work regularly, and cause all the orderly and regular compositions, dissolutions, changes and varieties in the infinite Parts of Nature: Besides, their perception and observation being more general, it lasts longer; for, the rational continue the Perception of the past actions of the sensitive, when as the sensitive keep no such Records.

Some say, That Perception is made by the Ideas of exterior objects entring into the organs of the Sentient; but this opinion cannot be probable to sense and reason:[1] For, first, If Ideas subsist of themselves, then they must have their own figures; and so the figures of the objects would not be perceived, but onely the figures of the Ideas. But if those Ideas be the figures of the objects themselves, then by entring into our Sensories,[2] the objects would lose them; for one single object, can have no more but one exterior figure at one time, which surely it cannot lose and keep, at one and the same time. But if it be a print of the object on the Air, it is impossible there could be such several sorts of Prints as there are Perceptions, without a notable confusion.[3] Besides, when I consider the little Passages, (as in the sense of

---

1 Seventeenth-century scholastic philosophers believed that perception entails the replication or "multiplication" of the object perceived, or the production of an incorporeal form that travels through the air and then "into the organs of the sentient." As Cavendish goes on to suggest, this leads to questions about how these forms could exist without substance and, if they were material, how they could endlessly replicate.

2 Our sensory organs.

3 For similar responses, see Kenelm Digby (1603–65), First Treatise: Sect. 32, Ch. 9; Joseph Glanvill (1636–80), *Scepsis Scientifica*, Ch. VI.

Touch) the Pores of the flesh, through which they must enter, I cannot readily believe it: nay, the Motions and Prints would grow so weak, and faint in their journey, especially if the object be a great way off, as they would become of no effect. But if their opinion be, That Ideas can change and alter, then all immaterial substances may do the same, and spirits may change and alter into several immaterial figures; which, in my opinion cannot be: for what is supernatural, is unalterable; and therefore the opinion of Ideas in perception, is as irregular, as the opinion of senseless Atoms in the framing of a Regular World.[1]

Again, Some of our Modern Philosophers are of opinion, That the subject wherein Colour and Image are inherent, is not the object or thing seen; for Image and Colour, say they, may be there where the thing seen, is not:[2] As for example, The Sun, and other visible objects, by reflexion in Water or Glass; so that there is nothing without us, really, which we call Image or Colour: for the Image or Colour, is but an apparition unto us, of the motion and agitation which the object works in the brain or spirits; and divers times men see directly the same object double, as two Candles for one, and the like. To which I answer, That all this doth not prove that the object is not perceived, or that an object can be without Image or Colour, or that figure and colour are not the same with the object; but it proves, that the object enters not the Eye, but is onely patterned out by the perceptive motions in the optick sense; for the reflection of the Sun in Water or Glass, is but a Copy of the Original, made by the figurative perceptive motions in the Glass or Water, which may pattern out an object as well as we do; which Copy is patterned out again by our optick perception, and so one Copy is made by another. The truth is, Our optick sense could not perceive either the Original, or Copy of an exterior object, if it did not make those figures in its own parts: and therefore figure and colour are both in the Object, and the Eye; and not, as they say, neither in the Object, nor in the Eye; for, though I grant that one thing cannot be in two places at once,

---

1 Cavendish disputes the existence of "senseless" or irrational atoms by claiming that these could lead only to chaos; see *Observations* 125–31.

2 Cavendish refers to mechanical philosophers like René Descartes (1596–1650) and Hobbes. Descartes suggests that the images and colors we perceive are merely ideas in our minds, while Hobbes claims that they are "phantasms." See Hobbes, *De Corpore*, Part IV: Ch. 25.

yet there may be several Copies made of one Original, in several parts, which are several places, at one and the same time; which is more probable, than that figure and colour should neither be in the Object, nor in the Eye; or, according to their own words, that figure and Colour should be there, where the thing seen is not; which is to separate it from the Object, a thing against all possibility, sense and reason; or else, that a substanceless and senseless Motion, should make a progressive journey from the Object to the Sentient, and there print, figure and colour upon the optick sense, by a bare agitation or concussion, so that the perception or apparition (as they call it) of an Object, should onely be according to the stroke the Agitation makes: As for example, the perception of Light, after such a manner, figure after such, and colour after another; for, if Motion be no substance or body, and besides, void of sense, not knowing what it acts, I cannot conceive how it should make such different strokes upon both the sensitive organ, and the brain, and all so orderly, that every thing is perceived differently and distinctly. Truly, this opinion is like *Epicurus*'s of Atoms;[1] but how absurd it is to make senseless Corpuscles, the cause of Sense and Reason, and consequently of perception, is obvious to every one's apprehension, and needs no demonstration.

[...]

As for Sleep, they call it a privation of the act of Sense:[2] To which I can no ways give my consent, because I believe sense to be a perpetual corporeal self-motion, without any rest. Neither do I think the senses can be lockt up in sleep: for, if they be self-moving, they cannot be shut up; it being as impossible to deprive self-motion of acting, as to destroy its nature; but if they have no self-motion, they need no locking up at all, because it would be

1 Epicurus, a Greek philosopher whose materialistic and atomistic account of nature became widely debated in seventeenth-century England. According to Roman poet and philosopher Lucretius (c. 99–55 BCE), who preserved Epicurean doctrine in his poem *De rerum natura*, Epicurus also suggested that perception occurs when these tiny particles penetrate our senses.

2 Cavendish refers to Hobbes's claim that "sleep is the privation of the act of sense." See Hobbes, *Elements of Law*, Part I: Ch. 3, Sect. 2. For more on dreaming, see his *Leviathan* 43–46. See also Descartes, *Principles of Philosophy*, Part IV: Sect. 196.

their nature to rest, as being moveless. In short, Sense being Self-motion, can neither rest nor cease; for what they call Cessation, is nothing else but an alteration of corporeal self-motion: and thus Cessation will require as much a self-moving Agent, as all other actions of Nature.

Lastly, say they, It is impossible for sense to imagine a thing past;[1] for sense is onely of things present. I answer, 'Tis true, by reason the sensitive corporeal motions work on, and with the parts of inanimate Matter; nevertheless, when a repetition is made of the same actions, and the same parts, it is a sensitive remembrance; and thus is also Experience made; which proves, there is a sensitive perception and self-knowledg, because the senses are well acquainted with those objects they have often figured or patterned out: And to give a further demonstration thereof, we see that the senses are amazed, and sometimes frighted at such objects as are unusual, or have never been presented to them before. In short, Conception, Imagination, Remembrance, Experience, Observation, and the like, are all made by corporeal, self-knowing, perceptive self-motion, and not by insensible, irrational, dull, and moveless Matter.

1 On "a thing past; which is impossible to sense," see Hobbes, *Elements of Law*, Part I: Ch. 3, Sect. 6. On "decaying sense" as it relates to memory and dreams, see *Leviathan* 41–44.

Appendix C: Selections from Contemporary Philosophers

[Starting in the Restoration period, Cavendish dedicated herself to reading and critiquing contemporary philosophy. In her 1664 *Philosophical Letters*, for instance, she assesses at length the philosophical doctrines of Jan Baptist van Helmont (1580–1644), Henry More (1614–87), Thomas Hobbes (1588–1679), René Descartes (1596–1650), Walter Charleton (1619–1707), and Galileo (1564–1642). In *Observations upon Experimental Philosophy* (1666; 1668), she critiques both speculative and experimental philosophy, targeting authors like Descartes, Hobbes, Robert Hooke (1635–1703), Henry Power (1623–68), and Robert Boyle (1627–91). Similarly, in *Grounds*, Cavendish pits her organic materialist view of nature and the human body in direct competition with the work of these learned men, especially van Helmont, More, and Hobbes. Although not widely known today, van Helmont and More were deeply influential in late-seventeenth-century England; Cavendish disagrees fundamentally with both of these thinkers on most issues, including the existence of spirits in nature and the commingling of philosophy and theology.

The English translation of van Helmont's work *Oriatrike* (1662), which Cavendish read sometime between 1662 and 1664, outlines his chemical-vitalist natural philosophy as well as his controversial views toward medicine (including magnetic healing).[1] As Cavendish noticed, van Helmont tended toward difficult, sometimes intractable prose, while he also unceremoniously exploded the foundations of ancient philosophy (including the doctrine of the four elements and the related humoral theory of medicine). Cavendish also found herself at odds with More, whose vitalist philosophy depended on the "Spirit of Nature," an immaterial, living substance that binds and controls the universe but does not itself know or perceive. However, we should note that More's interest in spiritual phenomena does not signal that he was not "modern": most thinkers of the period espoused spiritual entities of some kind and considered the rigorous materialism

1 See *Oriatrike* 756–93; Cavendish critiques this idea extensively in *Philosophical Letters* (e.g., 242, 290, 299, 320, 334).

of Cavendish and Hobbes as a form of atheism. Cavendish was familiar with a new edition of More's collected works published in 1662, which included *An Antidote against Atheism* and *The Immortality of the Soul*.]

1. From Henry More, *A Collection Of Several Philosophical Writings of Dr. Henry More* (London, 1662)

The Preface general.

... That there is a *Spirit of Nature*, that is to say, a substance incorporeal that does interesse it self in the bringing about some more general *Phænomena* in the World, I think I have demonstrated so evidently that nothing can be more evident in Philosophy. Nor can a man doubt but that it is an *Universal* Principle, if he consider the *nature of God* and the *Divine Fecundity*, and the *use of this Spirit* whereever there is Matter manageable to some serviceable end for the good of the whole Creation; besides those Testimonies of its Omnipresence, if I may so speak, it doing the same things at vast Distances. As for example, It remands down a stone toward the Center of the Earth as well when the Earth is in *Aries* as in *Libra*, keeps the Waters from swilling out of the Moon, curbs the matter of the Sun into roundness of figure, which would otherwise be oblong, restrains the crusty parts of a Star from flying apieces into the circumambient Æther,[1] carries along those large Regions of looser Particles of the third Element, together with the Comets, in their peregrinations from *Vortex* to *Vortex*, every where directs the magnetick Atoms in their right Rode; besides all the *Plastick* services it does both in Plants and Animals.[2]

This therefore being a mute copy of the eternal *Word* (that is, of that Divine Wisedome that is entirely everywhere) is in every part naturally appointed to doe all the best services that Matter is capable of, according to such or such modifications,

---

1 In ancient and medieval science, "aether," or ether, refers to the substance that fills the province of the universe that lies beyond the terrestrial sphere. In the seventeenth and eighteenth centuries, thinkers like Isaac Newton (1643–1727) draw on the concept of ether to explain motion at a distance (and, specifically, gravity).

2 More refers to Descartes's vortex theory of planetary motion; see *Principles of Philosophy*, Part III. By "Plastick services," he means the animating motions that allow creatures to live, grow, and change and that, for him, originate from the soul.

and according to that *Platform* of which it is the *Transcript*, I mean according to the Comprehension and Purpose of those Ideas of things which are in the eternal Intellect of God. Whence it is plain, That there need be no other ... *Seminal Forms*, th[a]n this one, which virtually contains all everywhere, and is therefore rightly styled *The Universal Spirit of Nature*: As also, That this Spirit need not be *perceptive* it self, it being the *natural Transcript* of that which is *knowing* or *perceptive*, and is the lowest *Substantial Activity* from the all-wise God, containing in it certain general Modes and Lawes of Nature for the good of the Universe. But the Eye of particular Providence is not therein. Else why does a tyle[1] fall upon the head of him that passes by in the streets, goe he to either Play or Sermon? And how come those bungles in monstrous productions, or those inept and self-thwarting Attempts of this Spirit in certain experiments about the finding out a *Vacuum*?[2] as I have particularly noted in my *Antidote*.[3] Wherefore neither Omnipotency nor Omnisciency acts in such cases, but this *imperceptive* Spirit of Nature. Whose *Imperceptiveness* is no more Obstacle to her *natural* and *plastical Operations*, then the Soul's having *no actual Idea* of a thing aforehand is an hinderance of her *occasional perceptions*, as I have already intimated in my * Preface to my Treatise of the *Soul's Immortality*.

Which things well considered and allow'd, that special Office of this *Spirit of Nature* in conducting of souls in their *State of Silence*, to actuate prepared Matter, and so to raise Animals into Life, will easily be conceived as becoming an employment as any of the rest, and not at all more difficult. For how much harder is it to apprehend that the *Spirit of Nature* may direct or carry down a *silent Soul*, then a *dead stone*, to their fit and natural abodes?[4] For the *liveless Spirit* and the *dead stone* are alike easy to be taken hold upon, the *Spirit of Nature* penetrating them both alike; and *body* slipping up and down so easily in this Spirit of the World, as that it cannot be imagined that any *Mechanical* power, but that only which is truly called

---

1 Tile.

2 In opposition to others like Hooke, More suggested that this spirit was necessary to explain the operation of a vacuum, or empty space.

3 *An Antidote against Atheism* (1655).

4 Essentially, More asks: If we believe that rocks fall to the ground, controlled by the spirit of nature, then why would it be difficult to believe that the spirit of nature can also convey human souls into the afterlife?

Sympathetical, must be the Tye where any hold is taken.[1] Which Tye catches and lets goe, for the direction and transmission of things to their proper places in the several parts of the World for the good of the Whole, according to that Essential Law which is the Form and Being of this *Spirit of Nature*, the last Ideal or *Omniform Efflux* from God.[2] Nor is it, as I have already said, any thing more marvellous that a *liveless* soul should by this *imperceptive* Spirit of Nature be carried away and conducted to duly-prepared Matter, then that a *dead* Stone or the *sensless* Magnetick Particles should be guided thereby. For that whereby the Soul is catched so fast by its particular Body is not the *perceptive* part thereof, but the *plastick* or *natural*; else in a pet[3] she might easily leave the body without either hanging, drowning or stabbing. Why then may not a Spirit, that has subtiler fingers then the finest Matter, I mean the *Spirit of Nature*, lay hold on that *imperceptive* part of the Soul, or on the Soul it self, in the state of *Silence* or *Imperception*, and by the *sympathy* and *coactivity* of its own Essence carry her away to such services as either her self had deserved or the Universe required? All which things though I will not assert as true, yet I dare pronounce them as intelligible as the Union of the Soul with the Body, which experience makes us understand whether we will or no....

An Antidote against Atheism, Book III, Chapter XVI

... I do not here appeal to the *Complexional* humors or peculiar Relishes of men that arise out of the temper of the *Body*, but to the known and unalterable *Ideas* of the *Mind*, to the *Phœnomena* of *Nature* and Records of *History*. Upon the last whereof if I have something more fully insisted,[4] it is not to be imputed to any vain credulity of mine, or that I take a pleasure in telling strange stories, but that I thought fit to fortifie and strengthen the faith of others as much as I could; being well assured that a contemptuous misbelief of such like Narrations concerning *Spirits*, and an endeavour of making them all ridiculous and incredible, is

---

1 That is, mechanism cannot explain all natural phenomena or the migration of souls.

2 Appearing or manifest in all forms.

3 Fit or tantrum.

4 More dedicated significant time to cataloguing stories of witchcraft and paranormal activity; e.g., see Book III of his *Antidote*. Later, he would contribute another register of such stories in his "Letter" to Glanvill's well-known *Saducismus triumphatus* (1681).

a dangerous Prelude to *Atheism* it self, or else a more close and crafty possession and insinuation of it. For assuredly that Saying is not more true in Politicks, *No Bishop, no King*; then this is in Metaphysicks, *No Spirit, no God.*

The Immortality of the Soul, The Third Book, Chapter XII

... *The Spirit of Nature therefore, according to that notion I have of it, is, A substance incorporeal, but without Sense and Animadversion, pervading the whole Matter of the Universe, and exercising a Plastical power therein according to the sundry predispositions and occasions in the parts it works upon, raising such* Phænomena *in the World, by directing the parts of the Matter and their Motion, as cannot be resolved into mere Mechanical powers.* This rude Description may serve to convey to any one a conception determinate enough of the nature of the thing. And that it is not a mere Notion, but a real Being ...

2. From Jan Baptist van Helmont, *Oriatrike* (London, 1662)

Chapter V: The Chief or Master-Workman.

I Have touched at the birth and Causes of Natural things, and least I may seem to have placed the efficient Cause, undeservedly within, I will the more fitly explain the Workman, the Vulcan or Smith of generations.

Whatsoever therefore cometh into the World by Nature, it must needs have the Beginning of its motions, the stirrer up, and inward directer of generation. Therefore all things however hard and thick they are, yet before that their soundness, they inclose in themselves an Air, which before generation, representeth the inward future generation to the Seed, in this respect fruitful, and accompanies the thing generated, even to the end of the Stage.[1]

Which air, although in some things it be more plentiful: yet in Vegetables it is pressed together in the shew of a juyce; as

1 For van Helmont, air and water are the only two primary elements. Generation occurs when the *archeus*, a spiritual entity, "stirs up" air and seminal matter, or seed, thereby creating new forms (with the next, "future generation" enclosed in all creatures at the time of its generation). This concept derives from Swiss physician and alchemist Paracelsus (1493/94–1541), who similarly maintained that the *archeus* was a vital or seminal power that made seeds fertile.

also in Mettals it is thickned with a most thick homogeniety or sameliness of kinde: notwithstanding, this gift hath happened to all things, which is called the *Archeus*, or chief Workman, containing the fruitfulness of generations and Seeds, as it were the internal efficient cause. I say, that Workman hath the likeness of the thing generated, unto the beginning whereof, he composeth the appointments of things to be done.

But the chief Workman consists of the conjoyning of the vitall air, as of the matter, with the seminal likeness; which is the more inward spiritual kernel, containing the fruitfulness of the Seed; but the visible Seed is onely the husk of this. This Image of the Master-Workman, issuing out of the first shape or Idea of its predecessour, or snatching the same to it self, out of the cup or bosom of outward things, is not a certain dead Image: but made famous by a full knowledge, and adorned with necessary powers of things to be done in its appointment; and so it is the first or chief Instrument of life and feeling. For example. For a Woman with Child, fashioneth a Cherry in her Young, by her desire, in that part, in which she moveth her hand in desiring.

A Cherry, I say in the flesh, true, green, pale, yellow, and red, according to the stations,[1] in which the Trees do promote their Cherries. And the same Cherry sooner waxeth red in the same Young, in *Spain*, than in the Low-Countries. Therefore a Cherry is made by Imagination: So through the Imagination of lust, a vitall Image of living Creatures is brought over into the Spirit of the Seed, being about to unfold it self by the course of generation.[2]

But since every corporeal act is limited into a Body, hence it comes to passe, that the *Archeus*, the Workman and Governour of generation, doth cloath himself presently with a bodily cloathing: For in things soulified,[3] he walketh thorow all the Dens and retiring places of his Seed, and begins to transform the matter, according to the perfect act of his own Image. For here he placeth the heart, but there he appoints the brain, and he every where limiteth an unmoveable chief dweller, out of his

1 Stages.

2 For van Helmont, imagination has real, physical effects. In this case, the female imagination produces a material excrescence or bud, which is then worked upon by the *archeus*.

3 I.e., creatures with souls.

whole Monarchy, according to the bounds of requirance, of the parts, and of appointments.

At length, that President, remains the overseer; and inward ruler of his bounds, even until death. But the other floating about, being assigned to no member, keeps the oversight over the particular Pilots of the members, being clear, and never at rest or keeping holyday.[1]

Moreover, as sublunary things, do express in themselves an Analogy or proportion of things above: So every thing, by how much the more lively it is, by so much the more perfectly it imitates the Stars, so that sick persons do seem to carry in themselves sensible *Ephemeries*, or daily *Registers*,[2] being skilful of future seasons. Indeed in the bowels, the planetary Spirits do most shine forth, even as also, in the whole influous[3] *Archeus*, the courses and forces of the Firmament[4] do appear.

But the first mover, hath no where had a member in men: but onely under the *Archeus* of the wombe, it meets by meditating by way of similitude, as it were in the last finishing of created things. For happily a Woman is therefore more stirred, or troubled in her first Conceptions, as she drawes with her, other Orbs, by her first motions. As often as the wombe being swollen, with the ascending Rule of Imagination, doth suffer an animosity, or angry heat, it snatcheth the particular *Archeusses* of the bowels into the obedience of it self, by striving to excel manly weaknesses, and for the most part, wretchedly deludes Physitians with a feigned Image.[5] The Archeusses of bruit[6] Beasts, are almost like unto man[']s. Neither shall we draw an unprofitable knowledge of the shop of simples, from the difference of Plants, and their Sexes. Because neither is it without a Mystery, that in creeping things and insects being born in corruption alone, Nature invariously sporting her self, intends nothing so seriously, as the proportionable differences of Sexes on both sides....

---

1 Observing holy days with rest.

2 Tables that chart the positions of celestial objects.

3 Likely "influential."

4 The heavens or sky.

5 Van Helmont describes morning sickness as the influence of the powerful *archeus* of the womb, which commands all other *archeuses* of the body.

6 Brute.

Chapter XIV: The Blas[1] of Meteours.

THE Stars are to us for signes, times or seasons, dayes and years. Therefore they cause the changes, seasons, and successive courses or interchanges. To which end, they have need of a twofold motion, to wit, locall, and alterative. But I signifie both these by the new name of Blas. And they do rather stir up a Blas by their mooving through a place, than by their light. Indeed in a dark night, the South winde oft-times followeth the blowing North-windes, and this likewise, it. Therefore because Blas breaths forth a luke-warm winde, it hath need, not of the heat or light of Heaven it self; but of place, direction and connexion. Whither, when the light of the Stars shall descend, the folding-doores do open and shut themselves.

Therefore let the Key-keeper of the folding-doores, be the motion of the Stars. Which also moveth the Peroledes[2] or Pavements of the Air. Therefore all heat is not made by fore-existing fire, or light, nor doth cold shew a naked absence of heat: But the motive Blas of the Stars, is a pulsive or beating power or virtue, in respect of their Journey through places, and according to their aspects. Which circumstances in the Stars, do cause the first qualities on these inferiour bodies; no otherwise than bashfulness, anger, fear, *&c.* do stir up cold and heat in men. And that thing the Stars have by the gift of Creation.

The Winde according to *Hypocrates*,[3] is a flowing Water of the Air: but I defining it by its causes, say, that the Winde is a flowing Air, mooved by the Blas of the Stars. And that for a naturall winde: but otherwise, it is often granted to an evill Spirit, that even without a Blas he should stir up windes, or increase a tempestuous Blas. Therefore the Air, unless it have a Blas, remains quiet, nor hath it the principle of motion from it self, but it comes to it from elsewhere. Therefore the motive Blas stirreth up Windes, Tempests, over-flowing of Waters, by running thorow the divers Peroledes of the Air, sometimes upwards, sometimes downwards, across, long-wayes, side-wayes, into all the Coasts

---

1 While van Helmont's concept of "blas," or elemental, celestial motion, is abstruse, the general idea that the motion of the stars controlled the mechanism of the universe was not unusual. Van Helmont also suggested that there was a "Blas of man," which has some overlaps with the *archeus*.

2 Layers.

3 Hippocrates (460–370 BCE), Greek physician.

of the Earth: although the Elements have no need of motion, yet man[']s necessity requireth that motion.

But seeing nothing was for mooving of it self (except the Archeus granted to seedes) it hath well pleased the Eternall, to place in the Stars, a flatuous, violent, motive force, not much unlike to the Command of his mouth. So that Blas is for a testimony to us, that God of his excelling goodness, hath made the Elements, and Stars for us, by measuring out bounds of these according to our Commodities. Blas therefore mooveth, not so much by light beames, and motion, as motion: but as the Stars have come down unto certain places, whereunto these Stars do owe their offices.... Blas therefore as a Masculine thing in the Stars, is the generall beginning of motion; it seemes no lesse to respect the Earth, than the Air and Water.[1] ...

Chapter XVIII: The Fiction of Elementary Complexions and Mixtures.

I Have said, that there are two primary Elements;[2] the Air, and the Water; because they do not return into each other: but, that the Earth is as it were born of water; because it may be reduced into water. But if water be changed into an Earthy Body, that happens by the force or virtue of the Seed, and so it hath then put of the simpleness of an Element. For a flint is of water, which is broken asunder into Sand. But surely, that Sand doth lesse resist in its reducing into water, than the Sand, which is the Virgin-Earth. Therefore the Sand of Marble, of a Gemme, or Flint, do disclose the presence of the Seed. But if the Virgin-earth, may at length, by much labour be brought into water, and if it was in the beginning created as an Element; yet it seemes then to have come down to something that is more simple than it selfe; and therefore I have called those two, Primary ones. I have denied the fire to be an Element and Substance; but to be death in the hand of the Artificer, given for great uses. I say, an artificial Death for Arts, which the Almighty hath created, but not a natural one.

But now I take upon me to demonstrate, that Bodies which are believed to be mixt are materially the fruits of water onely;

---

1 That is, it influences the earth as much as the atmosphere and oceans.

2 Unlike most other thinkers of his era, van Helmont rejected entirely the ancient doctrine of the four elements (air, water, earth, and fire).

neither that they have need of the Wedlock of another Element: to wit, that Bodies, whether they are dark, or clear, sound, or fluide, bodies of one and the same kinde, [...] or those that are unlike; Suppose them to be Stones, Sulphurs, Mettalls, Hony, wax, Oils, a Bone, the Brain, a Grisle, Wood, Barke, Leaves: lastly, that all things, and all particular things, are wholly reduced into a water, altogether without savour, and so that they do consist, and are contained in simple water onely ...

Works Cited and Select Bibliography

Adams, Marcus P. "Visual Perception as Patterning: Cavendish against Hobbes on Sensation." *History of Philosophy Quarterly*, vol. 33, no. 3, 2017, pp. 193–214.

Akkerman, Nadine, and Marguérite Corporaal. "Mad Science Beyond Flattery: The Correspondence of Margaret Cavendish and Constantijn Huygens." *Ashgate Critical Essays on Women Writers in England, 1550–1700: Vol. 7: Margaret Cavendish*, edited by Sara H. Mendelson, Ashgate, 2009, pp. 263–304.

Anstey, Peter. "Boyle against Thinking Matter." *Late Medieval and Early Modern Corpuscular Matter Theories*, edited by Christoph Lüthy, John E. Murdoch, and William R. Newman, Brill, 2001, pp. 483–514.

Boyle, Deborah. "Freedom and Necessity in the Work of Margaret Cavendish." *Women and Liberty, 1600–1800: Philosophical Essays*, edited by Jacqueline Broad and Karen Detlefsen, Oxford UP, 2017, pp. 141–62.

——. "Margaret Cavendish on the Eternity of Created Matter." *Early Modern Women on Metaphysics*, edited by Emily Thomas, Cambridge UP, 2018, pp. 111–30.

——. *The Well-Ordered Universe: The Philosophy of Margaret Cavendish*. Oxford UP, 2107.

Broad, Jacqueline. "Cavendish, van Helmont, and the Mad Raging Womb." *The New Science and Women's Literary Discourse: Prefiguring Frankenstein*, edited by Judy A. Hayden, Palgrave Macmillan, 2011, pp. 47–63.

——. "Margaret Cavendish and Joseph Glanvill: Science, Religion, and Witchcraft." *Studies in History and Philosophy of Science*, vol. 38, no. 3, 2007, pp. 493–505.

Cavendish, Margaret, Duchess of Newcastle. *The Description of a New World, Called the Blazing World*, edited by Sara Mendelson, Broadview, 2016.

——. *Grounds of Natural Philosophy*. London, 1668.

——. *The Life of ... William Cavendishe, Duke, Marquess, and Earl of Newcastle*. London, 1667.

——. *Observations upon Experimental Philosophy*. 1666. Edited by Eileen O'Neill, Cambridge UP, 2001.

——. *Orations of Divers Sorts*. London, 1662.

——. *Philosophical Letters*. London, 1664.

——. *Philosophical and Physical Opinions*. London, 1655.
——. *Philosophical and Physical Opinions*. London, 1663.
——. *Philosophicall Fancies*. London, 1653.
——. *Sociable Letters*, edited by James Fitzmaurice, Broadview, 2004.
——. "A True Relation of my Birth, Breeding, and Life." *Paper Bodies: A Margaret Cavendish Reader*, edited by Sylvia Bowerbank and Sara Mendelson, Broadview, 2000, pp. 41–63.
Cavendish, William, Duke of Newcastle, editor. *Letters and Poems in Honour of the Incomparable Princess, Margaret, Duchess of Newcastle*. London, 1676.
Clucas, Stephen. "'A double Perception in All Creatures': Margaret Cavendish's *Philosophical Letters* and Seventeenth-Century Natural Philosophy." *God and Nature in the Thought of Margaret Cavendish*, edited by Brandie R. Siegfried and Lisa T. Sarasohn, Routledge, 2016, pp. 121–40.
——. "Margaret Cavendish's Materialist Critique of Van Helmontian Chymistry." *AMBIX*, vol. 58, no. 1, 1995, pp. 1–12.
——. "Variation, Irregularity and Probabilism: Margaret Cavendish and Natural Philosophy as Rhetoric." *A Princely Brave Woman: Essays on Margaret Cavendish, Duchess of Newcastle*, edited by Stephen Clucas, Ashgate, 2003, pp. 199–209.
Cottegnies, Line. "Brilliant Heterodoxy: The Plurality of Worlds in Margaret Cavendish's *Blazing World* (1666) and Cyrano de Bergerac's *Estats et Empires de la lune* (1657)." *God and Nature in the Thought of Margaret Cavendish*, edited by Brandie R. Siegfried and Lisa T. Sarasohn, Routledge, 2016, pp. 107–20.
Cowley, Abraham. "To the Royal Society." *The History of the Royal-Society of London*, by Thomas Sprat. London, 1667. Sig. B[1r]–B[3v].
Cunning, David. *Cavendish*. Routledge, 2016.
——. "Cavendish on the Intelligibility of the Prospect of Thinking Matter." *History of Philosophy Quarterly*, vol. 23, no. 2, 2006, pp. 117–36.
——. "Margaret Lucas Cavendish." *Stanford Encyclopedia of Philosophy*, edited by Edward N. Zalta, 2017, plato.stanford.edu/archives/sum2017/entries/margaret-cavendish. Accessed 22 August 2018.
Descartes, René. *Meditations on First Philosophy*. 1641. Translated by Ian Johnston, edited by Andrew Bailey, Broadview, 2013.

——. *Principles of Philosophy*. 1644. *The Philosophical Writings of Descartes*, translated and edited by John Cottingham, Robert Stoothoff, and Dugold Murdoch, Cambridge UP, 1985, pp. 177–292.

Detlefsen, Karen. "Atomism, Monism, and Causation in the Natural Philosophy of Margaret Cavendish." *Oxford Studies in Early Modern Philosophy*, edited by Daniel Garber and Steven Nadler, Clarendon P, 2006, vol. 3, pp. 199–240.

——. "Margaret Cavendish on the Relationship between God and World." *Philosophy Compass*, vol. 4, no. 3, 2009, pp. 421–38.

Digby, Kenelm. *Two Treatises*. London, 1645.

Duncan, Stewart. "Debating Materialism: Cavendish, Hobbes, and More." *History of Philosophy Quarterly*, vol. 29, no. 4, 2012, pp. 391–409.

Fitzmaurice, James. "Margaret Cavendish on Her Own Writing: Evidence from Revision and Handmade Correction." *Papers of the Bibliographical Society of America*, vol. 85, no. 3, 1991, pp. 297–308.

——. "Margaret Cavendish Writing Fiction in Antwerp: Observers, Observation, and the Visual Arts." *Research Companion to the Cavendishes*. Unpublished.

——. "Some Problems in Editing Margaret Cavendish." *Papers of the Renaissance Text Society, 1985–1991: New Ways of Looking at Old Texts*, edited by W. Speed Hill, Medieval and Renaissance Texts and Studies, 1993, pp. 253–61.

Glanvill, Joseph. *Lux Orientalis*. London, 1662.

——. *Scepsis Scientifica*. London, 1665.

Grant, Douglas. *Margaret the First: A Biography of Margaret Cavendish, Duchess of Newcastle 1623–1673*. U of Toronto P, 1957.

——, editor. *The Phanseys of William Cavendish, Marquis of Newcastle, Addressed to Margaret Lucas, and Her Letters in Reply*. Nonesuch P, 1956.

Hobbes, Thomas. *The Elements of Law, Natural and Politic*. 1640. Edited by J.C.A. Gaskin, Oxford UP, 1990.

——. *Elements of Philosophy the first section, concerning body* [*De Corpore*]. London, 1656.

——. *The English Works of Thomas Hobbes of Malmesbury*. Vol. 4, edited by William Molesworth, London, 1840.

——. *Leviathan*. 1651. Edited by A.P. Martinich and Brian Battiste, Broadview, 2010.

——. *On the Citizen* [*De Cive*]. 1642. Edited by Richard Tuck and Michael Silverthorne, Cambridge UP, 1998.

Hutton, Sarah. *Anne Conway: A Woman Philosopher.* Cambridge UP, 2009.

——. "In Dialogue with Thomas Hobbes: Margaret Cavendish's Natural Philosophy." *Women's Writing*, vol. 3, no. 3, 1997, pp. 421–32.

——. "John Finch, Thomas Hobbes, and Margaret Cavendish." *Anne Conway: A Woman Philosopher*, edited by Sarah Hutton, Cambridge UP, 2009, pp. 94–115.

——. "Margaret Cavendish and Henry More." *A Princely Brave Woman: Essays on Margaret Cavendish, Duchess of Newcastle*, edited by Stephen Clucas, Ashgate, 2003, pp. 185–98.

Hutton, Sarah, and Marjorie Hope Nicolson, eds. *The Conway Letters: The Correspondence of Anne, Viscountess Conway, Henry More, and Their Friends, 1642–1684.* Clarendon P, 1992.

Keller, Eve. "Producing Petty Gods: Margaret Cavendish's Critique of Experimental Science." *ELH*, vol. 64, no. 2, 1997, pp. 447–71.

Killeen, Kevin. "Microscopy, Surfaces, and the Unknowable in Seventeenth-Century Natural Philosophy (from Lucretius to Margaret Cavendish)." *Journal of the Northern Renaissance*, vol. 8, 2017, www.northernrenaissance.org/microscopy-surfaces-and-the-unknowable-in-seventeenth-century-natural-philosophy-from-lucretius-to-margaret-cavendish/. Accessed 22 January 2019.

Lascano, Marcy P. Review of *The Well-Ordered Universe. Mind*, vol. 128, no. 509, 2018, pp. 1–9.

Lewis, Rhodri. "Of 'Origenian Platonisme': Joseph Glanvill on the Pre-existence of Souls." *Huntington Library Quarterly*, vol. 69, no. 2, 2006, pp. 267–300.

Locke, John. *An Essay Concerning Human Understanding.* 1689. Edited by Peter H. Nidditch, Clarendon P, 1975.

Lokhorst, Gert-Jan. "Descartes and the Pineal Gland." *The Stanford Encyclopedia of Philosophy*, edited by Edward N. Zalta, 2017, plato.stanford.edu/archives/win2017/entries/pineal-gland/. Accessed 22 August 2018.

Lucretius. *De Rerum Natura: The Latin Text of Lucretius.* Edited by William Ellery Leonard and Stanley Barney Smith, U of Wisconsin P, 2008.

Mendelson, Sara. "The God of Nature and the Nature of God." *God and Nature in the Thought of Margaret Cavendish*, edited by Brandie R. Siegfried and Lisa T. Sarasohn, Routledge, 2016, pp. 27–42.

——. "Introduction." Cavendish, *Blazing World* 9–49.

Michaelian, Kourken. "Margaret Cavendish's Epistemology." *British Journal for the History of Philosophy*, vol. 17, no. 1, 2009, pp. 31–53.

More, Henry. *A Collection of Several Philosophical Writings*. 2nd ed., London, 1662.

O'Neill, Eileen. "Introduction." *Observations upon Experimental Philosophy, by Margaret Cavendish*. Edited by Eileen O'Neill, Cambridge UP, 2001, pp. x–xxxvi.

——. "Margaret Cavendish, Stoic Antecedent Causes, and Early Modern Occasional Causes." *Revue philosophique de la France et de l'étranger*, vol. 138, no. 3, 2013, pp. 311–26.

Peterman, Alison. "Canonizing Cavendish." *HOPOS: Journal of the International Society for the History of Science*, vol. 8, 2018, pp. 191–97.

Poole, William. "Margaret Cavendish's Books in New College, and around Oxford." *New College Oxford*, vol. 6, 2015, www.new.ox.ac.uk/sites/default/files/6NCN5%20%282015%29%20Margaret%20Cavendish%27s%20books%20in%20New%20College%2C%20and%20around%20Oxford.pdf. Accessed 22 August 2018.

Sarasohn, Lisa T. "Fideism, Negative Theology, and Christianity in the Thought of Margaret Cavendish." *God and Nature in the Thought of Margaret Cavendish*, edited by Brandie R. Siegfried and Sarasohn, Routledge, 2016, pp. 93–106.

——. *The Natural Philosophy of Margaret Cavendish: Reason and Fancy During the Scientific Revolution*. Johns Hopkins UP, 2010.

Semler, L.E. "Margaret Cavendish's Early Engagement with Descartes and Hobbes: Philosophical Revisitation and Poetic Selection." *Intellectual History Review*, vol. 22, no. 3, 2012, pp. 327–53.

——. "Stories of Selves and Infidels: Walter Charleton's Letter to Margaret Cavendish (1655)." *Storytelling: Critical and Creative Approaches*, edited by Jan Shaw, Philippa Kelly, and L.E. Semler, Palgrave, 2013, pp. 191–210.

Sheppard, Kenneth. *Anti-Atheism in Early Modern England 1580–1720: The Atheist Answered and His Error Confuted*. Brill, 2015.

Siegfried, Brandie R. "The City of Chance, or, Margaret Cavendish's Theory of Radical Symmetry." *Early Modern Literary Studies*, vol. 14, no. 9, 2004, www.extra.shu.ac.uk/emls/si-14/siegcity.html. Accessed 8 August 2018.

——. "God and the Question of Sense Perception in the Works of Margaret Cavendish." *God and Nature in the Thought of Margaret Cavendish*, edited by Brandie R. Siegfried and Lisa T. Sarasohn, Routledge, 2016, pp. 59–76.

Stevenson, Jay. "Imagining the Mind: Cavendish's Hobbesian Allegories." *A Princely Brave Woman: Essays on Margaret Cavendish, Duchess of Newcastle*, edited by Stephen Clucas, Ashgate, 2003, pp. 143–55.

Tabor, Stephen. "The Bridgewater Library." *Dictionary of Literary Biography*, vol. 213, no. 47, edited by William Baker and Kenneth Womack, Gale, 1999, pp. 40–50.

Thell, Anne M. "Lady Phoenix: Motion, Imagination, and Cavendish's *Blazing World*." *Minds in Motion: Imagining Empiricism in Eighteenth-Century British Travel Literature*. Bucknell UP, 2017, pp. 41–74.

Van Helmont, Jan Baptist. *Oriatrike*. London, 1662.

Walters, Lisa. *Margaret Cavendish: Gender, Science and Politics*. Cambridge UP, 2014.

——. "Poems and Fancies, 1653." *Handbook of English Renaissance Literature*, edited by Ingo Berensmeyer, De Gruyter. Forthcoming.

Whitaker, Katie. *Mad Madge: The Extraordinary Life Of Margaret, Duchess Of Newcastle, the First Woman to Live by Her Pen*. Chatto & Windus, 2003.

Wilkins, Emma. "'Exploding' Immaterial Substances: Margaret Cavendish's Vitalist-materialist Critique of Spirits." *British Journal for the History of Philosophy*, vol. 24, no. 5, 2016, pp. 858–77.

——. "Margaret Cavendish and the Royal Society." *Notes and Records: The Royal Society Journal of the History of Science*, vol. 68, no. 3, 2014, pp. 245–60.

Wilson, Catherine. "Two Opponents of Material Atomism: Cavendish and Leibniz." *Leibniz and the English-Speaking World*, edited by Pauline Phemister and Stuart Brown, Springer, 2007, pp. 35–50.

Woolf, Virginia. *A Room of One's Own*. Edited by Mark Hussey, introduced by Susan Gubar, Harcourt, 2005.

From the Publisher

A name never says it all, but the word "Broadview" expresses a good deal of the philosophy behind our company. We are open to a broad range of academic approaches and political viewpoints. We pay attention to the broad impact book publishing and book printing has in the wider world; for some years now we have used 100% recycled paper for most titles. Our publishing program is internationally oriented and broad-ranging. Our individual titles often appeal to a broad readership too; many are of interest as much to general readers as to academics and students.

Founded in 1985, Broadview remains a fully independent company owned by its shareholders—not an imprint or subsidiary of a larger multinational.

For the most accurate information on our books (including information on pricing, editions, and formats) please visit our website at www.broadviewpress.com. Our print books and ebooks are also available for sale on our site.

broadview press
www.broadviewpress.com

This book is made of paper from well-managed FSC® - certified forests, recycled materials, and other controlled sources.